W9-BLE-388

You Can Do the Math

You Can Do the Math

Overcome Your Math Phobia and Make Better Financial Decisions

Ron Lipsman

Westport, Connecticut
London

Library of Congress Cataloging-in-Publication Data

Lipsman, Ronald L.
You can do the math : overcome your math phobia and make better financial decisions / Ron Lipsman.
p. cm.
Includes bibliographical references and index.
ISBN 0–275–98341–2 (alk. paper)
1. Finance, Personal—Mathematics. 2. Consumers—Decision making—Mathematics. 3. Investments—Mathematics. I. Title.
HG179.L525 2004
332.024'001'51—dc22 2004040053

British Library Cataloguing in Publication Data is available.

Library of Congress Catalog Card Number: 2004040053
ISBN: 0–275–98341–2

First published in 2004

Praeger Publishers, 88 Post Road West, Westport, CT 06881
An imprint of Greenwood Publishing Group, Inc.
www.praeger.com

Printed in the United States of America

The paper used in this book complies with the Permanent Paper Standard issued by the National Information Standards Organization (Z39.48-1984).

10 9 8 7 6 5 4 3 2 1

To my sons, Kenny and David,
In gratitude for their
love, respect and patience

Contents

Preface

This is one of innumerable self-help or how-to books with an emphasis on financial matters that you might browse through at your local bookstore or library. Why should you buy this one and not one of the others? There is an unending supply of books that teach you how to save your money, invest your money, stay out or get out of debt, minimize the taxes you pay, buy a house, finance a car, choose between insurance policies, win the lottery, beat the market, or retire rich. Most books focus on one, or at most a few, of these highly desirable goals. This book will discuss all of them.

Moreover, the emphasis in this book is different from most in the genre. There will be no grand strategies for guaranteeing you a 12% return in the market over a decade. Nor will there be a foolproof plan that you can follow to build an annual income of $200,000. And finally, you will not find any instructions for keeping your creditors at bay. Rather, I will demonstrate that in order for you to navigate the financial shoals of your life, you need to under-stand a few basic arithmetic concepts and learn how to do some simple arithmetic computations. Furthermore, recognizing that the overwhelming majority of the population is mathphobic, I will explain the concepts in the simplest possible layman's terms and provide you with an electronic tool for actually doing the computations. If you want to get a preliminary look at it, put down the book, crank up your wireless Web browser, and tune into http://www.math.umd.edu/~rll/cgi-bin/ finance.html.

If you don't have a gadget in your pocket that will transport you to the Internet, then read on and log in when you return home or to the office—with this book in hand, of course.

THE BASIC PREMISE OF THIS BOOK

There are certain simple computations, involving no more than rudimentary arithmetic and the very basic laws of chance, that the average American Joe and Jane should be doing in the course of everyday life. But these computations are often not done for several reasons. First, people don't realize how easy they are to do. Second, and more fundamental, the computations are not done because it does not occur to people to do them. Finally, and tragically, in most people's elementary, middle, or high school educational experience the importance of doing them was not stressed, and of course Joe and Jane were not taught *how* to do them. This is particularly ironic since modern calculators and computers make the computations very easy to do.

WHAT THIS BOOK IS

The goals of the book are to reveal to you what the computations are, make them readily understandable, and by means of a very easy-to-use companion Web site enable you to do them effortlessly and informatively. For example, I will explain compound interest, and how to compute it. There will also be simple explanations of: after-tax income versus before-tax income (on investments as well as salary); how an automobile lease works financially; the odds against winning your state lottery; and the difference between credit card debt and the balance due on your home mortgage. Moreover, in every case, I will explain in lay terms the math behind the issues, and then, with the aid of the Web site, lead you through instructive and representative computations of the numbers and answers you long to know.

WHAT THIS BOOK IS NOT

This book is not a recipe for financial success. I do not claim that after reading this book you will know how to become a millionaire. In fact, all of us are subject to the fickle whims of fate and the constraints of our own financial circumstances. Recessions arise through no fault of our own; job opportunities fail to materialize; parents and children turn out to be more needy than anticipated; or illness can strike unexpectedly, and so for that matter can extreme good fortune. The point is that life is hard and often unpredictable. What is certain is that we are constantly faced with decisions, many of which have financial content and implications. We ought to equip ourselves with the best possible ammunition for making those decisions. My primary goal here is to provide you with some of that ammo. Therefore, the main thing you should expect from this book is the arithmetic tools—more precisely, the electronic tools to do the arithmetic—that will help you to make those decisions. This may not be as good as guaranteeing you a million dollars, but it is more realistic and in the end, I believe, extremely helpful.

WHO SHOULD READ THIS BOOK

My guess is that the older you are and the more experience you have had in dealing with life's financial vicissitudes, the more of this book you will already know. So my intended audience is first and foremost young people. Young people: Pay attention! This stuff is not being taught in school, and you desperately need to know it. There are countless traps out there waiting for you to fall into them. Having the financial tools I intend to impart in this book will help you to avoid those traps.

Others who will likely profit (pun intended) from this book include young adults who are no longer in school but who have already encountered some of the early needs for the arithmetical wisdom to be found in these pages, thirty-somethings with young families and not enough time or energy to think through financial matters, middle-aged folks who suspect that maybe they have not learned the lessons I would hope they should have by this point in life, aging baby-boomers who have been too busy leading the good life to notice that Father Time is bearing down on them, and finally elderly folks who, despite the fact that they know this stuff, have not figured out how to teach it to their adult children and young grandchildren—in short, *everyone.*

WHAT YOU WILL GET OUT OF IT

You will get a rudimentary understanding of the basic concepts behind the arithmetic that governs the fundamental financial questions that challenge us in life. Your math skills may not improve. Sorry about that. This is because my goal is not to teach you any math but rather to help you put some newly understood arithmetical concepts to work for you in making financial decisions. As for the arithmetic computations, that is what the companion Web site is for. You can defer all the math skills you do or don't have to the wizardry of the software that underlies the workings of the Web site. So, in summary, you get two things: some basic understanding of the arithmetical concepts that underlie the financial questions of your life, and a tool for answering those questions.

WHY I'M THE ONE TO WRITE IT

I am not a stockbroker, an insurance agent, or an accountant, and I don't work in a financial institution. I am a university professor of mathematics and an academic administrator in the science college of my university. Moreover, like many people my age, although I have none of the "formal" qualifications listed above, I do have many years of experience buying and selling stocks and mutual funds, buying and canceling insurance policies, paying college tuition, paying taxes (lord help me, I am *really* experienced at that one), spending my salary, hurling epithets at my credit card company, obtaining and disposing of cars and homes, and worrying about how I can retire comfortably. I am also good with numbers—very good with numbers. They don't frighten me the way they do such a substantial portion of the population. I actually like them and enjoy working with them. And so when it comes to the arithmetic behind the decisions one confronts in doing all the things that I just mentioned, I don't mind crunching the numbers. I like to examine the numerical alternatives, investigate how different choices lead to different outcomes, speculate on possibilities, and act on past performance. I also have some experience in writing technical help books (I've written six of them). And finally, I have the training and experience of an educator. Therefore, all I have to do to fulfill the goals outlined in this preface is to distill the math into numbers and concepts that are simple and clear enough for you to understand—that, and design a simple-to-use Web site. When you are done breezing through this book and navigating the Web site, you can send me an email and tell me how well I succeeded.

HOW TO USE IT

The book is organized into three parts and thirteen chapters. In the first part, I discuss one of the most elementary monetary decisions that confronts a parent upon the birth of a child—namely, how to afford to educate this child. In that vein, we will investigate routine bank accounts, a phenomenon that involves the simplest and most fundamental arithmetic concept that we consider: *compound interest.* After that we will discuss inflation, and then we will explore the simplest aspects of taxes. Although taxes are one of the most painful and unpleasant features of our financial existence, the arithmetic required to understand them runs (for most taxpayers) no deeper than simple percent computations. In addition to compound interest, along with inflation (which is nothing more than a special kind of compound interest), the third fundamental topic of Part I is tax-deferred income. I will explain how it differs from income subject to normal income taxes and why it plays such a vital role in your quest for financial success.

In Part II of the book, I will discuss the seemingly routine, but often challenging, financial obstacles normally faced by American adults: your salary, and how the tax man pillages it and what you can do about that; buying and selling houses and cars (mortgage loans and vehicle leases); the gamut of insurance vehicles and how to evaluate them; and finally, credit. Then, in Part III, we advance to the most sophisticated issues that we shall explore in this book: gambling, stocks and bonds, and retirement.

There are six special types of paragraphs that you will encounter, each with a special symbol (or dingbat) so that you can identify them easily:

Paragraphs following this symbol contain a basic monetary principle. The principles are often self-evident, but I set them off like this so you will pay special attention and endeavor to remember and implement them. A simple example is: If you must choose between two bank accounts paying the same interest rate, the one that compounds most often is the better choice.

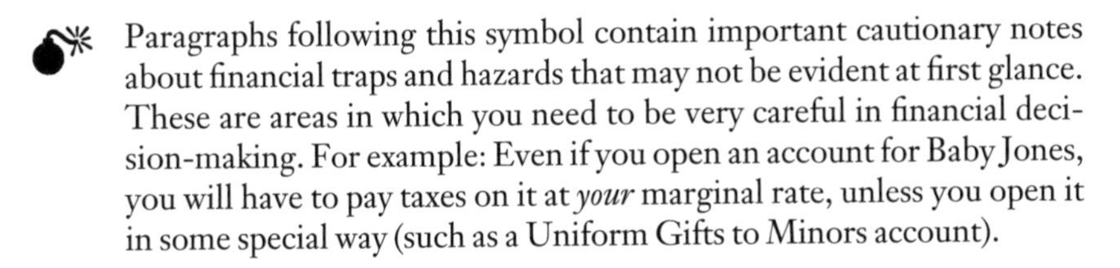

Paragraphs following this symbol contain important cautionary notes about financial traps and hazards that may not be evident at first glance. These are areas in which you need to be very careful in financial decision-making. For example: Even if you open an account for Baby Jones, you will have to pay taxes on it at *your* marginal rate, unless you open it in some special way (such as a Uniform Gifts to Minors account).

Paragraphs following this symbol contain fundamental questions that you should ponder and hopefully will be able to answer using the wisdom and resources found in this book and the companion Web site. An example might be: When you take out a mortgage on your first home, should you try to make your down payment as large as possible in order to keep your monthly payments as low as possible, or should you borrow as much as the bank will lend you, counting on your increasing paycheck and inflation to diminish the burden of your monthly payment as the years go by?

Paragraphs following this symbol contain useful tips or asides that may not be critical to the story but may prove useful or handy after you have mastered the fundamentals. For example: The marriage penalty (to be explained later) should not stop you from getting married, but you ought to compute what it will cost you before you walk down the aisle so that you can be prepared.

Paragraphs following this symbol point you toward a spot on the companion Web site where you can do a computation. The URL is http://www.math.umd.edu/~rll/cgi-bin/finance.html.

Finally, paragraphs following this symbol contain personal experiences or reminiscences that are germane to the topic at hand.

Each chapter concludes with a summary statement of the primary new computation that you learned to do, even if only with the help of the Web site. A synopsis of what is covered in each of the chapters is provided in the Outline section immediately after the Introduction.

A CONFESSION

You will notice as soon as you start reading that there are some mathematical *formulas* in the body of the book. Please do not be intimidated by them. At no point will I ask you to do any algebra or mathematics more advanced than relatively simple arithmetic. In fact, you can understand the book's contents even without doing any arithmetic, as any calculation that appears is easily checked or replicated with a basic handheld calculator. Those of you who are mathematically inclined will find some interesting crumbs to pick up and explore. For the vast majority of you who are not, I have provided explanations in English where the symbols might be confusing, and I have presented the results of all calculations. You do not have to do any of them by yourself—you can either take my word or check with your calculator. You don't need any special math background or ability to profit from this book. However, I would be less than honest if I didn't say that I do expect you, as you progress through the discussion, to recognize patterns, think logically, and appreciate coherent reasoning.

ACKNOWLEDGMENTS

I would like to thank my wife of thirty-nine years, Shelly, for reminding me periodically that my opinion is, after all, just my opinion. If indeed there is any financial wisdom in these pages, it has been distilled and purified by her sage advice and counsel. My children, Kenny and David, and their families have provided a wonderful window for me into the world of young people, just as my parents, aunts, and uncles have helped me to see the world through the eyes of the generation prior to my own. I am grateful to Arnie Lerman, of Ferris, Baker, Watts, who has been my broker for more than twenty years, during which time I managed to soak up a small part of his financial acumen. I've been inspired by the books of Ric Edelman, whom I met one time and found as sharp and witty in person as he is in his books and on television. My agent, John Willig, has been extremely helpful and solicitous of my interests, and my editor, Nick Philipson of Praeger Publishers, has been extraordinarily attentive. Finally, my hat's off to all the folks over the years who tried, sometimes successfully, to fool me, trick me, deceive me, cheat me, and generally relieve me of my money—as well as to the folks who were helpful, informative, generous, and gracious with their time, advice, and even their money.

Introduction

I began my public school career in September 1948 when I entered the first grade in P.S. 86 in the Bronx, New York. My graduation from the Bronx High School of Science in June 1960 concluded that career. In the intervening twelve years, I was privileged to encounter many dedicated and talented teachers who most diligently and patiently filled my head with an extraordinary amount of knowledge.

Very early on, I learned the names of the capital cities of every state in the forty-eight states of our great country as well as the names of the capitals of the one hundred or so countries in the world. I also learned to deftly manipulate numbers in various forms—for example, fractions, percents, and negative numbers—although the reasons for doing so were barely hinted at by my teachers. I could spell many obscure words, diagram complicated sentences, and retrieve antonyms and synonyms with ease.

As my career progressed, my storehouse of knowledge widened and deepened. I learned from my teachers, and from the wonderful books they made available, how to appreciate the plays of Shakespeare, the music of Beethoven, the novels of Dickens, and the poems of Keats and Shelley. I learned about the glorious history of Greece and Rome, the ignorance and backwardness of the Middle Ages, the reawakening of mankind during the Renaissance, and the modern triumphs of Western civilization.

My interest in mathematics and science originated in the halls of the Bronx High School of Science, whose teachers were justifiably famous for their devotion to student achievement. I learned there about DNA, the periodic table, Newton's Law of Gravity, mechanical drawing, slide rules, Euclidean geometry, and even a little calculus. Perhaps surprisingly, the humanities faculty there also managed to contribute something worthwhile to my growing wealth of information, as I also learned about the workings of our constitutional system and a little bit about economics. Regarding government and economics, I might mention that a bias toward the left among my teachers was already evident, although I didn't recognize it for many years. For example, we spent a great deal of time on the First Amendment but none on the Second. And I learned far too much about Marx and socialism and not nearly enough about a free market economy. The name Adam Smith may have appeared in my textbooks, but none of his writings were in the syllabus, and it goes without saying that the names F. A. Hayek and Ludwig von Mises (gurus of capitalism) were nowhere to be found.

And this leads me to my main point. We live in the greatest free market economy in the history of the world. This requires that each of us, as citizens, must continually make decisions that seriously affect our financial well-being. These include simple but life-critical matters, such as: Can I afford the payments on that car? If I need to borrow $150,000 to buy that house, what will my monthly payment be? If I bet this week's paycheck on that horse, what are my chances of winning? How much do I need to put away each month if I am going to pay for my daughter to go to Harvard in fifteen years? And then there are more sophisticated questions: How much should I contribute to my pension plan? Will my family be adequately protected by the amount of life insurance I am carrying? Is that stock overvalued?

I never learned the answers to any of those questions in school, and, I'll bet, neither did you. But if you are old enough, you certainly have had to learn them as your life has unfolded. And if you haven't, woe is you! If you are young and wise enough to be reading this book, then I am here to tell you that you are still not going to learn the answers in school. If you are in school, you may have found my litany of what I learned in school a little bizarre. In lieu of teaching you about the monumental achievements of the geniuses of Western civilization, today's public schools often concentrate more on multicultural subjects than on classical topics. But your teachers are still not about to teach you the answers to any of the fundamental life questions listed above or how to do some of the simple computations that would reveal the answers for you. The curriculum may have changed, but the economic facts of life are still not part of it. Read on, good friend, as I will so instruct you and provide you with a resource to do the math for yourself.

Outline of the Book's Content

In this outline, I provide a very brief chapter-by-chapter description of the topics and issues covered in the book. The main content of the book is organized in thirteen chapters within three parts:

I. Basic Money

1. *Saving for a College Fund*
   Bank interest; simple annual interest; compound interest; frequency of compounding; computing how much a single deposit will grow into over the years with compound interest; computing how much you must deposit in order to reach a predetermined goal in a certain number of years; dealing with changing interest rates.

2. *Investing for a College Fund*
   The difference between saving and investing; computing how much an account, into which regular deposits are made, will grow into over the years with compound interest; computing how much you must deposit regularly in order to reach a predetermined goal in a certain number of years; comparing account values of lump sum programs to regular deposit schemes; how to estimate answers to computations.

3. *Taking into Consideration Taxes and Inflation*
   Defining, measuring and understanding inflation; inflation as a form of negative compound interest; the effect of inflation on savings and investments; coping with inflation; income taxes, tax brackets and marginal tax rates; the effect of income taxes on savings and investments; coping with taxes.

4. *How Tax-Deferred Accounts Can Help*
How income taxes influence your behavior; the meaning of "tax-deferred"; comparing tax-deferred and taxable investments; measuring the effects on both low-income and high-income individuals.

II. The Facts of Life

5. *Your Paycheck: What Is Your Salary Really Worth?*
Deductions from your paycheck (taxes, nontax but mandatory, optional); gross pay, net pay, and after-tax pay; the freedom quotient (after-tax divided by gross); strategies for maximizing your freedom quotient; the "freebie," "pay yourself first," and estimated tax payments; the difference between deductions, exemptions, and credits.

6 *Buying a House or Car: Mortgages and Loans*
Home loans and car loans have the same structure; collateral; how to compute the monthly payment; the portions that are interest or principal; comparisons between financing and paying cash; a closer examination of the similarities and differences between car and home loans; loan balances over time.

7. *Buying or Leasing Your Car*
Three methods to purchase a car (for cash, finance, lease); an explanation of the lease concept; financial components of a lease and how lease payments work; the dealer's role; how residual values and lease lengths affect monthly payments; psychological factors; monetary comparison of the three methods; a surprising conclusion; coping with a lack of spare cash.

8. *Owning or Renting Your Home*
New homes versus existing homes; home ownership versus rental; monthly costs; a detailed monetary comparison of monthly expenses between home ownership and rental; values of homes you can buy for monthly expenses equivalent to a rental; nonfinancial considerations in the decision; a firm recommendation for ownership.

9. *Insurance*
A precise definition of insurance; insurance is a bet; factors that enter into the decision to buy insurance; the various kinds (health, automobile, home, life, disability, umbrella, business, long-term care); other products that you don't think of as insurance but qualify according to our definition (for example, extended warranties, stock options, prenuptial agreements); Social Security, Medicare, workers' compensation, unemployment insurance; the basic principles that should guide your insurance purchases.

10. *Cut Up Those #$^& Credit Cards*
Why we use credit cards; the history of credit cards; how they work; the main features and some of the dangers; credit cards as a weapon for you;

avoiding credit card debt; credit card facsimiles (debit cards, ATM cards, lines of credit).

III. Accumulating Wealth

11. *Gambling: Can I Win the Lottery?*
    The universal desire to "be rich"; gambling as a tempting method to fulfill the desire; different gambling scenarios; basic probability; the expected value of a game; understanding odds and how they are determined; the numbers game (or lotteries) are particularly insidious; why state-sponsored gambling is a tax; how to gamble if you must.

12. *The Stock Market and Other Investments*
    The basic axioms of a sustained investment program; stocks, bonds, and mutual funds; other investment vehicles; a mathematical model for a regular investment program (what you can expect to achieve); implementation and recommendations; some helpful observations.

13. *Retirement*
    The generally accepted wisdom on retirement income needs; sources of retirement income; the role of your investment program in building a nest egg; how much money you need to retire; how long your money will last; a mathematical retirement model; more on defined benefit plans; nonfinancial retirement advice; a final summary of the book's contents.

Part I

Basic Money

Chapter 1

Saving for a College Fund

You and your spouse are standing beside the crib of your infant child, born a week ago. Both of you are overwhelmed with powerful feelings of pride and joy. You are barely conscious of the fact that you are making ridiculous faces and noises at the baby, hoping to engender some reaction. Unbeknownst to you, the baby's immature digestive system is finding mom's milk a bit rich, and a small gas bubble has formed in the infant's tummy. Perhaps, if you hadn't blindly followed the pediatrician's advice to place the baby on its back at all times, the bubble might have been expelled by now. Alas, the baby's mind is occupied by the bubble, not your cooing. But finally the bubble exits, and at exactly the instant that your exhortations, designed to definitely elicit a response, reach a crescendo of babble. Of course, the baby has little adeptness at altering her or his facial expression, but the departure of the bubble actually instigates some change in the child's countenance, whereupon you and your spouse yelp in joint spasms of joy, firmly convinced that your offspring is undoubtedly a genius, or at least the smartest person ever born on either side of the family.

The glow of that moment will keep you enthralled for hours, maybe days. The warm feeling lasts until you suddenly realize the dire financial consequences of your baby's monumental intelligence. College! The local state university is clearly not equipped to handle *your* child. Only an Ivy League school such as Harvard or Princeton will be up to the challenge of engaging and developing that great intellect. The problem is that a year at one of those august institutions costs on the order of $35,000 at the beginning of the twenty-first century. What it will cost when your child is ready to enter its portals, even if your offspring's precocity means that said entrance might be in fifteen rather than eighteen years, is too horrible to contemplate. The thought that crashes through your head as soon as you formulate the problem is, "Where in heaven's name are we going to get that kind of money?" The baby may not be as athletic as he or she is smart, so a full scholarship is unlikely. "Well, we better start saving right now," you exclaim. "I agree," adds your spouse, "but how? Should we transfer all of our savings to a special education account? Should I ask my parents to give us money now? How much do we really need? How much can we afford to save each month?"

HOW CAN MOM AND DAD PAY FOR THEIR LITTLE GENIUS'S COLLEGE EDUCATION?

A hundred questions of this ilk are sloshing around in your minds. The problem can be confusing and daunting. Let's see if we can simplify the problem by simplifying the assumptions. Then maybe you and your spouse—Mom and Dad for this exercise—may be able to make some headway. Suppose we ignore inflation for the moment, and suppose that, unlike too many of today's college students, your child will be disciplined enough to complete her or his studies in four years. Then Mom and Dad need \$35,000 for each of the four years in college, that is, $\$35{,}000 \times 4 = \$140{,}000$. Mom decides that regardless of how precocious the baby may be, she wants her child to enjoy the full benefit of a social life in high school, so you have eighteen years before you need to start writing tuition checks to Harvard. Next, let's suppose that Grandma and Grandpa volunteer to pay for the baby's higher education and that they intend to do it with funds they already have. (This certainly simplifies the problem for Mom and Dad!) Furthermore, everyone agrees that there will be a sufficient number of unexpected events, life occurrences, and large purchases to occupy the parents' and grandparents' funds during the baby's journey from infancy to young adulthood, so no one will have the luxury of thinking about accumulating college funds during the next eighteen years. Let's take care of it all now! So Grandma and Grandpa open an unsophisticated bank account that pays 5% simple annual interest.

How much money must they deposit today so that the account will have \$140,000 in it in eighteen years?

Let's step back for a moment. Put a buck in the bank. It doesn't get any more basic than that. With the possible exception of forking over a buck in the grocery store, the act of depositing money in the bank is the most basic financial transaction in which we engage. It underlies every other transaction that we will discuss in this book, and so we had better get a good handle on it and the results that ensue.

THE ROLE OF A BANK ACCOUNT

Why do we put our money in the bank? In olden days people did it in great measure for security, and to some extent we still do so today. Not only can the highwaymen not get at it, but if we can't get at it too easily, then we aren't likely to spend it too casually. But the primary reason we deposit money in a bank account is that a bank account is a safe, reliable, and predictable way to make our money grow. That is true because the bank *pays interest* on our deposits. Assuming the bank pays a 5% simple annual interest, then exactly one year from the day we deposit, say, $100 in an account, the bank will credit our account with 5% of $100, namely $5. So at the end of that day, the balance on the account will read $105, as opposed to the $100 balance it showed throughout the year.

Why is the bank willing to do this, that is, pay you 5% for the privilege of parking your funds in their coffers? The company that manufactured your mattress won't pay you anything, even if you leave your money in it forever. The answer is because the bank *uses* the money during the year. More than likely, the bank will *lend* it to someone who will put it toward the purchase of a house or a car. And the bank will charge that person 8% for the service. So the bank winds up with a net profit of $0.03 on a dollar for the year. Of course, they do that for the millions and millions of dollars that people save in their bank accounts. Not bad! Want to go into the banking business?

COMPOUND INTEREST

Now pay careful attention. What comes next is really important! If you don't need the money you left in your account for the year, then you are likely to leave it in the account for another year. What happens at the end of the second year? The bank will again credit your account with interest. But, and this is crucial, the amount credited will *not* be $5. It will be 5% of $105, that is, $\$105 \times 0.05 = \$5.25$. You should verify this calculation, either by multiplying out the numbers by hand or cracking out your trusty calculator, or

Consult the Web site. (Try *arithmetic calculator*.) Once again, the URL is http://www.math.umd.edu/~rll/cgi-bin/finance.html.

So, your account balance after two years is $110.25, which includes the original $100 deposit, the $5 interest you earned in Year 1, and the $5.25 interest you earned in Year 2.

Here is a better way to analyze what happens annually to your bank account. At the end of each year, the bank adds to your account 5% of *whatever* has been in there for the whole year. Therefore, if you start with D dollars, the bank adds $D \times 0.05$ dollars to your account, thereby giving you a balance of $D + D \times 0.05$, that is, $D \times 1.05$ dollars. In summary, you can compute the amount you will have at the end of the year by multiplying the amount you start with by 1.05.

For an account paying simple annual interest of 5%, the amount in the account at the end of a year will be 1.05 times the amount in the account at the start of the year.

Assuming you continue to leave your money in the account, this happens every year, *no matter what amount you start with.* So, if you start with D dollars, you have $D \times 1.05$ dollars at the end of the first year. This also means you have $D \times 1.05$ dollars at the beginning of the second year, and therefore $D \times 1.05 \times 1.05$ dollars at the end of the second year. Math folks write 1.05×1.05 in the form 1.05^2 and recite the expression as "one point zero five squared." Your calculator will quickly show you that

$$1.05^2 = 1.1025.$$

Therefore, if you start with $100, then after two years you have $\$100 \times 1.1025$, that is, $110.25 as we saw above.

The arithmetic in the above discussion involves multiplication of decimal numbers. But the underlying concept is fairly simple. If you understand this concept, you will clearly see that after a third year, the account will contain

$$\$100 \times 1.05^3 = \$115.7625.$$

If perchance you did not follow the reasoning in the paragraph above, then you have two choices: either read it again to see if you can improve your understanding, or ignore the math, take my word for it, and rely completely on your calculator or the Web site for the computation. However, this example is so basic to what follows that I urge you to have another crack at understanding it if you need to.

In any event, after five years, the account will be worth $\$100 \times 1.05^5$, and then after ten years, $\$100 \times 1.05^{10}$, or as the math guys who love letters would say, after n years it will be worth $\$100 \times 1.05^n$, where n stands for an unspecified number of years. Therefore, to answer the question confronting Grandma and Grandpa, we need to solve the equation

$$D \times 1.05^{18} = 140{,}000$$

for the as yet unknown quantity D. Why? In fact, because if Grandma and Grandpa put an as yet undetermined amount D in the account, then we know that after eighteen years, the account will contain $D \times 1.05^{18}$ dollars. We need to find the number D so that $D \times 1.05^{18}$ equals 140,000.

Well, another round with your calculator will reveal for you that 1.05 raised to the eighteenth power, when rounded off to five decimal places, is 2.40662, that is,

$$1.05^{18} = 2.40662.$$

So the equation we have to solve now reads

$$D \times 2.40662 = 140{,}000.$$

Continuing to use our high school algebra, we see that the solution to the equation is obtained by dividing through by 2.40662. That is,

$$D = 140{,}000/2.40662 = 58{,}172.87.$$

If Grandma and Grandpa deposit $58,172.87 into a bank account paying 5% simple annual interest, the account will contain $140,000 after eighteen years.

This relatively simple example illustrates the power of compounding; the grandparents' money has multiplied nearly 2½ fold over the eighteen years. Albert Einstein is reputed to have said that the most powerful force in the universe is compound interest. Albert was very familiar with a few other very powerful forces, some of which he actually discovered. Who am I to argue with him? For our purposes, that is, financial edification, he is certainly correct. Compound interest is a potent force in the pursuit of growing one's financial accounts. Let's demonstrate that even more forcefully (pun intended).

Suppose the interest in the account was not compounded—that is, suppose the same interest that the initial deposit garnered is credited year after year, despite the continued presence of new interest in the account over the years. One year's interest on $58,172.87 is 5% of that figure, namely, $58,172.87 × 0.05 = $2,908.64. (Use your calculator to check if you like.) If the interest were not compounded every year, then the total interest paid in eighteen years would be eighteen times that figure, namely 2,908.64 × 18 = 52,355.52. Added to the original amount, that is, 58,172.87, this would yield a total of $52,355.52 + $58,172.87 = $110,528.39. So, without compounding the account would contain nearly $30,000 less than what it contains when the interest is compounded annually.

THE MAGIC NUMBER

Here's a good way to think about the model we have built for a bank account earning simple annual interest. What we saw above is that if you deposit D dollars in such an account that is paying an interest rate r (in decimal form) and leave it in the account for n years, then at the end of that period the final value of the account V is given by

$$V = D \times (1 + r)^n.$$

Now that's a nasty trick Lipsman, throwing in an equation full of variables. Please say it in English:

We refer to the quantity $(1 + r)^n$ as the *magic number*. It depends only on the interest rate and the number of years in which the money remains in the account.

For example, in the computation above, we had $r = 0.05$ and $n = 18$, so that the magic number was

$$1.05^{18} = 2.40662.$$

Then the final value of your account is obtained by multiplying the magic number by whatever you deposited initially. In our discussion above, we first had an initial deposit of $100, and later on one of $58,172.90. The amount does not matter—whatever amount you deposit in an account such as this, the value after eighteen years is arrived at by multiplying that amount by the magic number.

Table 1.1 gives the magic numbers for varying interest rates and varying number of years. It presumes simple annual interest. Remember: If a certain amount is placed in the account, then to compute the sum it grows into in the specified number of years at the specified interest rate, just multiply the original amount by the magic number.

To further reinforce your understanding of the magic number concept, let's use the numbers in Table 1.1 to compute a few illustrative examples. Thus, if you place $100 in a simple annual interest account paying 3% and leave it there for five years, then the account will grow to $\$100 \times 1.1593 = \$115.93$ in that time. The magic number 1.1593 is found in the table by looking in the column marked "5" under "Number of Years" and across the row marked "3%." Similarly, if you deposit $1,500 in a simple annual interest account paying 7% and leave it to accumulate over a ten-year period, then the resulting sum in the account will be $\$1{,}500 \times 1.9672 = \$2{,}950.80$. Finally, and more dramatically, if you commit $10,000 to a simple annual interest account paying 10% and leave it untouched for forty years, it will grow into a small fortune, namely $\$10{,}000 \times 45.2593 = \$452{,}593$.

Table. 1.1
Magic numbers for a simple interest account corresponding to a specific number of years at a specified interest rate

	Number of Years				
Interest Rate	**1**	**5**	**10**	**25**	**40**
3%	1.0300	1.1593	1.3439	2.0938	3.2620
5%	1.0500	1.2763	1.6289	3.3864	7.0400
7%	1.0700	1.4026	1.9672	5.4274	14.9745
8%	1.0800	1.4693	2.1589	6.8485	21.7245
10%	1.1000	1.6105	2.5937	10.8347	45.2593

COMPOUNDING MORE FREQUENTLY

Impressive, but some clever banker long ago thought, "Well, why don't we compound the interest more often than annually!" And so they did. Banks started compounding interest semiannually, quarterly, monthly, and even daily. The process is simple: Semiannual compounding means that instead of paying you 5% on your deposit at the end of the year, the bank pays you 2.5% after six months and then another 2.5% at the end of the year. But during the second half of the year, your account balance is enlarged by the interest paid on the first half of the year, so the amount you earn in the second half is somewhat greater than that earned in the first half. The bottom line is that you have more at the end of the year than you would have with 5% interest credited on the original amount. Matters improve further if the interest is compounded quarterly or more often. To illustrate, Table 1.2 gives the amount in your account after one year with simple annual interest, and then with semiannual, quarterly, monthly, and daily compounding. It assumes a $100 initial deposit and a 5% annual interest rate.

Table 1.2 also illustrates a feature of bank advertising of which you should be cognizant. Many newspaper and magazine advertisements for bank accounts, especially Certificates of Deposit (CDs), will say "effective annual yield—5.127%." That is the actual percentage that a daily compounded account paying 5% annually actually yields over the course of a year. (Actually, they would probably round it off to 5.13%.) If you wanted to do business with a competing bank that only paid simple annual interest, then that is the amount the bank would have to pay to match the account earning daily compound interest at a 5% rate.

A common acronym for the effective annual yield is APY, which stands for "annual percentage yield."

As you can see from Table 1.2, the difference between the amounts earned shrinks as the frequency of compounding increases. The gain from more than daily compounding is negligible, and in fact most banks pay daily compound interest on their normal accounts. Table 1.3 gives even more graphic illustra-

Table 1.2
Compounding at different periods, based on a $100 initial deposit and a 5% annual interest rate

Method of Compounding	Account Balance after One Year
Simple annual interest	$105.000
Interest compounded semiannually	$105.063
Interest compounded quarterly	$105.095
Interest compounded monthly	$105.116
Interest compounded daily	$105.127

Table 1.3
Amount that $100 grows to (with daily compounding) after specified number of years at specified interest rate

	Number of Years				
Interest Rate	**1**	**5**	**10**	**25**	**40**
3%	$103.05	$116.18	$134.98	$211.69	$332.00
5%	$105.13	$128.40	$164.87	$349.00	$738.80
7%	$107.25	$141.90	$201.36	$575.36	$1,644.02
8%	$108.33	$149.18	$222.53	$738.74	$2,452.39
10%	$110.52	$164.86	$271.79	$1,217.83	$5,456.82

tion of the power of compound interest. This time we will again assume that $100 is deposited in an account and that the interest is compounded daily, but we shall vary the interest rate and the number of years the money is left to accumulate. Historically, 5% is a fairly standard interest rate paid by banks. However, in times when inflation is very low (the situation at the time I am writing), banks may pay considerably less. And of course in times of high inflation, rates may be considerably higher. We will discuss inflation in Chapter 3

There are some very impressive numbers in Table 1.3. Even at the modest interest rate of 5%, your money multiplies more than seven times in the course of forty years. And if you can get a consistently high interest rate such as 10%, your initial stake is worth more than fifty-four times its original value after four decades.

Another way to look at Table 1.3 is that it supplies the magic number for daily compounded interest—at least for the interest rates and the number of years listed in the table. Even though the precise arithmetic formula for computing the magic number for daily interest is more complicated than for simple annual interest (OK, if you're that curious, look on the Web site), the principle is still exactly the same. Namely, once you specify the interest rate and the number of years, then there is a single magic number that works for *any* initial amount deposited—that is, you get the final value by multiplying the initial deposit by the magic number.

QUESTIONS RELATED TO COMPOUND INTEREST

The numbers in Table 1.3 above give the answer to the following kind of question: "If I place D dollars in a savings account earning r rate of interest (compounded daily), then how much will the account be worth in n years?" Earlier, in addressing Grandma and Grandpa's dilemma, we answered a related but slightly different question, namely "How many dollars must I place in a savings account earning a rate of interest *r* in order to reach a predetermined amount in a predetermined number of years?" Clearly, we are manipulating four gadgets in these questions:

1. Initial Deposit
2. Rate of Interest
3. Number of Years Invested
4. Final Worth of Account

The point is that if we know any three of them, then it is a relatively simple matter of arithmetic to compute the fourth. In the two questions we asked, the quantity we sought was #4 in the first instance and #1 in the second. You can easily pose problems that ask for either #2 or #3, provided you know the other three. For example, a famous problem that appears in many high school and college math books goes like this: If you place *D* dollars in a savings account paying *r* rate of interest, how many years will it take to double your money? In this case it is #3 that is the quantity we seek. Table 1.4 gives the answer to the question for varying rates of interest—as usual, assuming daily compounding.

TRUTH IN ADVERTISING AND THE LURE OF MONEY

Some folks have difficulty leaving their money untouched in an account. They withdraw funds for some "worthwhile" purpose, intending to replace it at the earliest opportunity. And sometimes they do. But now they confront the issue of whether the bank is truly compounding the interest on a daily basis. That is, is the bank paying interest from day of deposit to day of withdrawal or only on a minimum amount maintained in the account over the course of a month, a quarter, or even over a year? In the former case, each day you earn interest on what has been in the account during the last twenty-four hours. In the latter case, the bank is essentially paying monthly, quarterly, or simple annual interest on the lowest balance in the account over the period.

Table 1.4
Doubling your money

Interest Rate (Compounded Daily)	Number of Years for Money to Double
3%	23.1
5%	13.9
7%	9.9
8%	8.7
10%	6.9

You need to read the fine print when you open the account to know which circumstance you are in, that is, whether your money is truly earning interest from day of deposit to day of withdrawal.

Other folks find it hard to withdraw their money from their bank accounts for any reason. Those people are often misers, but not necessarily. To understand the phenomenon, consider the following recollection:

I spent the first seven years of my life in a five-story walk-up tenement building on Morris Avenue in the Bronx. It was a fifteen-minute walk from the hub of retail and commercial life in the borough, the intersection of Fordham Road and the Grand Concourse. The Concourse (as it was universally known) was a wide tree-lined boulevard that ran north-south through the west Bronx. Along it were a surprising number of stately apartment buildings, some of which bordered on elegant. However, in the vicinity of Fordham Road, the residential flavor of the street was given over to commerce, and along Fordham Road every manner of thriving retail establishment could be found. At the intersection was Alexander's Department Store, the Bronx's answer to R. H. Macy's. Nearby were Krum's and Jahn's, two of the most delectable and popular confectionary/ice cream/candy shops ever created to please the palettes of young and old; the Loew's Paradise Theatre, surely one of the grandest neighborhood theaters ever constructed, whose faux starlight sky ceiling was world famous; the impressive army-navy recruiting station, which always seemed to be doing a brisk business; and every conceivable type of retail establishment that kept the area alive with people shopping and socializing, eating and working.

But the establishment that I remember most vividly is the Dollar Savings Bank. It was a big building whose entire first floor was devoted to the public transaction activities of the bank. The room was enormous. The floors were marble, as were the walls. Along one side, behind a mahogany wood partition, were rows of impressive desks behind which sat impeccably dressed bank managers ready to discuss important financial matters with the eager public. Running the long length of the back wall was a marble half-wall topped by strong frosted glass, broken only by open window partitions that were fronted by brass bars behind which waited the efficient tellers who interacted with the depositors. It was a time before ATM machines, before phone or Internet banking, before credit cards. People went to the bank frequently to deposit and withdraw money, to buy money orders, to apply for loans. And when you entered the Dollar Savings Bank, you entered a very serious establishment where you and your money were treated with respect.

I remember many trips to that bank with my mother and my paternal grandfather. I loved walking into the lobby of that building. The grand

> feeling gave me a healthy respect for the importance of money. My maternal grandfather gave me a dollar once a week, every week for roughly the first fifteen years of my life. Having read this far in the book, you should not be surprised that every one of those dollars went into the Dollar Savings Bank and eventually paid for my honeymoon.

Whether you are the type who can't keep your fingers off your stash, or can't bear to part with a drop of it, or, hopefully, somewhere in between, I think you will find useful information in these pages. Whatever your monetary proclivities, you cannot avoid the financial questions and issues that we will explore in the chapters below.

VARIABLE RATES OF INTEREST

Before we close this chapter on the straightforward but profound effects of compound interest, let us take up what is likely to be an obvious objection to our presentation. Namely, everyone will agree that bank interest rates don't remain constant over several years, much less over forty years. The rates go up and down depending on various economic, and sometimes political, factors. Observation over a long period indicates that bank interest rates tend to average around 5% over an extended period. But they don't stay there; sometimes they are higher, sometimes lower. What implication does that have for the basic model of compound interest we have presented in this chapter? The answer is: minor, but not none.

Here's why. Suppose that in two successive years your account earned 6% and 4% respectively. Clearly the average for the two years is 5%. Are you better off or worse off earning 6% in Year 1 and then 4% in Year 2 than the person who earned 5% for both years? Can you guess the answer? Here's a hint: Which number is bigger, 6 times 4, or 5 times 5? I will explain now why the answer to that question answers the earnings question. Let's simplify the situation by assuming that both banks pay simple annual interest. The reasoning for interest compounded more often is in principle the same. Well, you know how to compute the interest. For the account paying different amounts over the two years, you get the amount in the account after one year by multiplying by 1.06, then you get the amount at the end of the second year by multiplying further by 1.04. In the account whose interest rate is held constant at 5%, you get the amount in the account at the end of the second year by multiplying the original amount by 1.05×1.05, or 1.05^2.

You can check easily that

$$1.06 \times 1.04 = 1.1024,$$

$$1.05^2 = 1.1025.$$

You should observe that the "24" came from multiplying 6 times 4, and the "25" came from squaring 5. These numbers show that the constant interest rate is better, but only very, very slightly so. The same principle will apply if your bank account rate varies slightly over the years but averages 5%. You only make a tiny error in the final numbers if you simplify the assumptions and assume a constant 5% rate. Let's illustrate with an example.

Suppose you open an account with $1,000. To make matters simple, we'll presume simple annual interest. Suppose the rates for five consecutive years are 4.8%, 4.9%, 5.0%, 5.1%, and 5.2%, respectively. The average rate over the five years is manifestly 5%. At the end of the five-year period you will have

$$\$1000 \times 1.048 \times 1.049 \times 1.050 \times 1.051 \times 1.052 = \$1,276.2758.$$

If you had bought a treasury bill that paid 5% every year instead, the amount in that case would be

$$\$1000 \times 1.05^5 = \$1,276.2816.$$

Note the small difference, namely $^{58}/_{100}$ of a penny.

On the other hand, if the rates are fluctuating wildly, then the error magnifies and the resultant drop in income can be more significant. To illustrate, try the pairs 7% and 3%, and then 8% and 2%. In fact,

$$1.07 \times 1.03 = 1.1021$$

$$1.08 \times 1.02 = 1.1016.$$

It is clearly better to earn 5% interest in two successive years than it is to earn 8% one year followed by 2% the next.

You may wonder whether reversing the order would change matters, that is, whether earning 2% in the first year and then 8% in the second would make any difference. In fact, there is no difference. In the first case you compute the amount in the account at the end of the second year by multiplying by 1.08 and then by 1.02. In the second case you first multiply by 1.02 and then by 1.08. But one of the fundamental principles of arithmetic you learned in grade school is that the order of multiplication *does not matter.* Eight times two is the same thing as two times eight.

Now consider an example where the interest rates fluctuate more substantially. Put $1,000 in an account, but now assume the interest rates in five successive years are 1%, 3%, 5%, 7%, and 9%. Again, the average is clearly 5%, but the variation is much wider. At the end of the five-year period, the account contains

$$\$1000 \times 1.01 \times 1.03 \times 1.05 \times 1.07 \times 1.09 = \$1{,}273.9670.$$

The difference this time is $2.31. This is not huge, but greater deposits or wider oscillations can magnify the loss of income.

The moral of the story:

If you want to save your money in a straightforward compound interest account, try to find a bank whose rates are as high as possible but fluctuate as little as possible, park the maximum amount of money you can afford to set aside in the account, and leave it alone for as many years as you can manage.

IMPORTANT NOTE TO THE READER

In Part I of this book, that is, in this and the next three chapters, I address you in the context of a young parent contemplating how to accumulate the money to fund a college education. The exact same arithmetic principles and financial advice apply to a person saving/investing in order to make a future major purchase (motorcycle, car, RV, home, pool, Caribbean cruise, what have you), fund a retirement account, or amass the capital to start a business.

DINGBATS

Before concluding this first chapter with the statement of the main computational skill I have taught to you, I would like to note that in the chapter I have used all six special paragraph styles (introduced by dingbats) described in the Preface. These special paragraphs should help to make the narrative more interesting and conversational. They should also provide places of special interest to which you can easily jump back and forth as you progress through the book.

YOUR NEW COMPUTATIONAL SKILL

How to compute the value of an account into which has been deposited a specific sum of money that has been accumulating interest for a specific number of years at a specific rate, compounded at a specific frequency.

CHAPTER 2

Investing for a College Fund

Let's put the baby back in the crib and ask the same questions that we did at the beginning of Chapter 1. But let's change the answers a little bit. Suppose Grandma and Grandpa need all of their money to support themselves in their retirement. And more than likely, not only do Mom and Dad—that is, you—not have any appreciable savings to speak of, you may be carrying an inappropriate amount of credit card debt (which we'll get to in Chapter 10). So, the only way little Einstein in the crib there is going to Harvard is if Mom and Dad can accumulate the money over the next eighteen years, one painful year at a time. You will have to put away money toward that goal on a regular basis—yearly, monthly, weekly if you can swing it. My purpose in this chapter is to explore the numbers so that you can see at a glance how much you would have to save on a regular basis in order to reach a predetermined financial goal. You are going to have to be systematic, disciplined, and aggressive. Yes, you will not only need to *save* to reach this goal, you will need to *invest!*

Before we go any further, we need to examine these two words: save and invest. What do they mean literally? What do they mean practically? When is a person saving, and when is he or she investing? What are the characteristics that differentiate between saving your money and investing your money?

WHAT'S THE DIFFERENCE BETWEEN SAVING MONEY AND INVESTING MONEY?

People often say that they are saving money to pay for a child's college education, for a rainy day, or for a down payment on a house or car, or that they want to be sure they have six months' wages saved in case of a dire emergency. On the other hand, we speak of investing for retirement, or investing in the market, and sometimes we say unfortunately that our investments are not appreciating in the way we had hoped. We can accumulate funds for college expenses either by opening a bank savings account or by regularly putting money in a mutual fund.

Are they both savings vehicles, or is the latter an investment? Similarly, we can accumulate funds toward our retirement needs by opening up a Certificate of Deposit (CD) in a bank or by buying technology stocks. Which of those is savings and which investing? Clearly, the monetary vehicle does not determine whether we are saving money or investing money. What does?

Let's turn to Webster for help.

More than forty years ago, when I entered college, my aunt gave me a copy of *Webster's New Collegiate Dictionary*, 1951 edition. It is barely holding together, but nary a week goes by that I don't seek help in its battered pages. Twenty-two years ago, when cleaning out my father-in-law's apartment after he passed away, I found a copy of *Webster's Seventh New Collegiate Dictionary*, 1972 edition. Even then, I worried that my original Webster might not survive much longer, so I kept my father-in-law's copy. It looks better than the original, but not by much. Let's see what these venerable sources have to say about saving and investing.

For *save*, we find "to keep from being spent, wasted or lost; to reserve (for a special purpose); to preserve by careful or sparing use; to put up as a store or reserve." Whereas for *invest*, the definition is "to lay out money or capital (in business) with the view of obtaining an income or profit; to convert into some form of wealth other than money, as securities or real estate, with the expectation of deriving income; to commit money in order to earn a financial return." So, clearly, the difference between saving and investing money is not the vehicle in which you do it, but rather the *purpose* intended for the money as well as the certainty of its future status. In short, we save money in a safe, reliable, predictable way for a very special use later on or just to keep it from getting lost or spent. On the other hand, we invest money in bold, aggressive, and sometimes risky schemes for the purpose of accumulating wealth.

The mind-set I want you to adopt is that you are virtually always *investing* your money and hardly ever *saving* it—assuming, of course, that you are not *spending* all of it. Putting money in the mattress is saving it. Stashing cash, gold, or other valuables in a safe deposit box is another form of saving. For me, even parking money in a low-risk savings account with the express purpose of accumulating a fixed amount by a fixed date for a specific expenditure is, if there is any return on the account, a form of investing. So in this book let's concentrate primarily on how you can grow your money via investments rather than preserve it via savings.

A SIMPLE INVESTMENT PLAN

Now back to the travail of Mom and Dad. The baby is staring up at you from the crib, ready to soak up the accumulated wisdom of the ages. Grandma and

Grandpa have bailed out on you. Nevertheless, you are determined that your child's intellectual gifts shall not go unattended. The fundamental quandary:

How much money must you deposit on a regular basis in order to accumulate $140,000 in eighteen years?

And so you contemplate an *investment* plan. You start with a basic annual scheme. Namely, you will place $100 in an account paying 6% simple annual interest. You expect to do this every year for eighteen years. How much will you have at the end of the eighteenth year? Of course, this is much too simplistic. You need to invest more, at more frequent intervals, in a better paying vehicle. We'll get to that. But the fundamental concepts will be the same, so let's do the math with the simplest possible model. Incidentally, I did offer one concession to Mom and Dad's (that is, your) increased sense of urgency. I gave you a better rate of return (6%) than Grandma and Grandpa had in the last chapter.

OK, here comes the math. At the end of the first year, the account is credited with 6% of $100, or $6. Therefore, when Mom and Dad show up at the bank on the first day of the second year, the account balance is $106. When they deposit their second installment of $100, the balance becomes $206. The second year goes by and the bank credits 6% on the balance of $206, namely $\$206 \times 0.06 = \$12.36$, yielding a total balance of $218.36. On the next day, the first day of the third year, Mom and Dad come in and drop off their third installment of $100, boosting the balance to $318.36. And so it goes. Another year evaporates, and it's time for interest to be credited; this time the amount is $\$318.36 \times 0.06 = \$19.1016$. The balance is now pushed up to $337.46 (if we ignore the fractional pennies). We could keep computing, but that would lengthen the number of irrelevant decimal places; instead, let's do something more enlightening.

MAKING "CENTS" OUT OF THE PLAN BY CHOPPING IT INTO CHUNKS

As we did in Chapter 1, we'll redo the analysis in a way that easily generalizes and helps us to see what's going on, while at the same time allowing the math wizards to develop a simple formula for computing the values in general circumstances. The key idea is to separate out the different chunks of money that you deposit in different years. If we think only about the fate of the original $100 deposited on the day the account is opened, well, we know how to compute what that will grow into over the course of the years. Again for simplicity, let's work temporarily with five years instead of eighteen. We know from our discussion in Chapter 1 that the original deposit of $100 will be worth

$$\$100 \times 1.06^5 = \$133.82$$

at the end of five years. But there is other money in the account. The $100 that was deposited at the beginning of the second year is working just as hard for you—it just hasn't had as much time as the original amount to grow. In fact, at the end of the fifth year, it will have been at work only for four years and so will be worth

$$\$100 \times 1.06^4 = \$126.25.$$

Now you see how to compute the value of the deposits that were made at the beginning of Years 3, 4 and 5. Each will have one less year to grow and so will be worth at the end of the five-year period

$$\$100 \times 1.06^3 = \$119.10$$

$$\$100 \times 1.06^2 = \$112.36$$

$$\$100 \times 1.06^1 = \$106.00,$$

respectively. The grand total in the account will be equal to the sum of these five different chunks, namely

$$\$133.82 + \$126.25 + \$119.10 + \$112.36 + \$106 = \$597.53.$$

Let's spell it out again. If you deposit $100 at the beginning of every year for five successive years in an account paying 6% simple annual interest, then the amount in the account at the end of five years will be

$$\$100 \times 1.06^5 + \$100 \times 1.06^4 + \$100 \times 1.06^3 + \$100 \times 1.06^2 + \$100 \times 1.06^1.$$

Now you should be able to see what will happen over the course of any number of years: you will have a sum of as many terms as there are years, and each term will be $100 times 1.06 raised to the powers 1, 2, 3, up to and including the number representing the total number of years. Mathematicians call such a sum a *geometric series*, and they have developed very nice formulas for adding them up. Since we have agreed that the purpose here is not to teach you math but rather to explain the arithmetic concepts underlying the computations you want to do—or more correctly, you want done for you—and then provide you with a tool to do the computations, I will not explain how to derive the formula for the sum of a geometric series. However, if you are brave enough to want to see the algebra:

Check out the Web site. (See "Mathematical Demonstrations and Special Features," *Geometric Series*.)

I will tell you what the formula yields in the case at hand. In fact, it tells you that after *n* years (be patient, we'll turn that nasty letter *n* into the number 18 in a moment), the amount in the account will be

$$\$100 \times 1.06 \times (1.06^n - 1)/.06.$$

Once again, $\$100 \times 1.06 \times (1.06^n - 1)/.06$ represents the total amount in an account paying 6% simple annual interest when equal deposits of $100 are made at the beginning of the year for *n* consecutive years.

OK, let's get that *n* out of there. After eighteen years the account contains

$$\$100 \times 1.06 \times (1.06^{18} - 1)/.06.$$

Your trusty calculator will reveal for you that

$$1.06 \times (1.06^{18} - 1)/.06 = 32.76, \qquad \text{(Formula 2.1)}$$

and so the investment program yields after eighteen years a balance of $\$100 \times 32.76 = \$3,276$. Yet again you see the power of compound interest. Over the years you deposited $100 eighteen times for a total of $1,800, but the account is worth almost double that because the money deposited earned compound interest.

HOW MUCH MONEY MUST THE BELEAGUERED PARENTS DEPOSIT EACH YEAR?

Now we are poised to answer the real question. How much must Mom and Dad deposit annually to have $140,000 at the ready when your brilliant child stands at the portals of Harvard University? There is nothing special about the amount of $100 that we selected for the above illustration. The number that really matters is 32.76 (see Formula 2.1). Presuming we deposit the same amount at the beginning of the year, every year for eighteen years, the value of the account at the end of the eighteen-year period will be the product of 32.76 times the regularly deposited amount. Therefore, to reach the desired $140,000, the amount we have to deposit every year is the amount that multiplied by 32.76 will yield $140,000. The answer is

$$\$140,000/32.76 = \$4,273.50.$$

The number 32.76 is playing the role of a *magic number* analogous to the role the number 2.40662 played in Chapter 1.

If Mom and Dad deposit $4,273.50 every year, then after eighteen years the account will contain $140,000.

Note that over the life of the exercise, Mom and Dad will deposit $4,273.50 eighteen times for a total of

$$\$4{,}273.50 \times 18 = \$76{,}923,$$

a little more than half of the $140,000 that they eventually will amass. For comparison's sake, note that Grandma and Grandpa only had to plunk down $58,172.87. But that full amount had all eighteen years to earn interest, whereas in Mom and Dad's scheme different amounts of money were at work earning interest over mostly shorter periods. And the key point, of course, is that coming up with four grand a year may be a lot easier than producing nearly sixty grand in one fell swoop.

Let's call the method employed by Grandma and Grandpa (in Chapter 1) the *lump sum method*, and let's call Mom and Dad's method described above the *regular deposit method*. We saw that the grandparents forked over a lump sum of $58,172.87, and the parents shelled out $76,923 in regular deposits—both to reach the same future goal of $140,000.

Quick: *What's the difference between the two amounts?* After you get over your surprise at this question, you rapidly realize that the answer will require some arithmetic. Namely, you have to do the subtraction:

$$\$76{,}923 - \$58{,}172.87.$$

Naturally, you reach for your calculator. Ah, but what if the calculator is unavailable, or the batteries are run down, or horrors, you have no immediate access to any electronic or portable device? You know the computation will be painful, and you are liable to get it wrong. After all, there are decimals in there, and borrowing (or is it carrying?) will likely be required. *Puleez!* What should you do? The answer is simple, although unfortunately it's usually only the mutants such as myself, who are comfortable with numbers, who think of it. The answer is: *Estimate*. The bigger number is about $75,000, and the smaller number is about $60,000; therefore, the difference is obviously *about* $15,000. Ninety-five times out of a hundred, that kind of rough figuring will be good enough to satisfy the needs that gave rise to the question that led to the arithmetic problem. Why more people don't think that way is one of the great mysteries of life to me. I suppose one reason is that you weren't taught how to estimate when you were in school, just like you weren't taught all the other useful stuff you are already learning in this great book. Oh, by the way, the difference between \$76,923 and \$58,172.87 is \$18,750.13. My estimate above was so-so, but at least it got me in the ballpark.

As you progress through the book and occasionally want to check an arithmetic calculation with your calculator, try a rough estimate first before plugging in the numbers. That is not a crazy suggestion. I have wide fingers; I often push the wrong key on my calculator or computer by accident without realizing it. To protect against that eventuality, I usually do a rough mental estimate anytime I plug in numbers on my calculator. You should consider doing the same. Why? Well, you may not know without the aid of a calculator that $16 \times 9 = 144$, but if you punch it in on your calculator and out pops the answer 5,432, you should know instinctively that that is the wrong answer. And if your arithmetic instincts are weak or nonexistent, you should still know it's wrong because you estimated: "Well, 16 is about 15, and 9 is about 10, and the product of those two numbers is obviously 150, so 16 times 9 had better be relatively close to 150." This kind of reasoning can be a lifesaver at the checkout counter, or when you balance your checkbook, or when the car salesman has you so befuddled that you can't think straight.

MAGIC NUMBERS AGAIN

Thus far we have developed a relatively simple model for the growth of an account into which regular deposits are made. Naturally, the final values are influenced by the regular amount deposited, the interest rate, and the number of years of investment. The analysis above shows that there will be a formula—involving the interest rate and the number of years—that will give a magic number, which multiplied by the regularly invested amount yields the final value. The formula is

$$(1 + r)\,[(1 + r)^n - 1]/r; \qquad \text{(Formula 2.2)}$$

where n is the number of years and r is the interest rate in decimal form. In the preceding example, r was 0.06 and n was 18.

If you deposit D dollars annually in a simple interest account, then in n years the account will be worth D times the magic number in Formula 2.2.

This is perhaps somewhat surprising—namely, that the principle of a magic number is just as valid for a regular deposit account as it was for a lump sum account. Nonetheless, it is true. The formula for this magic number is a little more complicated than the one in Chapter 1, but that should not concern you. You are not going to remember the formula in either case anyway. As long as you have access to the arithmetic machine on the Web site, you can do the computation. And so you can do whatever comparative analysis you desire in attempting to set up your college investment program. This illustrates the book's fundamental premise and is exactly the kind of financial decision-making you need to do. But nobody taught you why you should do it, much less how you should do it. My goal is to rectify that deficiency in many matters of your financial lives—not just your children's college fund. So read on.

A TABLE OF MAGIC NUMBERS

Table 2.1 gives the magic number for various interest rates and various numbers of years. The entries in the table signify what you have to multiply your regularly saved amount by to arrive at the final total amount accumulated if you invest for the number of years in the column at the interest rate in the row. After glancing through the table, what would you say is more critical: getting a higher interest rate or extending the plan over a greater number of years?

Here are two simple exercises that you can do to test your understanding of the table:

1. If the regular investment amount is $1,000 and the interest rate is 8%, how much will the account be worth in twenty-five years?
2. What would the regular investment amount need to be in order to accumulate $100,000 over ten years if the interest rate is 10%?

Check your answers at the link *Annual Deposit, Simple Annual Interest.*

Table 2.1
Magic numbers (for a simple interest regular annual deposit account) corresponding to a specific number of years at a specified interest rate

	Number of Years				
Interest Rate	**1**	**5**	**10**	**25**	**40**
3%	1.0300	5.4684	11.8078	37.5530	77.6633
5%	1.0500	5.8019	13.2068	50.1135	126.8398
7%	1.0700	6.1533	14.7836	67.6765	213.6096
8%	1.0800	6.3359	15.6455	78.9544	279.7810
10%	1.1000	6.7156	17.5312	108.1818	486.8518

LIFE IS MORE COMPLICATED THAN THAT

All of this is swell. It teaches you how the money in a regular investment program grows, but it depended on several simplifying assumptions. Let's remove those now. In fact, we know that banks normally compound interest daily rather than annually, so let's put that in the mix. Also, Mom and Dad should be able to make deposits more often than annually. Monthly is perhaps most likely, although many people use payroll deductions to implement biweekly or weekly saving—ahem, excuse me—investment programs.

Well, it turns out that although the arithmetic is a little more complicated, the nature of the underlying computation is essentially unchanged. A more complicated geometric series has to be summed. But at the end of the process, we find as before a magic number, which when multiplied by the regular investment amount yields the amount you find in the account at the end of the rainbow.

For any regular deposit investment program there is a magic number, which depends only on the interest rate, the method of compounding, the frequency of deposits, and the number of years, so that the amount accumulated in such a program is the product of the magic number times the regularly deposited amount.

OK, let's do some comparisons and see some real numbers. Table 2.2 gives the magic number and the amount accumulated for a 5% account, compounded daily, for twenty years, when $1,200 is deposited over the course of each year, with the following choices: one $1,200 annual deposit; twelve $100 monthly deposits; twenty-six biweekly deposits of $46.15; or finally, fifty-two weekly deposits of $23.08. Remember that the eventual worth of the account is the product of the magic number and the amount regularly invested. That product appears in the second column of the table.

Table 2.2
Regular deposit account with $1,200 annual deposit, paying 5% compounded daily, for 20 years

Frequency of Deposits	Magic Number	Amount Accumulated
Annual ($1200)	35.2305	$42,276.57
Monthly ($100)	413.2306	$41,323.06
Biweekly ($46.15)	894.3302	$41,273.34
Weekly ($23.08)	1787.8009	$41,262.44

Not surprisingly, we see that the more you deposit up fror [illegible] the final results. The principle is that the longer the money is at w [illegible] ter the compounding and the more favorable the outcome.

In fact, most people when setting up an investment prog [illegible] ot choose to invest forty-six dollars and fifteen pennies on [illegible] s. Working backward from an annual deposit of $1,200, th [illegible] e at the reasonable monthly alternative of $100. But then w [illegible] a biweekly alternative, they likely would keep the num [illegible] choose to put aside $50, and similarly the weekly contri [illegible] likely to be $25 than $23.08. In fact, if you run those nun [illegible] comes are $44,716.51 and $44,695.02, respectively. T [illegible] counterintuitive in that these choices lead to better outc [illegible] either the monthly or annual contributions. The answer [illegible] accounted for by the overall difference, on the one hand [illegible] total deposited via an annual or monthly program and, on th [illegible] the total deposited in a biweekly or weekly program. Namel [illegible] deposit gives you an annual total of $1,200, as does twelve $ [illegible] However, either twenty-six biweekly deposits of $50 or wee [illegible] of $25 add up to $1,300, a $100 bonus. This reflects the fact th [illegible] there are exactly twelve months in a year, there are neit [illegible] twenty-six biweekly periods nor exactly fifty-two weeks in a y [illegible] is an extra day. But, more seriously, there are not exactly tw [illegible] periods in a month or exactly four weeks in a month. The di [illegible] here is more crucial—it can vary anywhere from a day to severa [illegible]

These observations have an important analog for paying bill [illegible] explain. Virtually all of my household bills arrive on a month [illegible] This includes mortgage, utilities, car payments, insurance, cred [illegible] what have you. Others come on a seasonal or annual basis and so [illegible] ily reconciled with a monthly schedule. However, I, like many fo [illegible] paid biweekly. If I allocate two successive biweekly checks to [illegible] month's worth of bills, then I cover my annual expenses with tw [illegible] four biweekly paychecks. This leaves me with two "free" paycheck [illegible] the course of a year. In my family we call these paychecks *freebies*– [illegible] this concept has proven a great boon to our savings/investment [illegible] gram. I can't tell you how many vacations, special events, unexpe [illegible] bills, and investment opportunities have been funded at my house [illegible] those freebies over the years.

BUT YOU FORGOT THAT INTEREST RATES VARY

Continuing the conversation, we must, as we did in Chapter 1, take into account that interest rates fluctuate over the years. Hopefully, I convinced you in

Chapter 1 that if they fluctuate mildly, then the effect on the numbers is minimal. The perceived changes are substantial only when the fluctuations are wide. That is the case with regular investment accounts as well as with lump sum savings accounts. I could try to convince you with some concrete examples, but the numbers will get too complicated, and you are convinced already anyway. A more important point is the following: In the regular investment model, as opposed to the lump sum approach of Chapter 1, you have another serious variable—namely, the amount of the regular deposit. Being human, we sometimes cannot resist the temptation to deposit less than the regular amount. And the opposite does happen occasionally—a windfall, such as the small tax rebates that Uncle Sam distributed in the summers of 2001 and 2003, allows folks to deposit larger than normal amounts in their regular investment accounts. What is the effect of variable deposits?

As you might expect, it depends on the size of the variance. Small changes from the regularly deposited amount, especially if some are up and some are down, will have relatively little effect on the final value. Large changes, or many changes in the same direction, will have a greater effect. For illustrative purposes, Table 2.3 demonstrates these facts. The model is a five-year program with annual deposits of $500 and a simple interest rate of 5%. We'll allow for changes only in the second and third years. If you consult the table, you see that the numbers reinforce the statements made above. Namely, the $100 fluctuations result in at most a $5–6 variance, but the $500 fluctuations cause a distortion five to six times that magnitude.

The last point you may wish to raise is that people usually don't select one pure lump sum or one pure regular deposit model—typically, people combine the methods. That is, they start an investment program or account with some initial amount, and then at some point—maybe down the road a bit—institute a regular investment program on top of it. What kind of arithmetic model results? The answer is self-evident. Namely, compute the amount that the initial investment grows into using the magic numbers in Chapter 1, and separately

Table 2.3
Fluctuations in a regular deposit program

Contributions in Year					Total Accumulations
1	2	3	4	5	
$500	$500	$500	$500	$500	$2,900.96
$500	$400	$600	$500	$500	$2,895.17
$500	$600	$400	$500	$500	$2,906.75
$500	—	$1,000	$500	$500	$2,872.02
$500	$1,000	—	$500	$500	$2,929.90

Table 2.4
Combined lump-sum/regular deposit account

Initial Lump-Sum Amount	Regular Annual Deposit	Total Accumulations
$25,000	0	$215,577
$20,000	$200	$190,926
$15,000	$400	$166,276
$10,000	$600	$141,625
$ 5,000	$800	$116,975
0	$1,000	$ 92,324

compute the amount the regular deposits yield from their own magic number (developed in this chapter). Then just add the two amounts.

Again for illustrative purposes, Table 2.4 results from a combined program, with different initial amounts and different regular annual deposits, but with an assumption of 9% simple interest (it's an offshore account) and a twenty-five-year time frame. Note that the total dollar investment in each case is exactly $25,000.

The table reinforces the self-evident fact that the more you put in up front, the better your final results. It also highlights the following:

More up-front contributions help you to cope with another favorite bank trick. Namely, many accounts are advertised at an attractive rate of return, but only in small print is it mentioned that there are minimum deposits required to secure that rate. Amounts below that minimum only earn interest at some (perhaps substantially) lower rate. Watch out for that!

YOUR NEW COMPUTATIONAL SKILL

How to compute the value of an account into which has been deposited a specific sum of money at specified regular intervals for a specific number of years that has been earning interest at a specific rate, compounded at a specific frequency.

CHAPTER 3

Taking into Consideration Taxes and Inflation

Everyone has had the following experience: You head out to buy something that you have purchased previously. You have a good idea what the cost will be because you recall what you paid the last time or because you saw an ad for the item not long ago. But when you find it, you are surprised to see that it costs a few pennies, or a few dollars, or—if it's a big-ticket item—a few hundred or thousand dollars more than you anticipated. A wonderfully descriptive term to describe your surprise was invented about twenty years ago when the prices of automobiles skyrocketed in a relatively short period of time: *sticker shock*. The car showrooms of America were full of customers staring, with dropped jaws and unbelieving eyes, at the price stickers on the windows of new cars. An important contributing cause was the extremely high inflation rate that the United States experienced in the late 1970s.

Inflation. What is it? Why does it happen? What effect does it have on our personal finances? How do we cope with it?

Economists and politicians have debated the answers to those questions for generations. I am certain that debate will continue in a lively fashion long after I have stopped collecting royalties for this book. My opinion or yours will have little effect on the outcome. Therefore, my purpose here, after a few more words of explanation, is merely to examine how inflation impacts the numbers we worked out in the last two chapters. You will not like it, but as they say, "Forewarned is forearmed!" If you recognize that inflation is an unavoidable feature of the financial landscape, and if you have some reasonable idea of how it works and what it will do to your financial schemes, then you will be better prepared to overcome its negative effects. You may even come to see it as an ally in certain aspects of your financial planning.

Inflation is the (usually) slow but inexorable increase in the prices of goods and services.

That's what it is. I will not even attempt to offer any concrete reasons for why it happens. After all, as you know, I am not an economist. Besides, there are varying opinions on the cause of inflation. More importantly, why inflation happens doesn't matter for our purposes. It happens! Let's deal with it.

MEASURING INFLATION

The government has invented many statistics to measure inflation, referred to as *cost-of-living* indicators. Usually they are cited in terms of average annual percentages. The talking head on your network news station will blurt out a statement such as, "The Government announced today that the cost of living increased by 3.2% last year." This represents an *average* of the change in price of a sweeping basket of goods and services. It does not mean that gasoline prices are 3.2% higher today than they were 365 days ago; they might be even higher. It does not mean that television sets, or hotel rooms, or the cost to rent a truck for a day is 3.2% higher than it was last year; some of those costs might actually be lower. It means that, *on average*, the prices of goods and services in America are 3.2% higher than they were a year ago. Incidentally, having worked through the last two chapters, you know how to compute the current price of an item that went up by 3.2%—namely, you multiply last year's price by 1.032.

The immediate effect that inflation has on your personal finances is rather clear. Things cost more. You need more money than you did earlier to buy the same item. If your net salary hasn't increased by at least 3.2% during the year, then a severe consequence is that you cannot buy, during the coming year, everything that you bought in the course of the last year. Said otherwise: your *standard of living* has gone down. Not a pleasant thought. That prospect is the underlying reason workers, union negotiators, indeed all of us try mightily to ensure salary increases that are at least as large as the rate of inflation.

We'll have more to say about salaries in Chapter 5. For now, let us concentrate on how inflation affects the computations that we discussed in the first two chapters. So, baby is back in the crib again, and Mom and Dad are once again confronted by the fact that, *in today's dollars*, their child's college education will cost them $140,000 in eighteen years. They know how to get the dough, either using the lump sum method in Chapter 1 or the regular deposit method in Chapter 2, or maybe some combination of the two. The problem is that in eighteen years, the cost of that college education will have escalated due to inflation.

INFLATION, DEFLATION, AND HYPERINFLATION

It's time to start building a model. I shall assume 3% as the inflation rate, which is a pretty good approximation to the actual rate in recent years. There have been times in the past when the rate has been sharply higher (which is discussed later in this chapter). Unfortunately, there also have been times when it has been sharply lower, that is, when the rate has been negative. That situation, a continuing decrease in the prices of goods and services, is called *deflation*. It is not a good thing, as the citizens of Japan have been learning recently. The continually falling value of real estate, of established businesses, of goods and commodities shakes the populace's confidence and its faith in the society. All the experts agree: if America never again experiences deflation (as it did during the Great Depression), it would be a blessing. Sharply higher inflation is an even more insidious possibility. The citizens of Germany in the 1920s can testify to that. Along with other causes, severe inflation led them to make choices that the world will regret forever. By implication, therefore, a modest amount of inflation, such as 3%, is a desirable state of affairs. One reason for that is psychological: a steady (even if not steep) increase in salaries, which will follow as a natural consequence of a modest inflation rate, is extremely important to the morale of the workforce. Another reason is that inflation leads to a greater readiness to borrow—by consumers to buy houses and by businesses to develop products. A steady diet of modest inflation means that the dollars one uses to pay back loans are worth less and less, thereby making loans seem more affordable. That is definitely good for our economy.

THE EFFECT OF INFLATION ON YOUR COLLEGE FUND

OK, let's get back to the matter at hand. The baby's diaper is getting wet waiting for me to explain how inflation jeopardizes Mom and Dad's plans to accumulate the money for the little genius's education. You thought you had to come up with $140,000. But now that we have accepted inflation as a fact of life, we know that the $140,000 that it costs to finance a four-year Harvard education today will not be enough eighteen years from now. As I said, we'll take 3% as the inflation factor. And let's assume that the inflation in the cost of higher education follows that rate—a highly dubious assumption that I will comment on below. By now you should see that the rise in the cost of the Harvard education will work exactly like a 3% simple annual interest bank account. Indeed, the cost next year will be 3% higher than this year, which I can compute by multiplying $140,000 by 1.03,

$$\$140{,}000 \times 1.03 = \$144{,}200.$$

Then the second year, I can calculate the cost by multiplying the above amount by 1.03, that is,

$$\$144{,}200 \times 1.03 = \$148{,}526.$$

And so on. We've been down this path. Indeed, I can't resist my mathematician's impulse to throw in a formula: after n years, the cost of the Harvard education will be

$$\$140{,}000 \times 1.03^{n}.$$

Thus in eighteen years, the bursar at our esteemed Ivy League institution will bill Mom and Dad for

$$\$140{,}000 \times 1.03^{18} = \$140{,}000 \times 1.70243 = \$238{,}341.$$

What? $238,341! You are having a bad case of sticker shock. The cost of the education eighteen years hence will be 70% greater than it is today. You might have guessed that since $18 \times 3 = 54$, it would only be 54% greater. But just as compounding can be your friend, so can it be your enemy. The point is that 1.03 raised to the eighteenth power is (approximately) 1.70, not 1.54.

COPING WITH INFLATION

Oh well, it is what it is. Let's recompute the money needed to reach the desired plateau, both in the lump sum method and also the regular deposit method. In Chapter 1, we saw that if Grandma and Grandpa plunked down $58,172.87 as a lump sum in a simple interest account paying 5%, it would grow into $140,000 in eighteen years time. And in Chapter 2, we saw that if Mom and Dad invested $4,273.50 annually in the same kind of account, that too would yield the desired result. But now we know that inflation has increased the target amount from $140,000 to $238,341, a 70% increase. How can the higher target be hit? There are two tactics that can be employed: either increase the amounts contributed, or find a higher return on the investment, or perhaps some combination of both. Let's explore higher contributions first. In the lump sum method you would expect that Grandma and Grandpa will have to part with 70% more of their life savings, and you would be right. In fact,

$$\$58{,}172.87 \times 1.70243 = \$99{,}035.24.$$

Moreover, the magic number for Grandma and Grandpa is 2.40662. So we compute

$$\$99{,}035.34 \times 2.40662 = \$238{,}340.$$

Some of you are probably jumping up and down, exclaiming, "Ah, Lipsman, you dirty dog, I got you. There is a one-dollar discrepancy between the amount that is needed and what the computations revealed." Calm down, it's because of *round-off error.* Many of the numbers I have been multiplying involve long decimals. Naturally, I have not reported all the decimals—I have rounded off the answers in several places. After doing that a few times, the round offs can accumulate and cause minor inaccuracies. Tell me, when it comes to a quarter of a million dollars, are you so concerned with a measly one dollar?

Next, let's consider how the shortfall might be made up by finding a better rate of return, instead of by increasing the contributed amount. What is the necessary better rate of return? The answer seems obvious. You are getting 5% from the bank. Inflation is pushing up the target by 3%. You might guess that if you could get 8%, that would fill the bill (pun unintended). In fact, that is not quite correct. The reason has to do with the math, which basically says that it is not $0.05 + 0.03$ that determines the makeup amount, but really $1.05 \times 1.03 = 1.0815$.

For the algebra, see *Coping with Inflation* under "Mathematical Demonstrations and Special Features."

It is tempting to round off the latter number to 1.08, but if we use 8% for our computation, the math predicts that we will come up a little short. Let's see. The magic number for Grandma and Grandpa on an eighteen-year 8% simple interest account is

$$1.08^{18} = 3.99602.$$

And indeed,

$$\$58{,}172.87 \times 3.99602 = \$232{,}459.95.$$

I told you it would come up short. But maybe you expected to not be nearly $6,000 short. Hmm. Now let's see what happens if we run the numbers using an interest rate of 8.15%. Then

$$1.0815^{18} = 4.09711,$$

and

$$\$58{,}172.87 \times 4.09711 = \$238{,}340.65.$$

Right on the money (pun intended). Well, in the spirit of the above remark, when a quarter million dollars is at stake, we are content to ignore a dollar. But I am not sure that six thousand can be ignored so safely.

To summarize: A yearly 3% inflation rate means that the price for a four-year Harvard education will escalate from $140,000 today to $238,341 in eighteen years. In the lump sum method (using a 5% simple annual interest account), the amount required to generate that sum in eighteen years jumps from $58,172.87 to $99,035.34, a 70% increase. Alternatively, if the first figure—that is, $58,172.87—is all that is available to invest, then the return on the account must be increased to 8.15% to compensate.

REFLECTIONS ON INFLATION

Before we examine the unfortunate consequences that inflation imposes on the regular deposit method, let's make a few more observations and then indulge in some personal reflections concerned with the effects of inflation.

- Here's a bit of bad news. The cost of a college education has been rising during the last decade at a rate considerably in excess of the cost of living. Sometimes it has been as high as 6% or more, even when inflation remained down near 3%. The reason is not any more complicated than *supply and demand*, augmented by government subsidies. More and more people want a college education, and they and their families are willing to pay big bucks to get it. Also, the government has created many programs, loans, and tax credits to subsidize higher education, with the predicted effect on the price. But my primary purpose is not to explain the reason for inflation, but rather to figure out its cost and how to deal with it. I will prognosticate, however, that in our passage from an industrial age economy to an information age economy the demand for higher education is unlikely to decrease.
- In looking at the two alternatives described above for dealing with increased costs due to inflation, surely you prefer the second. Anyone would rather find a way to increase the rate of return rather than fork over more dough. The problem is that in order to secure a higher rate of return, you must take a commensurate increased risk. You won't find those increased rates of return in bank accounts—bank rates typically do not beat inflation rates by more than 2–3%, if that. You are going to have to explore riskier alternatives, such as stocks, real estate, limited partnerships, or other investment vehicles that we will discuss in Part III of this book.
- A hundred grand is a hefty sum to set aside for a single purpose, even if a worthwhile purpose such as a college education. And note that it is getting close to the amount you would need for the education today ($140,000). Most people don't have that kind of money lying around. Maybe the regular deposit model will offer some relief. In a moment we'll see how badly the annual four grand requirement is affected by inflation. But first:

Recalling Einstein's maxim that compound interest is one of the most potent forces in the universe, we can see now why inflation, which is nothing more than a form of compound interest, can, over a long period, dramatically increase the cost of goods and services. Here are two illustrations.

I am one of those guys who buys new cars and runs them into the ground. In my working life (a span of more than thirty-five years), I have only owned four cars. True, I've bought plenty of cars for my boys—especially during their teen years when they were smacking them up faster than I could buy them. Also, my wife has bought a few automobiles for which she has been the primary driver. But I have commuted to work in basically four vehicles in my life:

1. 1967 Dodge Dart
2. 1976 Toyota Corolla
3. 1987 Honda Accord
4. 1999 Lexus ES300

I bought them all new and kept them respectively twenty, thirteen, twelve, and *x* years (I am still driving the Lexus, of course). My eldest son, who was nearly born in the Dart, drove it for the last four years that I owned it. The amounts that I paid for those cars were:

1. $ 2,400
2. $ 3,500
3. $14,200
4. $31,000,

respectively. How about that for an illustration of inflation! Note that the so-called bad inflation of the early 1970s was not nearly as bad as the inflation of the late 1970s/early 1980s. (Richard Nixon dealt with the former by imposing wage and price controls—one of America's few flirtations with blatant socialism. Of course, it did not work. Jimmy Carter responded to the latter by declaring that America was suffering from "malaise." He was more successful in that his ineptitude led directly to the election of Ronald Reagan, whose tax-cutting policies of the early 1980s are still having a beneficial effect on our economy.) Inflation was under control in the 1990s. But obviously my taste in cars escalated more than did the rate of inflation.

My next story concerns the fear that inflation can generate. When I came to work at the University of Maryland (in 1969), the State of Maryland had in place a fantastic defined benefit retirement plan. I made modest contributions from every paycheck, and the state agreed to pay me an annual retirement benefit that was computed solely (and not ungenerously) on the basis of the number of years I worked and my three highest years of salary. The topping on the package was that it included an unlimited cost-of-living escalator—the state agreed to increase the benefit annually by an amount pegged to the U.S. government's cost-of-living numbers. Well, during the hyperinflation of the late 1970s, state officials suddenly realized that a program such as that could break the state's coffers. They weren't about to let that happen. So, of course, they passed a new law reducing the benefits unless employees agreed to substantially increase their contributions. There were various irrevocable choices that employees had to make, including one that kept the unlimited cost-of-living benefit but compensated for it by a dramatically increased contribution; a second choice imposed a 5% cap on the cost-of-living escalator in return for which no increased contributions were required.

At that time, as I watched the country's reaction to high inflation, I decided to bet that the population would not stand for long periods of high inflation and that Americans would make the political and economic choices necessary to rein it in. I chose the 5% cap. At this point in time, I look like a genius. Inflation has been under control, and I have had extra money in the last twenty years to invest because I did not increase my contributions. However, I am not retired yet; I will look like an idiot if my retirement happens to coincide with a sudden period of sustained high inflation in the country. We'll see. My point is that the perception and fear of inflation, as much as the raw numbers manifested by the inflation itself, governed the actions of the legislators who changed the law.

Now let's return to the effects of inflation on our plans for building a college fund, this time concentrating on the regular deposit method. In Chapter 2, we saw that Mom and Dad had to invest $4,273.50 annually in a 5% (simple interest) account to amass $140,000 in eighteen years. But they now know that inflation causes them to need $238,341. Recalling that the magic number for this kind of account (see Chapter 2) is 32.76, we compute that the amount required is

$$\$238{,}341/32.76 = \$7{,}275.37,$$

a rather hefty increase over the original figure of $4,273.50—indeed an increase of, what else, 70%. I will omit the analysis of what return Mom and Dad would need to earn if they can't afford to contribute any more than the original amount. You can be sure that it is in the neighborhood of 8%, but the same comments as made above about the difficulties and risks involved in seeking higher yields remain true.

Have you ever seen those ads touting long-term savings plans? For example, "put $10,000 in an account and it will grow to more than a *half-million*

dollars in forty years." Indeed, it is not a lie. If you consult Table 1.3, you will see that the forty-year magic number for a 10% (daily compounded) lump sum account is 54.5682. So $10,000 deposited into such an account will grow to $545,682 in the course of forty years. Of course, what they are failing to mention is *inflation.* (They are also forgetting taxes, but we'll get to that momentarily.) At the same time that your money is growing, inflation is eating away at it. Remember that the spread between the inflation rate and typical rates of return on safe investments is rarely more than 2–3%. Yes, the $20,000 you stash away today could be worth $1 million in the year 2040, but it's likely that if you have earned 10% consistently over that period (in a conservative investment vehicle), then inflation has probably averaged at least 7% in that time—meaning that in 2040, it will cost approximately $15 for a dozen eggs, $7,500 to fly across country, and a cool $450,000 to buy the equivalent of my Lexus. So don't be overly impressed by those ads. Compound interest—in the form of investment return, and in the form of inflation—is a two-edged sword. I'm not saying you should not invest for the long term. Absolutely you should. However, you need to know all the variables.

INFLATION BY THE NUMBERS

Next let's give a table that indicates escalation of prices due to inflation for several items that have been mentioned. In Table 3.1, we will vary the inflation rate but keep the eighteen-year time frame. If you want to try out different inflation rates, different commodities, and/or different time frames, then:

Check out the Web site. (Try the *Inflation Calculator.*)

A glance at the right two columns in Table 3.1 reveals the devastating effect of *double-digit inflation.* The figures in this table help to reinforce my assertion that

Table 3.1
Price rises in eighteen years caused by inflation

		Inflation Rate					
Item	**Today's Price**	**2%**	**3%**	**5%**	**8%**	**10%**	**15%**
Dozen eggs	**$1**	$1.43	$1.70	$2.41	$4.00	$5.56	$12.38
Plane ticket	**$500**	$714.12	$851.22	$1,203.31	$1,998.01	$2,779.96	$6,187.73
Lexus ES300	**$30,000**	$42,847	$51,073	$72,199	$119,881	$166,798	$371,264
College education	**$140,000**	$199,954	$238,341	$336,927	$559,443	$778,388	$1,732,564
Annual U.S. budget	**$2.0 trillion**	$2.86 trillion	$3.40 trillion	$4.81 trillion	$7.99 trillion	$11.12 trillion	$24.75 trillion

America will make whatever political choices it must to forestall any such eventuality.

WHY DO THEY CALL THEM *INCOME* TAXES WHEN IT'S ALL ABOUT *OUTGO*?

Now we turn our attention to taxes, like inflation an unavoidable force that affects your investment program, indeed your overall financial well-being. I shall focus on *income taxes*. Oh, there is no shortage of other taxes that have an impact on your standard of living. These include, but are not limited to, sales tax, real estate tax, personal property and excise taxes, transfer taxes (on the sale of homes), Social Security tax, Medicare tax, tobacco taxes, phone and other communication taxes, estate tax (or as it is infamously known, the "death tax"), capital gains tax, breathing tax. Huh? Just kidding on the last one, although I imagine if some loony politician proposed such a tax, it would instantly have its supporters. Anyway, the primary tax we are concerned with here is the income tax, in its federal, state, and local incarnations. All of them will siphon off some portion of the returns on your investments, unless you are astute enough to shelter the proceeds of your investments in tax-deferred vehicles. We will talk about that in the next chapter. For now, let's assume that whatever investment program you have, it generates income that is subject to the full range of income taxes.

VENTING MY SPLEEN ON INCOME TAXES

Of course the net effect of income taxes is that they reduce your rate of return. By how much? The answer depends on your *marginal tax rate*. In our society, income taxes are *progressive*, meaning that the more you make, the higher the percentage you pay in income tax. The rate of progression varies from state to state and municipality to municipality. Many states have fairly flat tax structures, some with substantial deductions and exemptions, others with much fewer. The tax structure that all of us pay the closest attention to, however, is the federal income tax—administered by the dreaded IRS, the Internal Revenue Service. The federal tax code, constituting the totality of laws passed by Congress that establish the rules and regulations by which the IRS administers the federal income tax, must be one of the most fiendish documents ever created by the human mind. It is ridiculously long, incredibly complicated, shot through with explicit and implicit contradictions, almost impossible to interpret in a consistent manner, changed far too often by its masters in the halls of Congress, and designed not only to fund the U.S. government but also to engineer myriad social, cultural, and political behavioral responses by the American people. The most favorable view of the monstrosity that the tax code has become is that it is a necessary evil, largely complied with by people and businesses, that provides to the government the money necessary to fund the many programs and services that the people demand of their government. A less charitable point of view would assert that the tax code and the IRS are coercive instruments that unjustly confiscate the wealth of American citizens in order to redistribute it according to the whimsical, often unproductive, and sometimes downright sinister motives of the lawyers who dominate the government. Whatever your view, you have three choices: cough up (the choice made by most, not that payroll withholding leaves you much of an option), emigrate, or resist (but be prepared for the consequences, such as fines and prison). I think coughing up is the only sensible choice, but you should do it with a clear view of what is transpiring and always with the hope that the beast might someday be tamed. Many sensible proposals have been made to simplify and streamline the tax code. But any one of them would require a retreat on the part of the government from the increasingly invasive, coercive, and pervasive role that it came to play in the lives of the American people during the course of the twentieth century—a role that continues in the twenty-first century. Simplifying and streamlining the tax code would require a massive sea change in attitude on the part of the body politic. I am not holding my breath.

INCOME TAX BRACKETS

Now that the polemics are out of the way, what about the numbers? Let's keep the analysis focused on two hypothetical models: a low-income tax bracket and a high-income tax bracket. For the former, let us assume that a low-income individual has a marginal federal tax bracket of 15%, and a local (state plus municipality) tax bracket of 5%. State taxes are deductible on federal income tax returns, but only if you itemize, and the low-income individual probably does not qualify. So I'll take 20% as the marginal tax bracket for a low-income individual. That does not mean that this person is paying 20% in tax on all his earnings. Remember, the income tax is progressive. In particular, up to a point, no federal income tax is due on income. That amount has gone up sharply in recent years so that a surprising number of low-income individuals and families incur no federal income tax. (They are probably paying Social Security and Medicare tax on virtually all of their income, but that is another story that I will delay until Chapter 5.) Moreover, Congress introduced a 10% federal tax bracket in 2001 but kept the band to which it applies quite narrow. For a married couple with two children, the 15% federal tax liability begins when taxable income reaches approximately $35,000 per year. Above that, and that is where we'll assume our hypothetical low-income wage-earner falls, every dollar of income—which is what Uncle Sam considers your return on your investments (including bank accounts) to be—is taxed by the feds at 15%. That is your (federal) marginal tax rate. Tacking on 5% for local income tax, we arrive at an overall marginal tax rate of 20%.

In our progressive system, as income rises there are a series of thresholds, and as you pass through them the percentage of income tax you incur climbs. The top rate was lowered in the 2001 tax legislation. There are some nuances (such as exemption phase-outs), but basically the top rate is approximately 33% (or will be when the legislation takes full effect). For our married taxpayer with two children, it kicks in somewhere in the neighborhood of $300,000. Now let's postulate a state (and municipal) tax that may be as much as 7%, even if you account for the fact that state taxes are offset to some extent by federal itemized deductions. Therefore, we shall take 40% as the marginal tax rate of our hypothetical high-income taxpayer.

The bottom line is that the low-income person gets to keep only 80¢ of every dollar earned in an investment program, while the high-income person is assaulted more aggressively, keeping only 60¢ of every dollar earned.

If your marginal income tax rate is x%, then to compute the true, or after-tax, rate of return on an investment paying y%,

$$\text{multiply } y \text{ by } (1 - x/100).$$

For example, if your marginal tax rate is 25%, then the true rate of return on an investment paying 8% is

$$8 \times (1 - 25/100)$$
$$= 8 \times (1 - 1/4)$$
$$= 8 \times 3/4$$
$$= 6,$$

that is, 6%.

Whether a person is rich or poor, income taxes definitely put a crimp in one's investment program. The effect of taxes on investment income is particularly pernicious when viewed in the context of the drubbing you are already taking because of inflation. For example, let us assume you are a cautious investor who is earning a 5% rate of return. If inflation is running at the modest rate of 3%, then your effective return is only 2%. But now suppose you are a hard-working bloke paying 20¢ of every dollar generated by your investments to the tax man. Then your 5% return is reduced by one-fifth, that is, to 4%. And so when coupled with 3% inflation, you are marching ahead to the grand tune of 1%. Those numbers can be very discouraging, but do not despair—we'll discuss better investment options in later chapters.

Of course, it is even worse for the "rich" gal. She is paying 40¢ of every dollar her investment returns to the tax man, so her net return is reduced by two-fifths, that is, to 3%. Now coupled with 3% inflation, you see that she is doing no more than treading water. Her effective annual yield is nada, a big goose egg. Is it any wonder that the "wealthy" in America seek to compensate for this awful state of affairs by risking their wealth in more aggressive investment vehicles; by lobbying Congress to create bizarre loopholes through which they can legally avoid what they view as confiscatory tax laws; or even worse, by surrendering to baser instincts and employing illegal schemes to "cheat" the tax man?

The double dagger of inflation plus income taxes poses serious difficulties for the investor. Actually, I consider taxes more lethal than inflation. If you view your investment program as the exercise of trying to hit a target in the distance, then inflation has the effect of moving the target back, but taxation is damaging the gun with which you are shooting. You may be talented and wise enough to hit the target, even if someone is moving it further away, but your chances of doing so will be severely impaired if the government limits the firepower of your weapon.

TAXES BY THE NUMBERS

Having slipped back into polemics again, let's crawl out and get back to numbers—it's table time. Let's take our cue from Table 1.4—the number of years it takes to double your money at different rates of return. Assume you put $10,000 in a simple interest investment. (See, I'm using the word "investment," even if the investment is no more than a bank account.) Let's see how many years it takes to not simply double your money, but for the money to grow to the point where you could, in the future, buy some stuff that will be worth the equivalent of $20,000 in today's dollars. A shorthand way of saying that would be: How long does it take for your money to double, inflation-adjusted? Allow for a steady 3% inflation rate, and let's deal with our low-income taxpayer first. If you consult Table 1.4, you see that, ignoring taxes and inflation, it took 23.1 years for the individual who relied on a 3% return to double a lump sum $10,000 investment. But if he is paying income tax, he only nets 80% of the 3% return, that is, $0.8 \times 0.03 = 0.024$, or 2.4%. But the inflation-adjusted amount he needs to amass is growing at a 3% rate. Not only is he never going to get to the target, he will actually fall further and further behind every year in that the inflation-adjusted worth of the account is actually declining by 0.6%. Because of the tax man, he needs a return of 3.75%, 80% of which is exactly 3%, just to stay even. In order to move ahead at an inflation-adjusted 3% rate, he needs a return of 7.5%, because 80% of that is exactly 6%, from which inflation skims off its 3%, leaving a true profit of 3%. The situation is worse for the high-income taxpayer. For her, the break-even point is 5%. And to move ahead at an inflation-adjusted

3% rate, she needs a return of 10%, because 60% of that is exactly 6%, which as we saw above is the amount she needs to garner a true profit of 3%.

OK, here comes a new table. Table 3.2 gives the number of years for your investment to double in inflation-adjusted dollars, depending on the rate of return and the tax bracket

I don't want you to take away the wrong message from this chapter. The numbers in Tables 3.1 and 3.2 certainly show that inflation and income taxes are not helpful in your efforts to grow your investments. As the years go by, inflation keeps increasing the target amounts you are aiming at, and taxes diminish the net return you receive on your investments. It is easy to become discouraged, but please try to avoid doing that. There are many things you can do to compensate. For example, you can consider investments that will supply better returns than bank accounts. We will discuss some of these in Part III of the book. Next, there are many investment vehicles that are *tax-deferred*, meaning that some or all of the income taxes that you normally incur do not apply to these investments. We will discuss some of those in the next chapter. Finally, it has been my experience that the raw data on inflation sometimes overstates its influence and is misleading in terms of its true effects. This is so for several reasons. First, many economists believe that the numbers the government supplies for the increase in the cost of living are inflated (no pun intended)—maybe by as much as a full 1%. Second, you must keep in mind that salaries are increasing, hopefully at a rate that at least matches inflation, and so if you are following a regular deposit model rather than a lump sum one, you will be able to increase the amount of your regular deposits relatively painlessly. Third, as mentioned previously, the loans you are paying off have fixed payment schedules, and so the amounts *seem* smaller as the years go by, again diminishing the pain of inflation. Finally, I certainly hope that you are succeeding in your career and that you are earning promotions and other advancements in your professional station. These will engender raises beyond normal cost-of-living adjustments (COLA as they are known). Such raises will afford you the opportunity to contribute substantially more to your investment programs and retirement plans, and thereby help to mitigate the

Table 3.2
Doubling your money, inflation-adjusted

Simple Interest Rate	Number of Years, No Tax Paid	Number of Years, 20% Tax Bracket	Number of Years, 40% Tax Bracket
4%	71.7	357.3	—
5%	36.0	71.7	—
7%	18.2	27.8	59.8
8%	14.6	21.3	40.0
10%	10.5	14.6	24.1

negative effects of taxes and inflation. Remember the famous Chinese proverb, "Even a thousand-mile journey begins with a single step."

Even if you start small, you must start somewhere—make sure that your household budget allows room for contributions to investment accounts and retirement programs. They will be critical for your financial health and family's well-being as the years go by.

YOUR NEW COMPUTATIONAL SKILLS

How to compute the precise future cost of an item knowing its current price and the projected rate of inflation, and how to compute the effect of income taxes on your rate of return on an investment using your marginal tax rate.

CHAPTER 4

How Tax-Deferred Accounts Can Help

We saw in Chapter 3 how the government, through the imposition of income taxes, impedes the progress of your investments. "That was a nasty crack," some of you might say. "Without those revenues," you would continue, "the government would not be able to fund the tremendous variety of social, health, defense, and many other types of programs on which we have come to rely." And you would be right.

USING THE TAX CODE TO INFLUENCE YOUR BEHAVIOR

But what the government taketh away, it also returns—albeit in a targeted fashion. There are many social goals favored by the populace. Those goals are fostered by the programs created by the legislators whom people elect to represent them. A favorite method of those legislators is to structure the tax code so as to encourage citizens to "invest" in those programs. One of the simplest such examples is the extremely popular income tax deduction allowing taxpayers to deduct interest payments on home mortgages, thereby encouraging the purchase of homes. Indeed, in its quest to teach us how to best structure our lives, the government has infused the tax code with deductions, exemptions, credits, and deferments—all intended to influence the decisions we make in organizing our lives. And they succeed! I will contribute to that success in this chapter as I concentrate on tax-deferred investment vehicles, which can ameliorate some of the negative effects that income taxes have on your investment returns.

TAX-DEFERRED ACCOUNTS

I will discuss deductions, exemptions, and tax credits in Chapter 5. Here let us focus on deferments. The principle of tax-deferred money is quite simple. As I have said, the interest or dividends that you receive on your various investments are considered to be income, and you must declare them as such on the income tax forms you file—that is, unless the accounts in which the investments reside qualify for tax-deferred status. The government says that because of some social objective it seeks to foster, the income tax due on certain kinds of accounts may be *deferred* to a later time. The most common kind of tax-deferred account is a retirement account. These come in many flavors: IRA, 401(k), 403(b), Keogh, SEP IRA, and others. My intention is not to explain and compare the litany of tax-deferred retirement opportunities that are available to taxpayers. I will leave it to you to explore the mechanics of these accounts with your employer, your accountant (if you have one), your brother-in-law (if you trust him), or the Internet (if you are so inclined). I will explain only the fundamental tax implications common to all of them and the resultant effect on your rate of return from your investments.

There are other kinds of tax-deferred accounts beside retirement accounts. These include education, child care, health care, dependent care, and others. In each instance, the government is attempting to foster some social good by using the tax code to induce you to steer your money toward the desired type of account. In every instance, the interest/dividends you receive from the money in the account is not subject to income tax until a later date. In retirement accounts, that later date will be pegged to your retirement and/or your age. In an education account, it will be when you use the money for educational expenses. You get the idea. But there is an even more beneficial aspect of these accounts. Namely, the original investment itself, that is, the money that you place in the account, is treated as tax-deferred. Most often that money comes from payroll deductions on your salary. The net effect is that the amount that goes into the account does not count as part of your salary when computing your income taxes at the end of the year. But even if you get the money from your mattress, the amount placed in the tax-deferred account is considered (temporarily) exempt from tax. That means you can subtract it from your taxable income when you prepare your income tax return at the end of the year.

Both the contributions of principal and the interest/dividends they earn in tax-deferred accounts can be subtracted from income when computing income tax.

The catch, of course, is that when you finally spend the tax-deferred money for the intended purpose (in retirement, to pay for college, whatever), you must declare it as income at that time—whether you spend principal or interest does not matter. That is why it is called tax-deferred, not tax-exempt. You still have to pay tax on the money, both on the original principal and on the interest earned; you just get to defer the payment to a later time. Why is this beneficial? Here are several reasons that are usually cited:

- First, you have more money in your hands now to invest or spend. If you invest wisely, you will see, as later tables in this chapter will reveal, that even after you pay the eventual tax, you come out ahead of the alternative—that is, paying the tax now.
- You may be in a lower marginal tax bracket later when you pay the bill. This is especially true of retirement accounts.
- The tax laws may—ha, almost certainly will—change between now and when you incur the tax. It's better to get your money while you can.

But nothing is ever cut and dried when it comes to Uncle Sam's tax code. There are some potential downsides to tax-deferred accounts as well:

- As I said, the tax laws *might* change in the future. Heavens to Betsy, lawmakers could even increase taxes, causing you to a pay a higher rate on the deferred income.
- When you do eventually pay the tax, it will be at your marginal income tax rate. That rate could be unfavorable compared to the capital gains tax rate for which some of your investments in the tax-deferred account might qualify.
- Finally, the sheer number and complexity of the tax-deferred accounts that individuals and couples now maintain is so vast that figuring out what you owe at the appointed hour will be a nightmare for all but accountants. There are Roth IRAs, and regular IRAs, and nondeductible IRAs, and so on—even worse, if you die with these accounts undepleted, knowing what to do with them may be impossible for your descendants who inherit your money and your debts.

In light of the above give-and-take, should you put money in tax-deferred accounts, and how aggressively?

Experts agree: You definitely should invest your money in tax-deferred accounts, and you should put as much into them as you can spare. The tables we present later will justify that assertion.

You should do more than put your money in tax-deferred accounts; you should welcome into those accounts any money that is offered to you by your employer. Many retirement plans include employer contributions or matches. Some employers will match, dollar-for-dollar, every cent that you invest in the company-sponsored retirement plan—usually a 401(k). By all means you should take maximum advantage of that opportunity. It is not only free money, but both it and the interest it earns are completely tax-free—ah, excuse me, tax-deferred—until your retirement. Such bonuses are hard to come by, and if one is in your path, you should not hesitate to scoop up as much as you can.

COMPARING TAX-DEFERRED AND TAXABLE INVESTMENTS

It's time finally to look at some numbers. In Table 4.1, we document what happens to a low-income taxpayer (marginal income tax bracket of 20%) who deposits $2,500 per year into a simple annual interest account. We will compare the amount accumulated, for varying interest rates and varying number of years invested, according to whether the interest on the account is taxable or tax-deferred. For consistency, we will use the same interest rates and years of investment that appear in Table 2.1. According to our well-established rules, the amounts in the tax-deferred account will be $2,500 times the magic numbers that appear in Table 2.1. As you will see, the numbers are considerably smaller in the fully taxed account.

You can see that the penalty of having to fork over some of your profit to income tax becomes increasingly more severe as the interest rate rises, but especially as the number of years in which the investment remains in force lengthens.

The numbers in Table 4.1 take into account the differences that accrue from treating the interest or return on your account in a taxable or a tax-free manner. But we have observed that in a typical tax-deferred account, the contributions

Table 4.1
Growth of $2,500 (for a simple interest regular annual deposit account) corresponding to a specific number of years at a specified interest rate, for both tax-deferred and taxable accounts (low marginal tax bracket)

		Number of Years				
Interest Rate		1	5	10	25	40
3%	tax-free	$2,575	$13,671	$29,519	$93,883	$194,158
	taxable	$2,560	$13,429	$28,549	$86,320	$168,773
5%	tax-free	$2,625	$14,505	$33,017	$125,284	$317,099
	taxable	$2,600	$14,082	$31,216	$108,279	$247,066
7%	tax-free	$2,675	$15,383	$36,959	$169,191	$534,024
	taxable	$2,640	$14,764	$34,151	$136,940	$369,700
8%	tax-free	$2,700	$15,840	$39,114	$197,386	$699,453
	taxable	$2,660	$15,115	$35,727	$154,431	$455,449
10%	tax-free	$2,750	$16,789	$43,828	$270,454	$1,217,130
	taxable	$2,700	$15,840	$39,114	$197,386	$699,453

of principal are also deductible. Therefore, to give a completely fair comparison, we should examine the final worth of both types of accounts after *all* taxes are paid. So, let's assume that the contributions to the account come from wages. Joan Smith contributes $2,500 per year from her salary toward a tax-deferred 5% simple interest account. She subtracts $2,500 from her gross salary when reporting her wages to the IRS and so is able to invest the full amount. None of the interest is reportable as income either. But at the end of the game, when she liquidates the account, she must report and pay tax on the full amount—all of her contributions and all accumulated earnings. John Jones, on the other hand, pays his taxes as he goes along. In particular, he pays 20% on the $2,500 he earns and invests the rest, also in a 5% simple interest account. Moreover, he pays income tax annually on the interest. At the conclusion of the epoch, everything he has accumulated in the account is his to spend, with no residual tax obligation.

You might think that Joan and John will wind up with the same money. They won't. To see that, let's trace through the events in a one-year epoch. Joan's initial $2,500 investment earns 5%, which is $125, so the account total becomes $2,500 + $125 = $2,625. She then pays 20% tax on the full amount, that is, 0.20 × $2,625 = $525, leaving a balance of $2,625 – $525 = $2,100. On the other hand, John pays tax on his $2,500, namely 0.2 × $2,500 = $500, leaving him with $2,000 to invest. That amount garners 5%, which is $100, out of which he pays 20% tax, so he only nets $80. His grand total is $2,080, or $20 less than Joan's.

In Table 4.2, we redo Table 4.1 to see how the numbers come out for variable interest rates and years. (We used the label "tax-free" in Table 4.1 because the tax was ignored. In the next two tables we use it purely to conserve space—the numbers reflect the tax-deferred status of the money.)

If you are curious, you could try to figure out why the amounts in rows seven and ten are identical.

If you want to try other rates or years,

Consult #4 on the Web site, "Tax-Deferred Accounts Can Help."

Note from Table 4.2 that tax-deferred investing definitely beats the alternative, although not as dramatically as in Table 4.1. The tax man still extracts his pound of flesh. Nevertheless, I reiterate:

You definitely should invest your money in tax-deferred accounts, whenever possible, and you should put as much into them as you can spare. If your employer is willing to match contributions to a tax-deferred account, that provides an even greater incentive to contribute as much as you are legally allowed into these kinds of accounts.

Table 4.2
Same comparison as in Table 4.1, but with all taxes paid on both accounts—up front for the taxable account and at the end for the deferred account

		Number of Years				
Interest Rate		1	5	10	25	40
3%	tax-free	$2,060	$10,937	$23,616	$75,106	$155,327
	taxable	$2,048	$10,743	$22,840	$69,056	$135,019
5%	tax-free	$2,100	$11,604	$26,414	$100,227	$253,680
	taxable	$2,080	$11,266	$24,973	$86,623	$197,653
7%	tax-free	$2,140	$12,307	$29,567	$135,353	$427,219
	taxable	$2,112	$11,811	$27,320	$109,552	$295,760
8%	tax-free	$2,160	$12,672	$31,291	$157,909	$559,562
	taxable	$2,128	$12,092	$28,581	$123,545	$364,360
10%	tax-free	$2,200	$13,431	$35,062	$216,364	$973,704
	taxable	$2,160	$12,672	$31,291	$157,909	$559,562

Let's turn our attention to the high-income individual now to see if the higher tax bracket diminishes the advantages of tax-deferred investing. This time Joseph, whose marginal bracket is 40%, will invest $5,000 annually in a simple interest, but tax-deferred, account; Josephine will invest with the same parameters except in a taxable account. In Table 4.3, we will go straight to the analog of Table 4.2, since that, unlike Table 4.1, factors in all parameters—namely, the taxes paid eventually by both individuals, on both the principal and the earnings.

Once again, tax-deferred investing is clearly superior to fully taxed (in the present) investing. Is the benefit better or worse for the taxpayer with the high marginal tax rate compared to the taxpayer with a low marginal rate? Table 4.3 reveals that in the short term the benefits are (percentage-wise) rather comparable, but in the long term the high-income individual benefits more proportionately.

FURTHER THOUGHTS ON TAXES

We have reached the point where more than half of all taxpayers now use a professional (firm or individual) to help them prepare their taxes. This is dramatic testimony to the exceedingly complicated—indeed impenetrable—nature of our tax laws. Simplification and streamlining are long overdue. But until that

Table 4.3
Same comparison as in Table 4.2, but with $5,000 invested annually and a high marginal tax bracket

Interest Rate		Number of Years				
		1	5	10	25	40
3%	tax-free	$3,090	$16,405	$35,423	$112,659	$232,990
	taxable	$3,054	$15,830	$33,136	$95,361	$176,667
5%	tax-free	$3,150	$17,406	$39,620	$150,340	$380,519
	taxable	$3,090	$16,405	$35,423	$112,659	$232,990
7%	tax-free	$3,210	$18,460	$44,351	$203,029	$640,829
	taxable	$3,126	$16,999	$37,881	$133,748	$311,448
8%	tax-free	$3,240	$19,008	$46,936	$236,863	$839,343
	taxable	$3,144	$17,303	$39,178	$145,982	$361,760
10%	tax-free	$3,300	$20,147	$52,594	$324,545	$1,460,555
	taxable	$3,180	$17,926	$41,915	$174,469	$492,143

day comes, you must live with the beast we have and do your best to coax it to your advantage (legally, of course). Tax-deferred accounts are one of the main weapons at your disposal. You should use them at every opportunity.

As I said in the personal note in Chapter 3, I started working at the University of Maryland in 1969, thirty-five years ago. Although I have held visiting faculty positions at several institutions, both domestic and foreign, I have had only a single employer in the last third of a century. I'm told that this is a state of affairs that is not likely to be duplicated very often in the future—individuals are likely to have many employers during their working years, with periods of self-employment occurring more frequently than in past generations. Therefore, mobile tax-deferred accounts, not tied to your place of employment, will be increasingly important in the future. This comment applies to retirement accounts of course, but it may also be applicable for health care accounts, dependent care accounts, and education accounts.

A natural question is, what happens if you pull money out of a tax-deferred account prematurely or for purposes other than the designated one? The answer is simple: Not only will that money count 100% as income on your tax return, but generally, you will incur an additional penalty—often 10%. If you change employers, as most of you young people appear destined to do (frequently), then instead of pulling the proceeds out of your tax-deferred accounts that were set up through your employer, you need to do what's called a *rollover*. I will leave it to your financial institution to explain to you the details of how to do a rollover, but basically it means that you ask the financial institution managing your current tax-deferred account to transfer the funds directly to a different institution that will be managing your account in the future. In this way, you don't get to place your grubby little paws on the money—in return for which the IRS holds you blameless (how nice of them) and the tax-deferred status of your account is undisturbed. Young people often make the mistake of cashing in their IRAs or 401(k)s for what may seem like a good reason (down payment on a house or car, for example). But the long-term financial sacrifice they make when initiating such a transaction is substantial, as the tables in this chapter should convince you.

A little bomb that the Congress and the IRS prepared for taxpayers is the *nondeductible IRA*. When IRAs proved immensely popular in the 1980s and people, especially upper-income people, were contributing to them aggressively, the government decided that the "wealthy" were benefitting too much. So lawmakers imposed income limits on IRAs—if one (or one's family) income was "too high," tax-deferred IRAs were deemed a no-no. Feeling a little guilty for what they had done, they created so-called nondeductible IRAs, accounts in which the principal contributed was nondeductible but the interest earned was deductible. And many people (yours truly for a while, I confess) participated in these plans before they realized that the administrative nightmare they were setting up was formidable. Many taxpayers commingled tax-deferred IRA accounts with nondeductible IRA accounts. The IRS even invented a tax form to try to keep track of this nonsense. It's a mess, and someday relatively soon, when people start withdrawing funds from these accounts, the accountants will have yet another reason to worship at the altar of IRS folly. The well-known financial adviser Ric Edelman was one of the first to point out the foolishness of nondeductible IRAs. Thanks to his wisdom, I ceased my participation in that counterproductive activity.

I want to raise an issue here that is deeply germane to the retirement discussion later in Chapter 13. I do so now because I want you to start thinking about the issue. It can be formulated as the following question: What are your eventual goals for the money you are accumulating in your tax-deferred retirement accounts? The obvious answer is that, supplemented by pensions and Social Security, it is the money you will use to live on in your retirement. But there are two ways to view your retirement stash. One is that you hope to have enough so that you won't have to "dip into your principal," as my mother says. That means that the interest thrown off by your investments in your retirement account (of course still supplemented by your pension and Social Security) is all you will need. As a corollary, you plan to leave the bulk, if not all, of the stash to your descendants. Alternatively, you plan to spend down the principal during your retirement years—you view not only the income from the retirement account but the account itself as fair game for pillage over the course of your retirement years. You can live a lot better in the second scenario, but your kids inherit nada, and if you spend too fast or you live too long, you could wind up in bad shape. This is a nasty dilemma for most people as they contemplate retirement. If you are young, it's beyond your ken to even pay attention to this now. But it's an important issue, and if you can formulate an opinion on the matter, even at a young age, it may govern how you structure your retirement investments as the years go by. I'll come back to this matter later, but I want to get you thinking about it.

YOUR NEW COMPUTATIONAL SKILLS

How to compute the future value of a regular deposit investment account when it enjoys tax-deferred status, and the role of both the principal and the interest in such an account on your income taxes.

Part II

The Facts of Life

CHAPTER 5

Your Paycheck: What Is Your Salary Really Worth?

The term is not commonly used, but *pay stub shock* is a phenomenon that is encountered at least as often as sticker shock. It strikes the teenager working part-time at a fast food restaurant, the baby-faced college graduate mounting the first rung of the corporate ladder in an entry-level job in the service sector, the school teacher who takes up a new position in the state to which he just relocated, the parent eagerly returning to the workforce after many years of child-rearing, or the elected politician ready to right all those wrongs she campaigned so assiduously against. For all of them, the pay stub that accompanies the first paycheck they receive on their new job hits them with the same force as those window stickers did auto consumers in the early 1980s in America's new car showrooms. The teenager shrieks, "I know that my salary rate is $6.50 per hour. I know that I worked a total of fifty hours in the last two weeks. My calculator tells me that 50 times $6.50 is $325. Dammit, why is the face value of this check only $261.39?" No less exasperated is the schoolteacher who complains, "They told me my monthly salary was $5,000. Why does this check for my first month's wages say $3,823.93?" And finally our vaunted politician, who is keenly aware that her annual salary is $100,000, is mortified to see that her first biweekly paycheck, during which period she earned $100,000/26 = $3,846.15, is payable for only $2,874.28. The figure $3,846.15 appears on the pay stub, but so do a host of other figures, all of which add up to the difference between her *gross* pay, $3,846.15, and her *net* pay, $2,874.28. Like I said, pay stub shock.

Assuming you have already entered the workforce, pay stub shock is an experience you have also likely encountered. Did you bother to figure out the reason for the seemingly cavernous gap between your gross pay and your net pay? Or were you so discouraged and disillusioned by the phenomenon that you threw up your hands in despair, emitted an utterance such as "Oh well, it is what it is,

I'll just have to deal with this net figure as my salary," and never again paid much attention to the discrepancy between gross and net pay?

DEDUCTIONS FROM YOUR PAYCHECK

Now that you have a good understanding of the three fundamental concepts discussed in Part I, namely, compound interest, inflation, and tax-deferred income, it is time to focus on the source of your money—which, of course, you hope to compound, inflate, and use to generate tax-deferred income. That source is, for most of you, your salary. Your salary! It is a wonderful thing. In exchange for your daily labors, an individual or organization issues you a paycheck on some regular basis. But as you have discovered, there are some nasty entries on your pay stub called *deductions*, and the figures next to those awful deductions add up to the difference between your gross pay (what you thought you had contracted your services for) and your net pay (what your employer actually dishes out to you). Our task in this chapter is to understand the nature of all those insidious deductions and to contemplate some strategies for minimizing the damage they do.

In fact deductions come in three flavors:

- *Taxes.* Almost always comprising the big three: income taxes, Social Security taxes, and Medicare taxes. For the record, income taxes refer to the taxes levied against your income (from salary, interest, dividends, capital gains, royalties, etc.) by federal, state, and local governments; Social Security taxes refer to the taxes assessed by the federal government to fund the Social Security program that supports the elderly and disabled; and finally, Medicare taxes are those, also levied by the federal government, that fund the national health care program for the elderly. The latter two are often referred to jointly as FICA, which stands for Federal Insurance Contributions Act—the enabling legislation that authorized the imposition of those taxes.
- *Mandatory.* What I have in mind here are items that are not taxes but that are conveniently, and perhaps economically, paid for by payroll deductions, and if you did not pay for them out of your salary through payroll deductions, you would almost certainly pay for them directly out of your personal funds. Some examples of this kind of deduction are health insurance, union or professional dues, parking fees, mandatory retirement contributions, and life or disability insurance.
- *Optional.* These are deductions that are completely within your power to choose whether to incur, for example, payroll savings accounts, health or dependent care accounts, education accounts, optional retirement accounts such as IRAs or 401(k)s, car loan payments to credit unions, membership fees in employer-related social organizations, and contributions to charity.

The line between *mandatory* deductions and *optional* deductions is sometimes a little blurry. For example, some folks choose to go without health insurance, whereas some employers make participation in retirement accounts mandatory. What is crystal clear, however, is the demarcation line between deductions for taxes and either of the other two types. If it looks, smells, and walks like a tax, then that's what it is. I can't think of a single instance of a deduction for taxes that might be mistaken for a deduction in one of the other two categories, and vice versa for that matter. Therefore, what I would like to propose is that the key number is not your net pay, but rather your *after-tax pay*—that is, you should pay close attention not so much to the number printed on your paycheck, but rather to the difference between your gross pay and the sum of all the taxes withheld from your paycheck. The money that comes from your mandatory and optional deductions goes directly to benefit you, your family, and the charities you support. On the other hand, the money that goes toward your tax obligations does not benefit you directly, but only indirectly in the sense that as a member of society you reap the rewards and penalties of the programs administered by the governments that are extracting the taxes from your paycheck.

INCREASING THE SIZE OF YOUR PAYCHECK

So what can you do about pay stub shock? How can you maximize your net pay? The most obvious answer is clearly *maximize your gross pay*. The more you earn, the more you keep. Although, as we learned in Chapter 3, income taxes in America are progressive, so the percentage you keep may actually decline as your income goes up. FICA, that is, Social Security and Medicare taxes, on the other hand, are *regressive*. Both are flat, and the former actually ceases to apply to income above a certain threshold (currently approximately $85,000). However, you would need to be in a very high marginal tax bracket before you might notice the percentage of your after-tax pay increasing as your gross pay goes up.

Before we answer the question posed in the last paragraph, we must ask another one: Is it really your net pay that you want to concentrate on maximizing? You are going to have to buy the items in the mandatory category anyway. As with any other purchase, you should shop around and compare prices. If you can buy life insurance at a better rate than that offered through your employer's plan, as is likely, then by all means do so. If you can buy health insurance at a better rate than that offered through your employer's plan—highly unlikely—then you should not hesitate to go that route either. You have even more flexibility with optional deductions. In these instances, you will probably have a wide variety of choices, and careful shopping will reveal whether you can save money. If you can't save any money (without sacrificing quality) or if you can only save a tiny bit, then you may decide that the convenience of payroll deduction makes worthwhile continuing to pay for these items directly out of your salary. In summary, with regard to nontax deductions, you are really buying products that you would buy anyway, and these products are for your personal benefit—thinking of the money that is coming out of your paycheck to buy them as not part of your "net pay" doesn't make sense.

Taxes are, of course, a different kettle of fish. You have absolutely no choice concerning whether to submit to these deductions, and the amounts that are withdrawn are determined by the law of the land, not by your desires or choices. Moreover, for most people, the deductions due to taxes are the largest deductions that impact their paychecks. Small wonder that we are so incensed by tax withholdings. Therefore, I think that the most important question you can ask yourself in addressing pay stub shock is:

How can I maximize my after-tax pay?

The key number inherent in your pay stub is the quotient determined by dividing your after-tax pay by your gross pay. That number represents the percentage of your salary that is not eaten up by taxes. In this book I will call that number the *freedom quotient.* For example, if your biweekly gross pay is \$5,000, and the taxes on your pay stub add up to \$1,500, then your after-tax pay is

$$\$5{,}000 - \$1{,}500 = \$3{,}500,$$

and your freedom quotient is

$$3500/5000 = .70.$$

YOUR FREEDOM QUOTIENT

Actually, you have several choices in deciding which data to use in order to compute your freedom quotient. You can use your current pay stub as implied above. But most pay stubs these days contain cumulative or year-to-date information. Therefore, you can use those figures, especially the ones on the last pay stub of the year. Finally, you can use your income tax return. This may be the most appropriate data to use; however, it will contain as part of your gross income items not subject to withholding from your salary. These include sources of income such as bank interest and stock dividends, or profit from a small home business you run, or royalties on a book. We'll talk more about these sources of income in Part III of this book. If you want to measure how much Uncle Sam and your local governments are extracting from your income, then your income tax form is the place from which to compute your freedom quotient; if you just want to see the damage done on your paycheck, then your pay stub contains the data to use.

My freedom quotient is approximately two-thirds. That means that one out of every three dollars that I earn goes to pay the big three taxes. *One out of every three*—about the same percentage that medieval serfs owed the noble whose land they worked. And that number is fairly typical for American workers. Of course, the quotient does not measure the other taxes that I pay, of which I gave you a partial list in Chapter 3. Some of these other taxes are not insubstantial, for example, sales taxes or the transfer taxes I paid on the new home that I purchased recently. Nevertheless, let us focus mainly on the big three (income taxes, Social Security, and Medicare). My freedom quotient means that from Monday morning when I arrive at the office until well into Tuesday afternoon, *all* the money I earn goes to the tax man. Another way of measuring the tax burden, publicized by Grover Norquist's organization Americans for Tax Reform, is Tax Freedom Day. It is the day roughly one-third of the way into the calendar year when we stop working for the government and start working for ourselves. Over the years, the day has been moving steadily later in the calendar as the tax man continues to take a proportionately larger bite out of American salaries. A potentially hopeful sign is that it has retreated recently, but currently the day is somewhere in the neighborhood of the one-third marker of May 2.

Regardless of whether you think that the money you pay in taxes is well spent or not, you must face the incontrovertible fact that Americans are spending a lot of money on taxes. This comment applies to low-income taxpayers as well as to high-income taxpayers. The latter are clearly paying a substantial amount because of the progressive nature of income taxes. But the low-income folks are also carrying a heavy load because of the regressive nature of Social Security and Medicare taxes. Many recent reports have documented that on average Americans spend more on taxes than on food, clothing, and shelter *combined.* This is a sobering fact, one you must keep in mind as you make whatever political choices confront you in the coming years.

I treasure the memory of my father. He grew up during the Great Depression, served his country for three years during World War II (seeing combat in the European theater), was married to my mother for fifty-three years, raised three children, worked for forty years as a laborer in the garment district in Manhattan, and led an honorable and productive life. I respect his accomplishments and value the many important lessons that he taught me. But in one respect, I think he had it wrong. I often heard him say, "There was no point in focusing on one's gross salary; the number printed on the paycheck was all that mattered." I doubt that his boss agreed with him. His boss still had to dish out all the money that bypassed my father's wallet on its journey to the tax man. In fact, his boss had to fork out a lot more. He had to pay, as do all employers, an amount to the government roughly equivalent to the amount my father paid in FICA taxes, as well as other mandatory employee benefit compensation items such as workers' compensation. These were dollars that my father's boss could have used to raise my father's salary, or hire more workers, or reinvest in his business, or—gasp—live better himself. Perhaps my father trained himself to ignore the increasing number of dollars for which he served only as a transit vehicle between his employer and the government. I assure you that his employer did not ignore them.

MAXIMIZING YOUR FREEDOM QUOTIENT

OK, it's finally time to answer the basic question: What are the specific methods for getting your freedom quotient up and maximizing your after-tax pay? Here are three broad tactics, each of which encompasses numerous possibilities.

1. The simplest and most obvious adjustment to make is to your withholding. When you began work at your current employer, you filed a so-called W-4 form. On it you listed your dependents, the number of which together with your salary (and maybe some other information such as the municipality in which you live) determines the amount that is withheld from your paycheck. The only other choice seemingly available to you on the W-4 form is the possibility of instructing your firm's accounting department to withhold *more* from your paycheck rather than *less.* Many people do exactly that, by either understating the number of legitimate dependents they have or by actually requesting that additional dollars be withheld from their paycheck. Are you one of those people? Why do people do that? Largely for one of three reasons: either (a) they worry that their nonsalaried income will cause them to owe some money to the tax man at the end of the year; (b) they are so fearful of the tax man that they want to be dead certain that they definitely will not have a balance due on their tax return (even if they don't have any nonsalaried income); or (c) (most common of all) they view it as a "forced savings" that will result in a windfall in the form of a tax refund at year's end. Which is your reason?

   So, lo and behold, for whichever reason, you are entitled to a tax refund. You are overjoyed at the prospect. Indeed, you should be dismayed. The refund is a return of your own money. By giving it to Uncle Sam, by giving the tax man more than you are legally obliged to send him in the year 2004, say, and waiting until the late spring of 2005 to get it back, you have given the government an interest-free loan. Moreover, on some of the money (the portion withheld in early 2004), the period of the loan approaches fifteen to sixteen months. Has anyone ever given you an interest-free loan for fifteen months? I doubt it. Well, maybe your parents. Uncle Sam is not your child; why should you give him an interest-free loan?

You should keep the amount withheld from your paycheck to the least amount legally possible. I try to arrange my withholding so that at the end of the year I owe Uncle Sam as much as possible, but just short of incurring a penalty. Roughly that means I fork over to the tax man, through withholding and estimated tax payments (for the latter, see the fourth item in the bulleted list in the next section, "You Are What They Pay You"), approximately 90% of the total tax due. Even if you pay less, the penalties are not so severe. It's the interest on late payments that is severe. I don't recommend that—you should pay the least amount you legally can, but always in a timely fashion.

"But," you say, "I count on the tax refund every year, and where would I get the money to pay the 10% that is due?" The answer is simple: instead of sending the extra $50, say, per pay period to the tax man, *save it*, or *invest it*, or *lend it out*. At the end of the year, you'll have enough to pay your tax balance, with an amount left over that easily exceeds what you would have received as a tax refund. Admittedly, this takes self-discipline—it's easier to let Uncle Sam pick your pocket all year long and then be grateful for the pittance he returns. Easier, yes, but much less profitable. And it's counterproductive to the goal of maximizing your after-tax pay.

So pull out your pay stubs and tax returns from last year to see how much you overpaid Uncle Sam per paycheck. Adjust your withholding as far as you can to reverse that trend. And make concrete plans to save/invest the difference. If you can't legally adjust your withholding to take care of the problem, then proceed to the next tactic.

2. The second tactic is to enhance your position in tax-deferred deductions. We have discussed this matter rather fully in Chapter 4. You should explore all the tax-deferred possibilities provided by your employer as well as other possibilities that you can implement on your own. Recall that the choices lie among retirement accounts, education accounts, health accounts, etc. Your employer, especially if you work for a big company or institution, probably has a *cafeteria plan* from which you can select a variety of tax-deferred purchases through payroll deductions. If you are going to buy these items anyway, you will decrease your taxable income and increase your freedom quotient by purchasing them through tax-deferred payroll deductions.
3. The third tactic is more of a general guideline than a precise method. Namely, you should switch as much of your income as possible off the basic Form 1040 and onto the various schedules, such as Schedules C, D,

and E. I am referring here to the most well-known forms and schedules that taxpayers encounter in their annual, unpleasant exercise of completing their federal income tax returns. We will have more to say about this in Part III. But simply put, the fellow on a straight salary is at a tax disadvantage when compared to the businessman, independent contractor, or self-employed individual. The main tool available to the normal employee on a salary, aside from tax-deferred deductions and various tax credits (which I will discuss in the next section), is the use of itemized deductions. That is where you get to claim various targeted expenses—for example, interest on your home mortgage, some local taxes, gifts to charity—as an offset to your gross income. However, the value of other traditional deductions, such as medical expenses and various miscellaneous deductions (e.g., union dues), that once were heavily invoked itemized deductions has been decimated through the imposition of fairly high thresholds, which rule these out for most taxpayers. But self-employed people who report income on Schedule C, investors who report income on Schedule D, landlords and authors who report income on Schedule E, and farmers who report income on Schedule F have a much greater latitude in offsetting their income through various expenses and deductions not available to the straight wage earner reporting the bulk of her or his income on Form 1040 and interest/dividends on Schedule B. This explains the rationale behind this guideline.

Implementing the guideline, however, may not be so easy. The vast majority of employment opportunities in your profession or trade may involve standard salaried positions. Abandoning the security of a salaried job for a more tax-advantaged career on one's own as a consultant or an entrepreneur requires a great deal of courage. It's a tough call, but it's your call. For now, let's content ourselves with the following observation. Namely, there are partial measures that you can take. For example, instead of putting in overtime on your current job, which only increases your salaried income, consider devoting the extra hours to setting up your own consulting firm, or starting your own business, or moonlighting as an independent contractor, or managing your own investments more aggressively. In this way, your additional income will trigger some of the benefits of nonsalaried income and thereby raise your freedom quotient.

YOU ARE WHAT THEY PAY YOU

In reading this chapter you will have noticed that there are far fewer computations than in previous chapters and correspondingly more "advice." This reflects in part the nature of the attitude many Americans have toward their salaries. Matters such as saving, investing, paying for education, coping with inflation, and even buying a home are very important to individuals. But these issues usually do not engage the ego the way that staring at one's paycheck does. For better or worse, Americans are overly focused on, if not obsessed with, the size of their paychecks. For many of us, the size of the paycheck is how we measure our success in life. Deep down we know it's not as important as our health, the quality of our family life, our commitment to our faith, or the way we regard and are regarded by our fellow human beings. But we can't help ourselves. We care deeply about the money we make—how much it is; how it compares to that of our coworkers, friends, and associates; and whether it is growing fast enough to accommodate our dreams for the future. That is why, in addition to the amount of your gross pay, your freedom quotient will remain a critical number for you throughout life, and why the emphasis in this chapter is on increasing your freedom quotient rather than on any computation you can do concerning the progress of your salary or on comparative numbers you could generate on the differing nature of salaries according to profession, region, or age. In that vein, here are some further comments and suggestions that are relevant to your salary.

- My suggestion in Chapter 3 to structure your pay and your bills in order to afford two freebies per year—that is, paychecks whose content is freed up from bill paying—is one I encourage you to take seriously. Implementing such a protocol will be of enormous financial benefit.
- How does your pay arrive: as cash in hand, in the form of a check, or as a pay stub that describes an electronic or direct deposit into your bank? If you can arrange it, I recommend the latter. Direct deposit makes for much easier budgeting. More importantly, it will help you to avoid impulse spending. The saying "The money is burning a hole in his pocket" is not without relevance here. Of course, you still can use the credit cards or ATM cards in your wallet to blow the dough—we'll address that eventuality in Chapter 10.
- Another famous adage is "Pay yourself first." Regardless of whether you get cash, a bona fide paycheck, or a pay stub that records the movement of electrons from your employers bank account to yours, when planning what to do with your after-tax pay, you should start with yourself and your family. Make sure that you budget for how much you plan to put away in payroll savings, sock into a 401(k) or IRA, or contribute to the company's profit-sharing plan. Then allocate for the mortgage, food and clothing, insurance, credit card debt, etc. If you budget in reverse, you may be sorely tempted to divert the personal payments to other "necessities" such as travel, entertainment, and hobbies, thereby leaving nothing for personal investment. I'm not saying that this is easy. But the long history of personal finance proves that "Pay yourself first" is the most important protocol you can establish on the road to fiscal solvency, and thence to personal wealth.

When setting up your household budget, make sure that you set aside monies for personal investment *before* you allocate funds to household necessities. Only then should you pay attention to luxuries and other optional spending needs.

- My final salary suggestion concerns *estimated tax payments*. You may find this suggestion as controversial as my opinion on how to structure your withholding. Most of you are used to paying your taxes by two well-established routes: withholding from your paycheck or paying any balance due when you file your income tax returns. But some of you have had the following experience. In a year where the balance due is surprisingly large—because you had an unexpected nonsalary windfall (for example, you hit the lottery or Aunt Sarah passed away and left you her dough)—the IRS has responded by sending you estimated tax forms to complete for the succeeding year. They request that you estimate quarterly your expected shortfall between salary withholding and tax due for the period. Then they demand that you remit the difference. That is to say, the IRS does not trust you with your own money. The law of the land compels you to send in the tax as you incur it, whenever the income materializes, as the income materializes—you are not allowed to wait until the end of the year to pony up.

A common reaction to the arrival of estimated tax forms, after the anger has passed, is, "Omigod, I better increase my withholding so I can avoid filing these forms." Mistake! Already explained. In fact, here are two reasons that filing regular estimated tax forms might not be such a bad thing. First, I would hope that the main reason you might need to file estimated tax is not because you hit the lottery or because your favorite aunt kicked the bucket, but rather because your investments are doing so well that they are throwing off enough income to have substantially increased your tax obligations. Another possibility is that you are doing so well as an independent consultant, contractor, or entrepreneur that you are paying virtually all of your taxes through estimated tax. Certainly, not having to settle up with the tax man until the end of the year would be better, but you should view your quarterly estimated tax forms as a badge of accomplishment, attesting to your personal financial achievements. Second, estimated tax can give you the opportunity to fine-tune the amount you fork over to Uncle Sam during the year, with the goal of narrowing it down to where you are just below the penalty as I outlined earlier.

When I was eighteen, I was a student at the City College of New York (CCNY). I lived with my family in the Bronx. During the summer following my freshman year, I worked as a clerk in the life insurance division of the Bowery Savings Bank in Manhattan. I earned $55 per week, plus a free lunch. Of course, there is never a free lunch; sans that benefit, they likely would have paid me $60 per week. Out of that salary, taxes were less than $10. Then my parents took $5, which they used to pay my school expenses for the following year. Those expenses were devoted to little more than books and supplies since my parents covered my room and board, and there was no tuition at CCNY then. Tuition-free higher education! Another "free lunch" that of course was not free; the taxpayers of New York City and New York state subsidized the education of a select group of the city's high school pupils. Of course, I am grateful for the "free" higher education I received; it made my parents' and grandparents' financial planning a lot simpler than that of the folks in Chapters 1 and 2 of this book. However, I can't escape the feeling that some sort of Ponzi scheme was in play here. Naturally, the citizens of the city and the state eventually balked at the idea, and tuition was initiated despite the fact that many of today's poor high school students in New York City are just as deserving as I and my comrades were back in mid-century. But I digress.

The point of my story is that I had about $40 per week of discretionary money left that summer. My personal expenses were not too high: commutation, some clothing, books to read on the subway, gas for my dad's car on the weekend. But before I paid for any of that, I made sure to sock $15 per week into a savings account, which netted me about $200 "profit" for the summer. What did I use that money for? It afforded me about $5 per week of entertainment funds for the forty weeks of the school year. My girlfriend (today my wife) and I had a great time that year because $5 easily bought dinner and a movie (even a Broadway show on occasion) in 1961. Thus I was able to devote myself full-time to my studies during the school year (no part-time job like too many of today's students), and I had the money I earned during the summer to woo the lady of my dreams. Pretty good application of "Pay yourself first."

This story is a little less cheery. My first job after receiving my Ph.D. was as an instructor at Yale University in 1967. My salary was $11,000 for the year, and I was paid monthly. The appointment was for two years, and I received no raise during that time. However, the inflation of the early 1970s that I referred to in Chapter 3 really began in the mid- to late 1960s, certainly instigated in part by President Lyndon Johnson's foolish "guns and butter" economic policy. Prices began to escalate noticeably during my tenure at Yale. Moreover, shortly after our arrival in New Haven, my wife and I had our first child, purchased our first new car, and furnished a two-bedroom apartment. Our favorite expression at the time was "There's too much month in our money," reflecting the fact that the money ran out before the month did. What little savings we had managed to accumulate during my years in graduate school were rapidly depleted. For some inexplicable reason, we blamed our situation on the fact that I was paid monthly. "If we could have gotten the same check biweekly instead of monthly," we reasoned wistfully, "then we would be OK." The reasoning is silly, of course. But there were two consequences of our difficult financial time in New Haven. First, when I did get a biweekly paycheck in my next job, I latched onto the freebie scheme with a vengeance. Second, our financial plight definitely played a role in my decision-making with regard to my next job. I had several offers, but I accepted the position at the University of Maryland in part because it was the most lucrative offer. Thirty-five years later, I am still here. I don't regret the decision at all, but I am disturbed by the thought that my motivation was financial rather than scientific or cultural.

Almost any financial adviser will tell you that regardless of your plans for investment, retirement, or future purchases, you should have an untouchable six months of salary in the bank for dire emergencies. What they have in mind is an unexpected period of unemployment, an unexpected catastrophic illness or injury, your kid or your parent needing to be bailed out of jail, or someone kidnapping your spouse and you needing to pay a ransom. It's good advice but not always easy to implement. Even if you could set aside 10% of your after-tax salary, which may be no more than 75% of your gross salary, toward such a stash, it would take you six years to reach the goal—and that's without accounting for inflation. I think the way to deal with this recommendation is to count all of your financial assets as the "collateral" for your dire emergency. The financial people will not be happy with that because many of those assets may not be liquid, that is, easily converted into cash. My response: It does not matter; if it's really a dire emergency, then you will pay the 10% penalty to withdraw funds prematurely from your IRA, or you will forfeit a quarter's interest to get your hands on the money in your Certificate of Deposit, or you will refinance your home mortgage to get out extra cash, etc. Stocks and bonds can be sold, and real estate can be liquidated. You may have to do so on unfavorable terms, but if it's that or the kidnappers keeping your spouse—well, you decide.

Here comes the promised discussion on tax credits. I don't think either of us wants this chapter to degenerate into a lesson on filling out your income tax return, so let's keep this brief. The majority of taxpayers receive a salary and have a relatively straightforward chore in filling out their federal tax returns. State and municipality returns are in principle easier and even more straightforward once you have finished your federal return. You list your salaried income (Form 1040), you add your interest and dividends (Schedule B), you subtract an amount based on your personal exemptions, and then you subtract your standard deduction. That's your taxable income. Look up the tax due on that amount in a table. Finally, subtract what your employer has withheld in payroll deductions. Send in the rest. If your income is low, your income tax obligation will be quite small—but of course Social Security and Medicare are another story. If your income is modest and you are following the above scenario, you are getting beat up pretty badly. Matters only improve if you can itemize deductions instead of taking the standard deduction. As described earlier, this is where you get to subtract things such as interest on your home mortgage, local income and real estate taxes, contributions to charity, and—subject to some severe restrictions—medical and other miscellaneous expenses. The only other way to beat the tax man is with various tax credits. You need to look at the back page of Form 1040 to see the list of all the possibilities. Let me mention a few: earned income credit (for very low-income individuals), child or dependent care credit, foreign tax credit, adoption credit, and certain education credits. Tax credits are better than deductions or exemptions in that they are straight subtractions from your tax due, whereas deductions and exemptions are only subtractions from your income, thereby reducing your tax due, but less on a dollar-for-dollar basis than a tax credit. However, for the generic taxpayer, it is usually much easier to come up with itemized deductions or to divert income from Form 1040 to the various schedules than it is to generate much in the way of tax credits.

WHAT IS YOUR SALARY REALLY WORTH?

We have seen that this is an emotional question that strikes at the heart of an individual's measure of her self-worth. My focus in this chapter is to get you to do two things: focus on your freedom quotient and try to improve it, and pay attention to a few other important points as outlined in the bulleted lists above. The final point is that there are some outside forces that can influence the worth of your salary besides your own individual psyche. These include:

1. *Geography.* Life is serene (some would say sedate) in Winchester, Virginia, or Flagstaff, Arizona, while it is frenetic and exciting in Los Angeles or Washington, D.C. Which do you prefer? The size of your salary may mean less than the quality of your surroundings.
2. *Commutation.* Driving twenty miles from your home to your office along the coast of Maine is very different from a trip of similar mileage on the Long Island Expressway.
3. *Local cost of living.* Have you checked out real estate prices in Honolulu lately? They eclipse those in Mobile, Alabama, by more than a little bit.
4. *Culture.* If you're an opera buff, then a big salary in Butte, Montana, will be of little use, but if it's big sky you crave, then any salary there is heaven.

In fact, all of these pretty much amount to the same thing. The value of your salary is a subjective thing that only you can determine. Whether you measure that value primarily in dollars and cents or alternatively in the social, geographical, or familial context in which you earn it, I ask only two things: (1) Remember that "man does not live by bread alone," and (2) keep that freedom quotient in mind and see what you can do about elevating it.

YOUR NEW COMPUTATIONAL SKILLS

How to compute your freedom quotient, that is, the quotient of your after-tax salary divided by your gross salary or, alternatively, the quotient of your after-tax income (the difference between your gross income and the total tax you paid) divided by your gross income.

CHAPTER 6

Buying a House or Car: Mortgages and Loans

So you have a job that pays a salary. In the last chapter, we examined what happens to your salary even before you get the chance to spend it. Then we explored several strategies for maximizing your after-tax pay, always keeping in mind the maxim "Pay yourself first!" Now, at last, it's time to start thinking about how to spend some of what's left—after taxes, after your nontax deductions, after you've paid yourself. Much of what you spend will be devoted to the basics of life: food, shelter, clothing, transportation, and communication. Implicit in that list are two of the most important purchases you will ever make, and not coincidentally, two of the most expensive—a home and a car. Most people buy homes and cars not by laying out the cash equivalent of the full price of the home or car, but rather by taking a loan to finance a large portion of the cost. The loan you take to (help) pay for a home is commonly called a *mortgage*.[1] There is no special name attached to car loans.

HOME LOANS AND CAR LOANS ARE FINANCIALLY ALIKE

In fact, the financial arrangements for home loans and car loans are structurally identical. Generally, the amount borrowed in a home loan is substantially larger (five to ten times as large typically) than in a car loan, and the length of a home loan usually lasts fifteen to thirty years, while the life of a car loan is more typically only three to five years. Other than those differences, the financial mechanisms are basically the same. I will describe those mechanisms momentarily, but first let us note several other features in which home and car loans resemble each other.

1. My trusty Webster informs me that the noun *mortgage* signifies "a conveyance of property on condition that it becomes void on payment or performance according to stipulated terms" and that its etymology is the French words "*mort*" and "*gage*," meaning death and pledge, respectively.

Your lender (a bank, credit union, or mortgage company) does not lend you money to buy a house or a car out of the goodness of his heart. He does it to make money. Namely, he charges you interest on the outstanding balance of the loan. But before he does that, he will want to check out a few things: Is the item you are buying actually worth the price you agreed to pay for it? Do you have the income and/or assets to afford the loan payments he will extract from you? What is your credit history? He will ask the same questions for a loan on either a home or a car. Another way, a most important way, in which the two loans are structured similarly is that the purchased item will serve as *collateral* for the loan. This means that if at some point during the life of the loan you are unable or unwilling to continue making the loan payments, then the lender has the legal right to take possession of the item, that is, the house or car. Once again, there is special language to describe this eventuality—*foreclosure* in the case of a home, *repossession* in the case of a car. Continuing with special language, we say that a home or car loan is a *secured* loan—the lender's money is secured by the collateral, which he can take possession of if you default on the loan payments. A secured loan differs drastically from an *unsecured* loan, which is what you essentially trigger when you don't pay the full balance on your credit card bill. We'll have much more to say about that in Chapter 10.

HOW A LOAN WORKS

OK, it's time to explain as simply as possible how a home or car loan works. The discussion will be surprisingly similar to that of compound interest, and we'll see that a magic number appears again. As usual, we start with very simple numbers and then generalize. Let's assume that you buy a new car for $20,000; you intend to make a 20% down payment of $4,000 and then borrow the balance of $16,000 and pay it off in exactly five years. Finally, suppose the lender's loan or interest rate is 8%. Virtually all loans such as this are paid off monthly, and the amount you pay every month remains the same. Since there are sixty months in a five-year period, you will make exactly sixty equal payments. Our task is to compute the amount you will pay monthly. If your lender was your dad and he did not charge you any interest, then your monthly payment would be

$$\$16{,}000/60 = \$266.67.$$

At this moment, we don't know the exact amount your real lender, who is charging you 8% interest on the loan, will bill you each month, but clearly it will be *more* than $266.67. Here's how the amount is computed. On the day the loan starts, the lender hands you a check for $16,000. You turn it over to the auto dealer together with your $4,000 deposit, and you drive out of the showroom. (I am ignoring sales tax, tag and title fees, etc., or alternately assuming that these taxes and fees are included in the $20,000 price.) You don't hear from the lender for a while, but then he sends you a bill, payable one month from the start of the loan (or loan origination date, to engage in a bit of jargon). He charges you one month's interest, which is 8% divided by 12, multiplied by the outstanding loan amount. Thus

$$0.08/12 = 0.00667,$$

and

$$0.00667 \times \$16{,}000 = \$106.67.$$

Now if that were all he asked, then after you pay $106.67 for the first month's use of the original loan amount of $16,000, you would still owe $16,000. So if you continued to pay the lender $106.67 each month, you would never pay off a nickel of the loan. This is not surprising—we knew the true monthly payment was going to be at least $266.67.

Now, for the sake of argument, suppose you paid $300 each month. Let's see what would happen. The lender would credit your account as follows:

$106.67 (interest)

$193.33 (principal).

The portion of the $300 that is in excess of the $106.67 interest charge, namely $193.33, goes toward repayment of the principal; that is, it reduces the outstanding loan balance. Therefore, after your first payment is credited, and as the second month of the loan begins, you now owe the lender

$$\$16{,}000 - \$193.33 = \$15{,}806.67.$$

Another month goes by, and the interest due at the end of that second month is

$$0.08/12 \times \$15{,}806.67 = \$105.38,$$

a little less than was due at the end of the first month when the loan balance was slightly larger. The lender credits the second $300 payment as follows:

$105.38 (interest)

$194.62 (principal),

and the loan is now reduced to

$$\$15{,}806.67 - \$194.62 = \$15{,}612.05.$$

And on it would go. The key question is:

Will the loan balance drop to exactly *zero* after precisely the sixtieth monthly payment?

We have to call in the math troops to figure it out.

COMPUTING A LOAN PAYMENT: MAGIC NUMBERS AGAIN

I won't take you all the way through the math. But I think you have enough experience to follow the reasoning partway. At a certain point you will see a geometric series (as in Chapter 2), and a magic number will pop out at the end. If the next few paragraphs look too scary, then please skip ahead to the point where the text says RESUME HERE. For the stouthearted, read on.

Let's go right to the letters. We assign the variables as follows:

B = the amount borrowed
r = the interest rate
n = the number of months in the life of the loan
P = the monthly payment.

After one month and the first payment, the new loan balance is

$$B + (r/12)B - P,$$

the three terms representing, respectively, the original loan, the first month's interest, and the first month's payment. We rewrite the above as

$$(1 + r/12)B - P.$$

Then the same process repeats at the end of the second month, leaving a loan balance of

$$(1 + r/12)\,[(1 + r/12)B - P] - P$$

$$= (1 + r/12)^2\,B - (1 + r/12)P - P$$

Can you see what the loan balance will be one month later at the end of the third month? Good guess!

$$(1 + r/12)^3\,B - (1 + r/12)^2\,P - (1 + r/12)P - P.$$

And after n months?

$$(1 + r/12)^n B - (1 + r/12)^{n-1} P - \ldots - (1 + r/12)P - P$$

$$= (1 + r/12)^n B - P[(1 + r/12)^{n-1} + \ldots + (1 + r/12) + 1].$$

Do you see the geometric series? The point is that the loan balance after n months is supposed to be exactly zero. So,

$$(1 + r/12)^n B - P[(1 + r/12)^{n-1} + \ldots + (1 + r/12) + 1] = 0.$$

If you call in the math army to add the geometric series and then solve the equation for P, you get the following intimidating formula:

$$P = \frac{B(r/12)}{1 - \dfrac{1}{(1 + r/12)^n}}$$

The quotient

$$\frac{r/12}{1 - \dfrac{1}{(1 + r/12)^n}} \qquad \text{(Formula 6.1)}$$

is a *magic number*. Its value depends only on the interest rate r and the length of the loan n. Once you have the magic number, you can compute the monthly payment on any loan with those parameters (that is, n months and interest rate r) by multiplying the amount borrowed by the magic number.

The monthly payment on a loan amount of B dollars, at interest rate r for n months, is obtained by multiplying B by the magic number specified by Formula 6.1.

Now going back to the example at hand, the magic number for an 8% loan for sixty months is

$$\frac{0.08/12}{1 - \dfrac{1}{(1 + 0.08/12)^{60}}} = 0.020276.$$

Multiplying that number by $16,000, we obtain

$$0.020276 \times \$16{,}000 = \$324.42.$$

TOTALING UP YOUR LOAN PAYMENTS

RESUME HERE The monthly payment on your car loan is $324.42—not only more than $266.67 as expected, but also more than the $300 that we guessed. If you pay the lender less than $324.42 each month, there will still be a loan balance after sixty months; if you pay more than $324.42 monthly, then you will pay off the loan in less than sixty months.

You may be wondering why we kept so many decimal places in the magic number. The answer is that since car and home loans usually involve large amounts, represented by five-, six-, or even seven-digit numbers, we need to keep lots of decimal places to ensure accuracy. For example, if we rounded off the number 0.020276 to 0.0203, a seemingly reasonable thing to do, then when we multiply it by $16,000 we get

$$0.0203 \times \$16{,}000 = \$324.80,$$

resulting in a 38¢ mistake. You and I may not care about such a small amount of money, but lenders *care.*

Now notice that you actually pay the lender, over the full life of the loan,

$$60 \times \$324.42 = \$19{,}465.20.$$

That amount is $3,465.20 more than you received from the lender at the start of the process. That's his profit on the loan. As a percentage of the original loan amount, it is

$$3465.20/16000 = 0.2166,$$

or 21.66%. But spread over five years, it translates into an average of 21.66%/5 = 4.33%—actually quite a modest return on his "investment." Of course, one must temper that remark by the observation that he is continually getting more and more of his original money back. Indeed, at any instant, he is earning an annual rate of 8% in return on the loan amount outstanding at that moment. Viewed that way—and that is the correct way to view it—the loan is an excellent investment for the lender. It works out well for you, too, so everyone is happy.

CAR LOANS AND MAGIC NUMBERS

Here are two tables for you to contemplate concerning car loans. Table 6.1 gives the magic number for varying loan rates and varying loan lengths. You can use it to compute the monthly payment on a car loan by multiplying the appropriate magic number by the amount of the loan. If you need the magic number for a loan rate or loan length not in the table, then

Consult the Web site. (Click on the *Loan Calulator*.)

You might object to the 12% rate as too high to be realistic except in a time of severe inflation. Think of it as a loan rate on a boat instead of a car; lenders often won't give as favorable a rate for nautical vehicles as they will for land vehicles.

Let's illustrate how to use Table 6.1. We have already seen one instance in the case of an 8% loan for five years. The corresponding magic number (from the table) is 0.020276, as we saw earlier, and the payment for a $16,000 loan in that case was obtained by multiplying the magic number 0.020276 by $16,000. Similarly, a three-year loan of $10,000 at 6% will yield a payment of $10,000 times the magic number 0.030422 (read from the table), that is,

$$\$10{,}000 \times 0.030422 = \$304.22.$$

Or, a six-year loan of $25,000 at 10% yields a payment of $463.15, obtained by multiplying $25,000 times the appropriate magic number, which in this case is 0.018526,

$$\$25{,}000 \times 0.018526 = \$463.15.$$

Next let's fix the variables in the magic number formula and give a table of values for varying loan amounts. You can easily use the Web site to make similar

Table 6.1
Magic number for a car loan at a loan rate in the designated row for the number of years in the corresponding column

	Number of Years				
Interest Rate	**2**	**3**	**4**	**5**	**6**
5%	.043871	.029971	.023029	.018871	.016105
6%	.044321	.030422	.023485	.019333	.016573
8%	.045227	.031336	.024413	.020276	.017533
10%	.046145	.032267	.025363	.021247	.018526
12%	.047073	.033214	.026334	.022244	.019550

comparisons. A fairly typical new car loan rate is 6%, and a common loan length is four years. The magic number for such a loan (from Table 6.1) is 0.023485. Table 6.2 lists monthly payments on varying amounts borrowed with such a loan.

The magic number can also work the following magic for you. Consumers often know how much they can afford to pay each month toward car payments but don't know how much car that will buy. Here's the solution:

If you *divide* the amount you want to pay each month by the magic number, then the result is the amount you can borrow.

For example, if you can afford a monthly payment of $225 for three years and the car dealer has a special loan rate of 5%, then the corresponding magic number from Table 6.1 is 0.029971, and the amount you can borrow is

$$\$225/0.029971 = \$7,507.26.$$

HOME LOANS AND MAGIC NUMBERS

As I said, home loans, or mortgages, work the same way. But typically, the loan lengths and the amounts borrowed are much bigger, five to ten times bigger. Making general statements about loan rates is more difficult. Sometimes long-term rates are lower than short-term rates; sometimes the reverse is true. At the time this is written, the latter situation is in force, since the Federal Reserve engaged in a sustained period of cutting short-term rates during 2002. Perhaps by the time you read this, the situation will have been reversed.

Now let's give two tables like those above, but I will switch the order. Typical home loan rates for thirty-year loans hovered around 7% for a long period (they were much lower in 2002–2003). The magic number for such a loan (i.e., 7% for thirty years) is 0.006653. This yields the data in Table 6.3.

Table 6.2
Car loan payments for a 4-year loan at a 6% loan rate

Amount Borrowed	Monthly Payment
$3,000	$70.46
$5,000	$117.43
$10,000	$234.85
$15,000	$352.28
$24,000	$563.64

Table 6.3
Home loan payments for a 30-year loan at a 7% loan rate

Amount Borrowed	Monthly Payment
$50,000	$332.65
$100,000	$665.30
$135,000	$898.16
$200,000	$1,330.60
$350,000	$2,328.55

Most mortgages, especially for first-time, new-home buyers, are for thirty years. For resales of older houses, especially to veteran home buyers, a fifteen-year term is more common. Much less common, but not unheard of, are terms of twenty or twenty-five years. Table 6.4 gives the magic numbers for those mortgage lengths and several loan rates.

TOTAL INTEREST PAID ON A LOAN

As we did above for car loans, let's give some illustrative examples for interest paid on a home loan. I will then use those examples to answer some common questions that arise in the minds of consumers shopping for loans. Three hypothetical home purchases—low-level, mid-level, and high-level—might be configured as follows:

- *Loan 1.* Home price $80,000; cash down payment $4,000, or 5%; amount borrowed $76,000; thirty-year mortgage; loan rate 8%.
- *Loan 2.* Home price $150,000; cash down payment $15,000, or 10%; amount borrowed $135,000; thirty-year mortgage; loan rate 7%.
- *Loan 3.* Home price $350,000; cash down payment $87,500, or 25%; amount borrowed $262,500; fifteen-year mortgage; loan rate 6%.

We can get the magic number for the three mortgages from Table 6.4. They are 0.007338, 0.006653, and 0.008439, respectively. Therefore, the monthly payments are, respectively,

$$\$76{,}000 \times 0.007338 = \$557.69$$

$$\$135{,}000 \times 0.006653 = \$898.16$$

$$\$262{,}500 \times 0.008439 = \$2{,}215.24.$$

Table 6.4
Magic number for a home loan at a loan rate in the designated row for the number of years in the corresponding column

	Number of Years			
Interest Rate	**15**	**20**	**25**	**30**
5%	.007908	.006600	.005846	.005368
6%	.008439	.007164	.006443	.005996
7%	.008988	.007753	.007068	.006653
8%	.009557	.008364	.007718	.007338
10%	.010746	.009650	.009087	.008776

Table 6.5 computes two pieces of data for each of these loans: (1) the total amount that the borrower pays on the loan and (2) the total interest paid on the loan.

You can use the Web site to compute these data for any home or car loan. (Click on *Total Payments* and *Total Interest* under #6.)

You will notice that the longer higher-rate loans entail a much higher percentage of interest paid (as a percentage of the total payments) than the shorter lower-rate loans. Which do you think accounts for that, the longer period or the higher interest rate? The answer is the former.

You can check that claim using the Web site. For example, try cutting back Loan 2 to fifteen years (without changing the loan rate) and then cutting back the loan rate to 6% (without changing the number of years). Compare your results with Loan 3.

Regardless of the loan rate and length, clearly the total cost of a loan is substantial—the totality of payments is often double and even triple (for rates higher than 8%) the amount of the loan itself. But always bear in mind that at

Table 6.5
Total loan payments and interest

Loan	Total Payments	Total Interest	Amount Borrowed
Loan 1 (30 yrs, 8%)	$200,758	$124,758	$76,000
Loan 2 (30 yrs, 7%)	$323,337	$188,337	$135,000
Loan 3 (15 yrs, 6%)	$398,722	$136,222	$262,500

any given moment, you are paying the stated interest rate on the outstanding loan balance. Loans are fair to lender and borrower, and in some sense they form the glue that holds our economy together. Of course, in most instances the borrower does not have a choice. She does not have the spare $35,000 for the Lexus and certainly does not have $250,000 lying around to plunk down for a house. Well, some people do—but most don't.

SHOULD YOU PAY CASH FOR YOUR HOME OR CAR?

But suppose she did! A legitimate question: If you can afford to pay cash for your house or car, should you? Naturally, there are two schools of thought—yes and no. Those who urge "yes" would tell you to pay for it in cash because (1) you won't have to worry about loan payments; (2) you'll own the car instead of the bank owning the car (which is not really correct reasoning—you really do own the car, although it is serving as collateral for your loan); and (3) you would probably make the payments out of your salary, so instead use that money for another purpose such as investments. Those who would counsel "no" would counter that you should take a loan because (1) home and car loan rates are fairly low, so borrow as much as you can and invest the cash you would have used to pay for the car to generate a higher rate of return than the loan rate; (2) besides, you'll be paying off the loan with deflated dollars; and (3) at least for the house, you'll get a major income tax break on the interest you pay on the loan.

I don't think there is an easy answer. In some sense the question is moot because most folks are not in a position (don't have the cash) to be able to ponder the dilemma. But if you are one of the lucky ones, then I think you have to consider personal inclinations and preferences as well as financial details. For example: (1) If your loan is at 7% and you can get 10% on an investment, then don't pay cash, but you may not be comfortable with the aggressive and risky investment required to earn the 10%; (2) the part of the loan payment that covers interest is indeed deductible (at least on a mortgage), but the money you earn in your investment is liable to be taxable; (3) the loan payments are in depreciating dollars, but so are the investment returns; and (4) yes, the interest payments on a mortgage are tax deductible, but you may be able to place your investment in a tax-deferred vehicle.

It's not an easy call. My father, with his Depression-era mentality, would not conceive of borrowing a nickel to buy something for which he could afford to pay cash. Ric Edelman, on the other hand, would borrow as much as he could and invest the cash aggressively. What would you do? I hope that someday you are privileged enough to encounter this exquisite dilemma.

COMPARING CAR AND HOME LOANS

I would like to point out some further similarities and also some differences between car loans and home loans. As we have seen, the financial mechanics of the two kinds of loans are identical. Other features in which the two resemble each other are:

- *Insurance.* You will have to purchase insurance to cover both your house and your car. (More on that in Chapter 9.) In some loan arrangements, the fees for those products are incorporated within the loan payment. This is a bad practice, if for no other reason than it obscures what you are paying for what, and should be avoided.
- *Maintenance.* Houses have to be maintained; so do cars. These expenses are rarely ever structured to be included in your loan payment, but you had better budget for them.

Now here are three areas where the dissimilarities outweigh the similarities:

- *Taxes.* There are up-front taxes you will have to pay for both products—various local and state transfer taxes when you buy a house, sales tax when you buy a car (in most states). But for a house you will have continuing annual taxes in the form of real estate or property tax. While some states have property or excise taxes that apply to your car every year, for the most part cars, unlike houses, do not generate ongoing tax costs.
- *Fees.* A home purchaser usually encounters a slew of fees, which when added to the transfer taxes (and a few other things such as attorney's fees), are usually summed up in the phrase "closing costs." Those costs can be as much as 3–5% of the purchase price of the house. While there are some fees associated with the purchase of an automobile (e.g., title and tag fees), they are trivial when compared to the closing costs of a home purchase.
- *Appreciation/Depreciation.* The major financial difference between homes and cars is that with very rare exceptions, a home is an appreciating asset (one that will increase in value) whereas a car is a depreciating asset (one that will decrease in value). Typically, at the end of a five-year new car loan, the value of the car will have fallen to half, or less, of its original purchase price. On the other hand, the value of the house you purchased thirty years ago will have gone up appreciably (pun intended). By how much? Well, let's say that house prices go up 5% per year. Now we're back in familiar territory. To get the appreciation on the house, I only need compute 1.05^{30}. In fact,

$$1.05^{30} = 4.32194.$$

The house that you bought for $200,000 in the year 2000 will be worth

$$4.32194 \times \$200{,}000 = \$864{,}388.$$

in 2030.

Inflation in home prices tends to be highly spasmodic—long periods of little or no appreciation interspersed with short bursts of severe jumps in real estate prices. The years 2001–2002 constituted one such period.

In any event, because of this fundamental difference between homes and cars, thinking of a home purchase as an investment, but a car purchase as an expenditure, makes sense. In fact, until recently, many people had to pay capital gains tax on the profit they gleaned when they sold their homes. Recent tax changes have allowed taxpayers to apply very high deductibles against the profit on the sale of their homes. Essentially, unless you realize more than a half-million dollars profit on the sale of your home,[2] no capital gains tax on it will be due. Uncle Sam never allowed a capital loss deduction when you sold your depreciated automobile, although fifteen years ago (ending in 1986) he did allow a deduction for local sales tax.

LOAN BALANCES OVER TIME

Now let's answer two simple arithmetic questions that might arise when you contemplate selling your home or car *before* the loan is paid off. The two questions are:

1. What is the point in the life of your loan at which you have paid off exactly one-half of the principal?
2. How much have you paid off at the midway point of the loan?

What do you think? Clearly, as the loan balance decreases the interest charge also decreases, so as the months go by, more and more of your payment applies to principal and less and less to interest. That means your loan balance decreases slowly at first and then rapidly later on. This suggests that a qualitative answer to the first question is "well past the midpoint in time of the loan," and a qualitative answer to the second question is "considerably less than half of the loan." The precise answers will clearly depend only on the interest rate and the length of the loan. Tables 6.6 and 6.7 give the answers for varying interest rates and loan lengths.

Not surprisingly, the longer the life of the loan and the higher the interest rate, the less you pay off in the first half of the loan span. That last entry, 18.34%, is quite dramatic. Clearly, that kind of loan is not the way to build equity quickly.

THE PERSONAL SIDE OF HOME MORTGAGES

Since I've told you my car history, I might as well also tell you my house history. My wife and I have bought three homes in the last thirty years:

2. For married couples filing jointly; for singles, a quarter-million dollars.

Table 6.6
How long it takes, in months, to pay off one-half of a loan

	Number of Years (Months)			
Interest Rate	**3 (36)**	**5 (60)**	**15 (180)**	**30 (360)**
5%	19	32	107	242
6%	19	33	110	252
7%	19	33	113	261
8%	20	33	116	269
10%	20	34	121	283

Table 6.7
Percentage of a loan that is paid off at midpoint

	Number of Years			
Interest Rate	**3**	**5**	**15**	**30**
5%	48.13%	46.89%	40.75%	32.12%
6%	47.76%	46.27%	38.96%	28.95%
7%	47.39%	45.65%	37.20%	25.98%
8%	47.01%	45.03%	35.48%	23.22%
10%	46.27%	43.81%	32.15%	18.34%

1. In 1972, we bought a new three-bedroom split rambler on a quarter-acre for $42,200. We took a $31,650 mortgage on the house for thirty years at 7.5%. We sold that house in 1977 for $67,500.
2. In 1977, we bought a five-year-old four-bedroom colonial on a quarter-acre for $80,000. We took a $43,000 mortgage on the house for thirty years at 8.25%. In 1991, we did extensive remodeling of the kitchen and bathrooms and took out an additional $49,900 second mortgage for fifteen years at 8.74%. We sold that house in 2001 for $310,000.
3. In 2002, we bought a new three-bedroom *luxury* townhouse for $341,000. We took a $100,000 mortgage for fifteen years at 6.25% (which we have since refinanced).

If you want to know what my monthly payments were, you can use the above data and the Web site to figure it out. Are there any interesting stories in the above data other than the obvious fact that we were making the classic trek through family life—getting into a house shortly after our kids were born, getting a bigger house as the kids grew, downsizing now that the kids are gone? You'll recall that the 1970s was a period of rampant inflation, and the numbers above reflect that. Actually, our $80,000 house escalated in value to nearly triple that figure in the first decade that we lived in it, but then the stagnant real estate market of the 1990s caused the value to tread water, even decline a little. Real estate prices shot up again recently, and that is reflected in the 2002 sale price—not to mention the price of my new townhouse. Also, you can see that my mortgage strategy is somewhere in between my father's and Ric Edelman's—although probably closer to Dad's than Ric would approve of. I know people in similar circumstances to mine who bought houses comparable to mine and paid cash, and I know (a lot more) people whose mortgage amounts were substantially larger than mine. Ric would probably say that I have too much equity in my townhouse. Well, retirement is looming larger, and I am getting more cautious. The same comment applies to my investment portfolio—that is, what is left of it after the carnage of 2000–2003. More on that in Part III.

If you've done the math, you will have figured out that I put down more than $10,000 on my first house. When you throw in closing costs, I had to write a check for nearly $12,000 in June 1972 on the day I closed on my first house. Now, it may be that since Hurricane Agnes had just turned my new basement into a swimming pool, I was overly nervous that day. But I do remember being awestruck at the size of the check. (Recall that I had bought my first car only five years earlier for $2,400, and I had financed it.) Moreover, although the monthly payment was paltry by today's standards, I had grave doubts as to whether my wife and I were going to be house-poor. However, if I had been thinking then like I am trying to teach you to think now, then I should have been able to anticipate the much greater prices that I would encounter thirty years later. The combination of inflation and improved personal financial circumstances easily account for the growth. There is a lesson in this, of course. You can afford to stretch yourself a little when you are scouting out the parameters of your (first) house. Neither the original sale price nor the monthly mortgage payment will seem so large on the day that you sell the place. So it won't surprise me when I sell my townhouse—er, ah, that is, it shouldn't surprise my children when they sell my townhouse—for something between $1.5 million and $2.5 million in 2030.

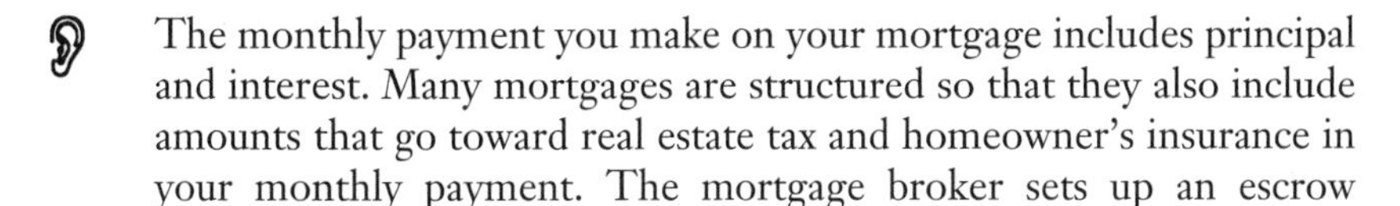

The monthly payment you make on your mortgage includes principal and interest. Many mortgages are structured so that they also include amounts that go toward real estate tax and homeowner's insurance in your monthly payment. The mortgage broker sets up an escrow account, a place where the portion of your payment allotted to taxes and insurance is parked until the money is due at the local government or insurance agent, respectively. I don't think this is such a good idea. You should park the money monthly in your own bank account and pay the bills when they are due. *You* will get the interest earned during that time rather than the lender. Also, whenever escrow accounts such as this are set up, the lenders demand that you deposit *up front* 6–12 months of taxes and insurance in the escrow account. This is to protect them, not you, in case you have trouble keeping up your payments. As far as you are concerned, the money in your escrow account is idle; it's not working for you. So avoid escrow accounts by paying your own taxes and insurance. Well, like lots of other financial suggestions that I have made, this one requires self-discipline—but you should do it. If you don't, then the acronym that has been dreamt up to describe these kinds of payments, *piti*—for *p*rincipal, *i*nterest, *t*axes, and *i*nsurance—is an accurate adjective to describe the poor practice you are engaged in.

Here's another less-than-wonderful trick that lenders and bankers employ. Lenders will be happy to withdraw your monthly piti from your bank account so that you don't have to write them a check every month. Moreover, the bank will give you the added bonus of *overdraft protection.* That is, if when the lender goes to take the money out of your account you have insufficient funds, then the bank automatically floats you a loan rather than bounce your hypothetical check. In this way, they supposedly save you from the attendant charges, which can be substantial. But the loan rate they impose on you for the float is pretty awful too. It may be as high as 20% per annum. Not such a great protective device.

Now that you know how car and home loans work, you should get out there and buy one of each. Too rich for your blood? Too much hassle? Well, you *have* to have a car, and you *ought* to have a house. Maybe you could rent them. Buy or rent—that's the topic of the next chapter.

YOUR NEW COMPUTATIONAL SKILLS

How to compute the monthly payment on a typical home or car loan, given that you know the amount borrowed, the loan rate, and the length of the loan.

CHAPTER 7

Buying or Leasing Your Car

To paraphrase William Shakespeare, "A car! A car! My kingdom for a car!" Americans love their cars as much as any medieval knight loved his horse. This has been true since shortly after Henry Ford rolled his first Model-T off the assembly line, and every indication is that this love of cars will continue into the foreseeable future. At the risk of waxing philosophical, I think that Americans love their cars in part because the act of driving, especially alone, reinforces the sense of individual freedom and personal accountability that is so characteristic of our nature as a people. But we love more than the freedom and power that our cars provide—we love every gadget, modernization, safety device, and upgraded mechanical capability that automobile manufacturers develop to satisfy our motoring desires. And that ensures that the prices we pay for our cars will continue to be hefty. One could argue that given the automobile's sophistication and what it does for us, the actual annual cost of ownership and maintenance is remarkably inexpensive. Nevertheless, for most of us, buying an automobile will be the second most expensive purchase that we make during a lifetime. Yes, we have to have it—even if we can't afford it. So if we can't afford it, can we arrange to rent it? And even if we can afford it, and since auto dealers are aggressively promoting car leases, car buyers will routinely be confronted with the decision:

Should I buy my car, or should I lease it? Which will be better for me financially?

THE WAYS TO GET A NEW CAR

In this chapter, we will compare the three common methods that consumers use to secure the keys to that vehicle they crave:

- Buying a car for cash,
- Buying a car by financing a substantial portion of it,
- Leasing a car.

Our comparisons will be primarily financial, but I will comment on some of the psychological considerations that enter into the decision.

My dad never considered leasing a car. In fact, he never seriously considered financing the purchase of a car. He bought five new cars in his life, and he paid cash for all of them.

He bought his first car in 1956 when he was in his mid-thirties. It was a black and pink Plymouth Belvedere with massive tail fins. G-d, I loved that car. He bought it when I was entering my teen years, and I loved to ride in it. Never did he have to worry about keeping it shiny, as every weekend I was eager to wash and polish it up. It had an automatic transmission, but instead of a shift lever on the drive shaft (like most automatics had in those days) or a stick shift on the floor (in today's style, which would be incompatible with the bench seats that were commonplace in midcentury), it had push buttons. The clunking sound that emitted from the engine when the transmission was shifted via those buttons was fearsome; nevertheless, the crazy thing worked.

But I digress. The only decision my dad ever confronted in buying a car, aside from which brand to select, was whether to buy a new car or a used one. He always opted for a new car, fearful that he could be buying "someone else's headache" if he bought a used car. I will not attempt to engage in a financial analysis of the decision between new and used vehicles—there are just too many variables. In this chapter, we will only evaluate the financial implications of the different methods of obtaining a *new* car.

Incidentally, my dad's last car was a 1990 Ford Taurus. I did not like it very much—certainly nowhere near as much as I loved that Belvedere.

THE LEASE CONCEPT

The leasing of a new car is becoming more and more a common phenomenon, but leasing is still unfamiliar to many Americans. So let's begin our analysis by examining the word *lease*. It's not such a commonly used word in the American consumer's lexicon. The concept, of course, is that by paying a regular fee you obtain the temporary right to or possession of an article that is actually owned by another. The presumption is that at the end of a previously agreed-upon and clearly specified period, you will return the object to its rightful owner, after which you will cease to pay any further fees. This is a familiar process to all of us. But we usually use the word *rent* to describe the process. For example, we rent an apartment for a year, a vacation cottage for two months, a power tool for several days, a snow blower or rug cleaner for several hours, a video tape or DVD to play at home for anywhere from several hours to several days, and even a car, usually for several days. In every instance, we take possession of the object for only the rental period; pay an agreed-upon rental fee, which may be paid daily, weekly, or perhaps in one lump sum; and return or vacate or surrender the object at the end of the rental period to the entity that rented it to us, affording the owner the capability of repeating the process with another consumer. In some rentals, we may have to put up a deposit or collateral of some sort against the possibility that we might damage, lose, or otherwise render the owner's property significantly less valuable than when it was given to us. Typically, the collateral is returned to us when we return the property undamaged.

In fact, there is nothing in the obvious features of a car lease that differs in any way from the parameters of a rental that I have just laid out. When you lease a car, you take possession of the car for a specified period, pay a monthly fee, return the car at the end of the period and cease paying the fee, and you and the car dealer go on your merry ways. The main difference is in the method of computing the monthly fee. In the vast majority of rentals, the owner of the property sets the rental fee roughly as follows. She computes what it costs to own and maintain the property during the period of the rental. The nature of that computation may vary tremendously depending on the type of object to be rented, the nature of the local market, the length of the rental period, and the way the owner arranges her financial affairs. After that, she tacks on a certain amount of profit to the computed figure and announces the total as the rental fee. You might not like the arithmetic if you actually saw it, but it's the owner's right to set the fee; you are under no obligation to engage in the rental. However, once you do, you are legally bound to live up to the terms of the rental contract.

To reiterate, a rental fee is determined in a manner that suits the owner. It may be methodical, or it may be whimsical. And it may be totally opaque to the consumer—although, if she completely ignores the proclivities of her rental customers, she is not likely to remain in the rental business for too long. Now, unlike rental fees, the fee for a car lease is determined in a much more formulaic manner. In fact, it is always set by a well-determined formula, which should be known to the average car lease consumer. Unfortunately, that is rarely the case since the formula is a little mysterious. It is my purpose to explain that formula now.

COMPUTING THE MONTHLY PAYMENT FOR A CAR LEASE

Here are the definitions of the relevant terms. The math will come afterward. There are four terms that influence the computation of a lease payment:

1. Capital cost
2. Residual value
3. Money factor
4. Lease length

I venture that if you have never explored how a car lease works, the first three of those terms conjure up little for you. Here are the explanations:

1. Capital cost (C) is essentially what you agree to as the price of the car. You negotiate with the dealer as if you were buying the car, or you accept what she informs you is the price of the car. The capital cost is then that figure minus any down payment you choose to make on the vehicle. Car dealers call your down payment a *capital cost reduction*. I will comment on the wisdom of capital cost reductions below, but first here is a typical example. You negotiate that the purchase price of a vehicle is $22,000; you give the dealer $2,000 as a down payment; the capital cost of the lease will then be $20,000.
2. Residual value (R) represents an expert estimate of the market worth of the car at the conclusion of the lease. It is always computed as a percentage of the sale price, said percentage depending on two things—the length of the lease and the resalability of the car. The latter depends on the ratings of the car and its consumer demand. Residual values for luxury cars will typically be much higher than for, say, routine sedans. A *very* rough estimate is that a car depreciates in value 10% per year. So the residual value of your $22,000 car after four years will be 60% of the original price, namely $\$22{,}000 \times 0.60 = \$13{,}200$.
3. Money factor (M) is essentially the interest rate in disguise. In fact, the money factor is exactly the nominal interest rate that the dealer is charging on the lease divided by 24. Thus, an interest rate of 6% translates into a money factor of $0.06/24 = 0.0025$.
4. Lease length (n) is the number of months in the lease. For example, a four-year lease translates into a lease length of forty-eight months.

Now for the formula. It has two pieces. First, the car dealer charges you for the depreciation in the value of the car over the life of the lease. The depreciation is represented by the difference between the capital cost and the residual value. The monthly fee for depreciation is therefore that difference divided by the number of months in the lease. In symbols, the monthly depreciation fee (D) is specified by

$$D = (C - R)/n.$$

That's pretty straightforward, and pretty reasonable—you are reimbursing the owner of the car for the loss in value that the property suffers while it is in your hands. Next comes the mysterious piece. It is a finance charge. The dealer has to buy the car from the manufacturer before she can lease it to you. Naturally, she does not pay cash but rather finances the purchase. To come up with the cost of the money the dealer shells out would require a complicated annuity computation involving declining balances. Instead, the industry has developed a simplified formula that yields almost identical results to what the complicated calculation would produce. The formula is as follows: the money factor is multiplied by the *sum* of the capital cost and the residual value. This amount is called the monthly finance charge (F), and in symbols it is specified by

$$F = (C + R) \times M.$$

Your monthly lease fee is the sum of the depreciation and the finance charge, or $D + F$. If we let P denote as usual the monthly payment, then

$$P = D + F = (C - R)/n + (C + R) \times M.$$

I will now explain the rationale behind the finance charge. The dealer finances the car, initially borrowing the capital cost amount (C). The finance deal is structured so that at the end of the lease her loan balance is the residual value (R). During the life of the lease, her balance declines from C to R. Instead of keeping track of that declining balance, one focuses on the average amount borrowed, which is $(C + R)/2$. If the annual interest rate is r, then the monthly interest rate is $r/12$. Therefore, the average monthly finance cost to the dealer is the product of the previous two numbers

$$\frac{C + R}{2} \times \frac{r}{12} = (C + R) \times \frac{r}{24} = (C + R) \times M = F.$$

DEALING WITH DEALERS

Your next question is likely to be, "How does the dealer make any profit? I am reimbursing her for the depreciated value of her auto, and also for the finance costs she incurs in buying it so she can lease it to me. Where's her profit?" The answer is exactly the same as it is when you buy the car for cash or finance it with a loan. Namely, the profit is in the difference between what the car dealer pays the manufacturer for the car and what you pay her. Many consumers, especially those who have become savvy by reading car-buying manuals—either in magazines or over the Internet—recognize that price differential as the one between the MSRP (manufacturer's suggested retail price) and the dealer invoice; both numbers are widely available on all new cars. Indeed, that is a good initial approximation to the amount of dealer profit on a new car. Classically, that price range is exactly your wiggle room as you haggle over the price of your new car.

But consumers should be aware that there are additional devices—sometimes hidden—that pad the dealer's profit. Manufacturers often use promotional subsidies, incentives, and rebates, sometimes given to buyers but more typically to dealers, to boost car sales. Extended warranties are another profit-maker for both dealers and manufacturers. Dealers also count on you to service your car in their service shops—often at much greater cost than you would incur at your local service station. Finally, there are special features of leases that increase dealer profit. These include excess mileage charges, unwarranted initiation and/or termination fees, bogus security deposits, and other tricks. I do not mean to suggest that car dealers are generally unscrupulous and duplicitous, although most have managed to maintain an aura of mystery around leases.

(One method of maintaining that aura of mystery is hiring sales personnel who themselves do not understand how leases work.) Nevertheless, most dealers are reasonably fair businesspeople, and the pleasure and convenience you get out of their product has few comparables in your other consumer purchases. Still, car purchases—and especially leases—are often difficult, tedious, and confusing, giving the dealer a tremendous advantage over the consumer in the transaction.

Everyone has their favorite horror story of a new car purchasing experience:

- Salespeople tell you that they have the model you want in the color and trim you crave; they just have to get it shipped from a dealership in Schenectady. When it arrives, it's the wrong color and is loaded with $3,000 worth of options you don't want.
- They keep you waiting for hours in the salesperson's cubicle after you've supposedly closed the deal, when the manager suddenly appears to tell you why it will cost another grand or so to drive the car out the door.
- They don't tell you about the manufacturer's rebate but try to maneuver you into signing a paper that will kick the rebate back to them.
- They tell you it's a lease when it's really a financed purchase with a balloon payment at the end.

After you finish haggling, you wonder if you haven't stumbled into a Middle Eastern bazaar instead of a mid-America showroom. Through it all you must remember: they are pros and you are an amateur; they do it every day, and you do it a few times per decade. The more you educate yourself about the process, the better you will do—especially with leases. And to help you,

Consult the *Lease Calculator* to compute the monthly payments on a car lease, provided you know the four relevant factors: cap cost, residual value, money factor, and length of the lease.

VARYING THE COMPONENTS OF A LEASE

Returning now to the mechanics of a lease, how the cap cost and money factor affect the cost of a lease should be completely evident—an increase in either one will entail a higher monthly payment. The tables below will help you see how the other two factors, residual value and lease length, impact lease costs. In Table 7.1, you lease a car with a $20,000 cap cost, a money factor of 0.002917 (which is equivalent to a 7% interest rate, 0.07/24 = 0.002917), a lease term of four years, and different possibilities for residual value. We compute four pay-

Table 7.1
Car lease payments for different residuals, based on a $20,000 cap cost, 7% interest rate, and 4-year lease

Residual Value	Monthly Payment
$12,000	$260.00
$11,000	$277.92
$10,000	$295.83
$9,000	$313.75

ments based on residual percentages of 60%, 55%, 50%, and 45%. Obviously, the higher residuals save monthly costs.

In Table 7.2, we use the same cap cost and money factor, but we allow the lease length to vary between two and five years. We keep the residual value constant by using a fixed rate of depreciation per year (12.5%).

Going out the extra years doesn't save as much per month as you might expect, especially when compared to the payments for a car loan (see, for example, any row in Table 6.1). This is because the residual value is declining steadily as the number of years is increasing. So,

When leasing a car, focus on the automobiles, in the class of car you are considering, that have the highest residual value.

FEATURES OF A LEASE

Now that you have the basics down, let's make some further, less obvious, observations about the components of a car lease.

Table 7.2
Car lease payments for different lease periods, based on a $20,000 cap cost, 7% interest rate, and 12.5% annual depreciation

Lease Length in Years	Monthly Payment
2	$310.42
3	$303.13
4	$295.83
5	$288.54

- Although lease arrangements remain mysterious to many car consumers, the mathematical formula for a lease payment is actually much *less* complicated than the formula for a loan payment. You need only compare the formula for a lease payment in this chapter with the formula for a loan payment in Chapter 6 to see that.
- The capital cost of a new car in a lease is the price that *you* agree to pay the dealer for the car. That number is usually between the MSRP and the dealer invoice, although there are rare occasions when it lies outside that range. The capital cost could be higher if the car you seek is really hot and you are willing to pay an exorbitant amount to get it; the capital cost could be lower if the dealer is really hurting and needs to move some stuff off his inventory.
- Making a down payment on a car you purchase and finance is common practice. It renders the amount borrowed lower and so keeps down your monthly loan payments. It also increases your equity in the car. And a bigger down payment may entice the lender to give you a more favorable interest rate. Even if not, you will generally be required to put down some minimal amount to even qualify for any loan. So down payments on financed car purchases are sensible, and usually mandatory. But down payments on leases are much less sensible. True, a down payment will lower your monthly payment, but I still think it is a bad idea for the following reasons:

    1. You are not building any equity in the car as you do when you finance a purchase. In principle, you get back some of your down payment on a financed car when you sell it. Your down payment on a lease is *gone*.
    2. The monthly amount you pay for a given car in a lease is already considerably less than what you would pay if you bought it—even with a sizeable down payment. Why do you need to lower your monthly payment even more?
    3. As mentioned above, the size of your down payment on a car loan may influence the interest rate. I have never heard of such an advantage to a down payment for a lease.

- In the computations that went into Tables 7.1 and 7.2, I have taken the depreciation to be linear, that is, a fixed rate of depreciation each year. More typically, new cars depreciate substantially the first year or so, and then the rate of depreciation declines as the years go by. In fact, for some cars, especially low-end vehicles, the car may depreciate as much as 50% in the first three years. That doesn't make for very good lease terms, particularly for short leases.
- On the other hand, the depreciation rate for high-end vehicles is markedly less than for low-end vehicles. Because of that, one can often get a very attractive lease on a luxury automobile. In particular, the monthly rate on a lease for

a luxury vehicle will generally be much less than the monthly payment on a loan for that vehicle—unless you make a very large down payment. Given the taste for fancy cars among many Americans, the number of Mercedes, Lexus, and Cadillac leases out there should be no big mystery.

BUY OR LEASE

At last it is time to take up the fundamental question of this chapter: Should you buy or lease your next vehicle? Since there is more to life than the size of your bank account, psychological considerations may play a significant role in your decision. I can't hope to fathom your psyche on this issue. But here are some typical personal considerations that arise when people wrestle with this decision.

Reasons to lease rather than purchase:

- You get the pleasure of a new car with much greater frequency. Most folks own their cars for five to eight years, some (such as myself) quite a bit longer. But if you are trading in your new car every three years or so because you *must* have the newest features and can't get by without the wonderful new car smell in your nostrils regularly, then leasing is for you.
- If you are a hand-to-mouth fellow with little or no cash on hand, then scrounging together a substantial down payment is, as the saying goes, "not happening." You may need to lease.
- If you hate maintaining your car—an interminable session in the service shop of your local new car dealer is not your idea of a day well spent—then consider a lease. Although the maintenance costs of a new car that is leased are the same as those for a purchased car, most people who lease, knowing they will return the car while it is still relatively new, put less money into maintenance of the vehicle than they would if it were purchased. And of course you won't have the car when it gets old enough to make more regular visits to the repair shop.

Reasons to buy rather than lease:

- When the payments are finished, you have a car, unlike with a lease where you have *nothing*. You can drive that car for another five or more years without making payments. True, you will have increased maintenance costs, but nowhere near what car payments would be.
- Leases always have mileage restrictions, sometimes fifteen thousand miles per year, often as little as ten or twelve thousand. If you drive in excess of that, you have to pay a mileage charge when you surrender the car. With your purchased car, you can drive to your heart's content.
- You feel better about a car that you own rather than one the dealer or a bank owns. Pride in ownership is an intangible feeling but is quite palpable to some.

MONETARY COMPARISON OF A PURCHASE WITH A LEASE

OK, let's get down to the nitty-gritty, a monetary comparison of leasing versus buying. We will entertain three scenarios, keeping as many variables constant as possible to make the comparison meaningful. We postulate the existence of three consumers looking to obtain the same new car. The purchase price of the car will be $20,000. Taxes and fees at the point of sale will be $1,000. We will assume that the value of the car depreciates 10% per annum over a ten-year period. Finally, we shall ignore insurance but take into consideration maintenance, which we will assume is incurred according to the following ten-year schedule:

- Years 1–2—no cost
- Years 3–4—$500 per year
- Years 5–7—$1,000 per year
- Years 8–10—$1,500 per year

The three consumers each have an initial stash of $21,000. They obtain their cars in the following ways:

- Larry buys a car for cash; he blows his entire stash up front on the purchase price, taxes, and fees.
- Moe also buys a car, but in addition to the taxes and fees of $1,000, he only puts down 20%, or $4,000, out of his stash and finances the rest, $16,000, at 6% over four years. His stash is reduced to $16,000.
- Curly leases a car for four years, also at 6%, which as you know translates into a money factor of 0.0025. Curly's up-front cost is only the grand for taxes and fees. His cap cost is $20,000, and from the assumption on depreciation, the residual value of his auto at the end of the lease in four years will be 60% of $20,000, that is, $12,000. His stash is reduced slightly to $20,000.

We assume that each of the three stooges plans to devote $5,000 per year, taken entirely from salary, to car payments and maintenance, with any left over being placed in an investment that contains the unspent portion, if any, of the original stash and returns 6% per year (just to keep things hypothetically even). We need to keep track of two balances for each stooge: the stash and the equity in the car. Before we do the math, let's make sure we understand qualitatively how things will unfold for each stooge. Larry will pay maintenance costs according to the above schedule, but the vast majority of his $5,000 annual allotment will be invested for his benefit. His equity in the car will slowly but steadily diminish. Moe will initially have to devote most of his $5,000 allotment to car payments and maintenance expenses, but the $16,000 left in the stash after purchase will grow. After Year 4, his equity in the car will match Larry's, and he'll be able to invest much more of his $5,000 allotment. Finally, Curly's $20,000 will grow, but he will always have substantial monthly expenses and never any equity in the car.

Next, let's be a little more quantitative. Larry will invest $5,000 in his stash at the beginning of Years 1–2, then $4,500 at the beginning of Years 3–4 (because he has to set aside $500 each year for maintenance), and finally $4,000 per year in Years 5–7 and $3,500 in Years 8–10. His equity in the car will decrease $2,000 per year from $20,000 to $0 over the course of the ten years. As for Moe, a simple application of the loan formula in Chapter 6 reveals that his monthly payment on the $16,000, four-year loan, at 6%, will be $375.76, yielding an annual expense of $4,509. This means that he can invest only $5,000 – $4,509 = $491 in his stash in Years 1–2, and in fact he has to borrow $9 per year from his stash in Years 3–4. After that, his investment will match Larry's. As for his equity in the car, after two years it would normally decrease to $16,000, but one must also subtract the outstanding loan balance at that time, which is $8,478. So the actual equity at the end of Year 2 is $16,000 – $8,478 = $7,522. As we noted, from Year 4 on, his equity in the car matches Larry's. Finally, what about Curly? Using the lease formula developed in this chapter, we compute that the monthly payment on his $20,000, four-year lease, at 6%, will be $246.67, yielding an annual expense of $2,960. This means that he can invest only $5,000 – $2,960 = $2,040 in his stash in Years 1–2. Then accounting for maintenance, his investment in Years 3–4 will be $1,540. But now the question arises as to how we shall track Curly's assets and expenses after Year 4 when he surrenders his leased vehicle. Of course, Curly will lease another vehicle, as he will yet again after Year 8. He never obtains any equity in any car. And his $20,000 continues to grow. But his expenses associated with each succeeding car will be subject to the forces of inflation. At 3% per year, since $1.03^4 = 1.1255$, we shall adjust his expenses in Years 5–8 by that amount, and since $1.03^8 = 1.2668$, we shall adjust his expenses in Years 9–10 by that amount. I will spare you the arithmetic and just tell you that

in Years 5–6, the amount available to Curly for investment is $1,669;
in Years 7–8, it is $1,106; and
in Years 9–10, it is $1,250.

Next, I present Table 7.3, which summarizes the three stooges' finances—taking into account their equity in the car and the balance of their investment stash—at the end of Years 2, 4, 8, and 10. The data was compiled by making use of the formulas in this chapter for lease payments, the formulas in the previous chapter for loan payments, the formulas in Chapter 1 for the growth of a stash, and the formulas in Chapter 2 for the growth of a regular deposit account. My Bronx High School of Science teachers would be proud of me for tying together all these seemingly unrelated formulas.

Table 7.3
Equity and cash for car buyers and lessees

	Consumer								
	Larry			Moe			Curly		
Years Elapsed	Equity	Cash	Total	Equity	Cash	Total	Equity	Cash	Total
2	$16,000	$1,0947	$26,947	$7,522	$19,147	$26,669	0	$27,150	$27,150
4	$12,000	$22,194	$34,194	$12,000	$21,534	$33,534	0	$33,832	$33,832
8	$4,000	$46,314	$50,314	$4,000	$45,479	$49,479	0	$49,549	$49,549
10	0	$59,881	$59,881	0	$58,942	$58,942	0	$58,602	$58,602

Surprise! Amazingly enough, the totals for the three stooges, in every year in the table, are very close. From a purely financial view, it does not matter very much whether you buy for cash, finance through a loan, or lease—your near-, mid-, and long-term financial worth will be about the same. However, there are definitely some qualifying comments to be made:

- As I mentioned earlier, the assumption of linear depreciation is somewhat of an oversimplification. Typically, automobiles depreciate rapidly at the outset, then slower but more steadily in midlife, and then often even more slowly in old age.
- One consequence of my linear depreciation assumption is the assignment of a rather good residual value to Curly's leased auto. The number is reasonable for a high-end car, but many lower ranked autos will have lower residual rates, thereby negatively impacting the finances for the lease option.
- The maintenance costs I have postulated are fairly modest. If you buy a car that turns out to be a lemon, then the negative impact is on the buyer, whereas a leased lemon can be returned and the lease agreement voided or renegotiated. Even if the car is not a lemon, maintenance costs in the out years could be substantially higher than I projected, again disadvantaging the buyer compared to the lessee.
- The imposition of the same 6% rate on all three mechanisms—investment rate, loan rate, and lease rate—is idealistic. A significant disparity among the rates will have obvious consequences: a high investment rate hurts the individual with a small initial stash, that is, Larry; a high loan rate hurts Moe; and a high lease rate hurts Curly.
- The model assumes that Larry, and Moe eventually, have the self-discipline to maintain regular investments with the money that they, unlike Curly, are not devoting to car payments.
- Finally, the table indeed reveals that with reasonable assumptions on the financial parameters that influence the outcome, the choice among paying

cash, financing, and leasing can comfortably be made based on nonfinancial considerations. In this regard, please refer to the lists in the previous section "Buy or Lease."

From a strictly financial point of view, assuming that you have the cash equivalent of the purchase price of a new car and that you are disciplined about investing unspent cash, then your financial resources down the line remain almost the same regardless of whether you obtain your new car by paying cash for it, financing it, or leasing it.

What if you don't have the cash up front, either to plunk down at the dealership or to invest while you pay off a loan or lease? Too many Americans find themselves in that unfortunate position. Their only choices then—provided they have an income that can carry payments—are to lease or to finance as much of the car as the dealer will permit. Let's run another financial comparison of these options only.

In Table 7.4, Larry is now out of the game, but Moe and Curly are still playing. Let's keep the same parameters as previously but assume a stash of only $2,000—enough to cover fees and taxes ($1,000), and a 5% down payment ($1,000). (Sad to say, even this may be too generous an assumption for some folks. But there is scarcely a dealer who will let you out the door with a vehicle on 0% down.) To keep matters equal, we'll assume that Curly uses $1,000 as a cap cost reduction. So, Larry and Curly are financing or leasing on the same $19,000 basis instead of $16,000 as in the previous case. The monthly lease payment is then $223.33, for a total annual expense of $2,680. The monthly loan payment is $446.22, for a total annual expense of $5,355. We keep the maintenance costs as before and use the 3% inflation factor for the renewal leases (every four years). Now we shall keep track of the out-of-pocket money for the

Table 7.4
Equity and cash for car buyers and lessees with little down

	Consumer					
	Moe			Curly		
Years Elapsed	Gross Expenses	Equity	Net Expenses	Gross Expenses	Equity	Net Expenses
2	$10,710	$5,932	$4,778	$5,360	0	$5,360
4	$22,420	$12,000	$10,420	$11,720	0	$11,720
8	$26,920	$4,000	$22,920	$24,911	0	$24,911
10	$29,920	0	$29,920	$31,701	0	$31,701

two stooges, and in Moe's case we'll decrease that amount by the amount of equity he has in the car. As before, the only complicated figure to compute is Moe's equity after two years—namely, $16,000 minus his outstanding loan balance at that time, which is $10,068.

The results in Table 7.4 aren't quite as neutral as in the last comparison. There is a slight but perceptible bias in favor of the buyer. It may not be enough to overcome personal proclivities and nonfinancial considerations, but I leave that to you, gentle reader. Also note that at the end of the game, both of them shell out approximately $30,000 for a $20,000 car.

FINAL THOUGHTS

My personal experience belies the supposition that the value of a new car depreciates to nothing in about a decade. If you look back at Chapter 3, you will see that I have kept several new cars for more than a decade. I donated both the Dart and the Corolla to charity at the end of their days, whence I was able to deduct the so-called blue book value, which, although measured in hundreds of dollars, was not zero. I actually sold the Accord after twelve years for more than $2,000. Not bad.

Although leases are becoming more common, the arrangements continue to be less understood by consumers than those for purchases. At the risk of repeating a few things from earlier in the chapter, some of the pitfalls are:

1. Lease payments are generally due at the *beginning* of the month, unlike loan payments, which are due at the *end* of the month. That is why you need to make your first lease payment before you escape the dealer's showroom. This mitigates against leases in comparison to purchases.
2. A typical loan contract is foreboding enough, but lease contracts are often worse. And some of the mysterious entries often have numbers next to them, meaning your dealer may be charging you for obscure things such as a dispensation fee, a security deposit, an abomination called "tax on cap cost reduction," and other ripoffs—mechanical breakdown protection, life and/or disability insurance, guaranteed automobile protection, and last but not least, an overpriced unneeded extended warranty agreement.
3. Lease deals almost always include mileage limits, sometimes as low as ten thousand miles per year with attendant charges of 10¢ per mile or more for excess mileage. This can add up, especially given that many motorists drive twelve, fifteen, or even twenty thousand miles per year.

4. Too many customers don't realize that they have to negotiate the sales price of the car before they conclude a lease agreement. They simply accept whatever monthly payment the dealer conjures up without understanding the components that went into it. Reading this chapter should forestall that problem for you.
5. Sales tax is another mystery for lease customers. Practices vary from state to state. In some, you pay it up front as you would in a purchase. In others, it is factored into the lease payments, essentially by adding it to the cap cost. The latter arrangement is particularly unappetizing to me, as you are then essentially paying interest on a tax.

The moral of the story: When leasing, make sure you understand how a lease deal works, arm yourself with as much information as you can about your desired vehicle (MSRP, dealer's invoice, residual value, etc.), and above all, don't fall in love with the car before you complete the deal—if you do, you'll be putty in their hands.

YOUR NEW COMPUTATIONAL SKILLS

How to compute the monthly payment on a typical car lease, given that you know the capital cost, the residual value, the interest rate or money factor, and the length of the lease.

CHAPTER 8

Owning or Renting Your Home

Now that we've thoroughly analyzed the second biggest financial transaction of your life (buying a car), we will turn our attention to the biggest (buying a home). We have already explained the finances underlying a loan—for either a car or a home—in Chapter 6. In Chapter 7, we examined the relative costs and conveniences of buying a new car versus leasing one. In this chapter, we shall do something similar for a home.

There were two rationales for the discourse in the last chapter: either you just didn't have the cash on hand to purchase a new car or even to make much of a down payment, so renting, that is, leasing, was the only financial option available to you, or there were certain nonfinancial considerations that impelled you toward temporary possession rather than ownership. Either rationale led you, as a new-car consumer, to the logical and reasonable alternative to buying that leasing offers. Furthermore, the financial analysis in the chapter revealed, surprisingly, that the financial consequences of the choice were actually rather minor.

KEY FACTORS IN THE DECISION

Are there similar considerations at work in the quest for a home? Indeed, we shall see that there are many nonfinancial factors that can influence a house seeker, some toward buying, others toward renting. On the other hand, we shall also see, quickly and easily, that the financial factors point overwhelmingly in one direction:

You should buy a home, not rent one. The actual financial analysis will come later, but I will state right at the outset that there are three extremely powerful reasons for the fact that, from a financial standpoint, ownership is far wiser than tenancy.

- The income tax laws of this land are very heavily skewed to give enormous tax advantages to the owner over the renter.
- Homes, unlike cars, are appreciating assets, not depreciating assets.
- Rents rise with inflation, but mortgage payments remain fixed.

NEW HOMES VERSUS EXISTING HOMES

Before I venture into any comparative analysis—financial and otherwise, I want to dispose of the new-versus-used issue. In the case of cars (see Chapter 7), I concentrated exclusively on new cars. I did so for many reasons, but the three primary ones were as follows:

1. There is virtually no leasing of used cars, and since I wanted to feature the leasing concept, I needed to avoid used cars.
2. There is a vast difference between the sale of a new car by an automobile dealership and the sale of a used car by an individual. The list of points where significant differences appear is very long: advertising, paperwork, formality, financing, warranty issues, monetary transfers, registration and title, incentives, deposits, interaction with the state motor vehicle administration, and on and on. Of course, dealers also sell used cars, and in doing so they have managed to combine the worst aspects of each of the dealership and individual sale phenomena. In order for me to say anything consistent in the last chapter, it was helpful to restrict myself to new cars.
3. Finally, predictability of maintenance and depreciation costs, at least in the short term, is much better for new cars than used ones.

There are also significant differences between new and used homes. (Incidentally, the common phrase used to refer to used homes is "existing homes.") But each of the three reasons listed above are ameliorated to a great extent. There is no lease concept for homes, at least not in the formulaic sense that it exists for cars. Second, although there is quite a difference between dealing with a new-home builder and an individual or family selling a single-family home, those differences are not nearly as vast as they are between a new-car dealer and an individual selling a used car. The presence of a realtor in both cases has a homogenizing effect. Finally, residence in a home usually occurs on a long time scale, much longer than the life of an automobile, so short-term predictability is much less important.

For these reasons, I shall not, when analyzing the differences between renting and owning a home, make any distinction between a new home and an existing one. For the fundamental points I examine, both financial and nonfinancial, whether the house is new or not will usually not be very important. That said, the basic question we are concerned with in this chapter, analogous to the corresponding question on the first page of Chapter 7, is,

Should I buy my home, or should I rent it? Which will be better for me financially?

HOMES AND APARTMENTS

I am using the word "home" in a broad sense to stand for single-family houses, attached homes (as in townhouses or row houses), condominium apartments, co-op apartments, regular rental apartments, trailers, etc. The physical layout and surrounding topography is not important—the point is that the space in which you dwell can either be rented or purchased. Which makes the most sense for you, financially and otherwise?

My four grandparents came to this country at various times between 1890 and 1915. They lived all their lives in rented apartments in New York and Florida. My parents lived most of their lives in rented apartments in New York. Only relatively recently did they buy a condominium in Florida. Most, but not all, of my friends, relatives, and acquaintances with whom I grew up in New York lived in rented apartments. The same was true for my wife, whose parents immigrated to America in 1938 and 1940. Therefore, when my wife and I spent the first eight years of our married life living in rented apartments in four different states, nothing whatsoever seemed amiss to me.

It came as something of a shock to me in 1972 when my wife informed me that it was time to buy a house. Why in heaven's name would I want to do that? Mowing lawns, paying to fix broken utilities, paying real estate tax, not having neighbors down the hall to drop in on, owing all that money to a bank—these did not seem like desirable goals to embrace. Thank goodness she brushed aside my objections and persevered. Aside from the pleasures I have come to enjoy in my home (the privacy; the room to spread out; wonderful space for my children to grow, learn, and play; the deck and garden; the chance to improve it in ways that suited my family's lifestyle), the financial consequences for us would have been dreadful if we had continued to rent for the last thirty years.

My point is that unless you have compelling personal reasons, which may or may not be financial, that mandate tenancy, you need to very seriously reexamine any decision to forego home ownership.

COSTS OF HOME OWNERSHIP

In order to lay some meat on the last assertion, we need to start examining the financial aspects of home ownership. There are two initial points to be made. First, there are some heavy start-up costs just to get into a house. These are borne by you at the closing. They include the amount you put down toward the purchase price and all the other legal fees, taxes, and various one-time payments. These costs can easily run into thousands of dollars, sometimes tens of thousands and even hundreds of thousands. On the other hand, when you enter your rental apartment, there may be some relatively insignificant start-up costs such as a security deposit, moving expenses, and perhaps one to two months of rent in advance. Generally, these are trivial in comparison to the start-up costs for Harry Homeowner.

The second point to raise is that you will incur monthly and annual expenses in the home you own that do not arise in a rental apartment. In the latter, you will have to pay rent, utility bills, insurance, and not much else. But the homeowner will incur the latter two as well as a mortgage payment (in lieu of rent), real estate tax, homeowner association or condo fees (if applicable), nontrivial maintenance costs, and a potential whopper, property improvements.

SETTING UP A MEANINGFUL COMPARISON BETWEEN OWNERSHIP AND TENANCY

At first glance whether to own or rent looks like no contest—the monthly expenses on a home you own will outstrip those on a rental property. (Instead of continuing to refer to "rental apartments," and in recognition that people rent houses and trailers too, we'll use the phrase "rental property.") But before we test that assertion with numbers, we bring to bear the first two of the bulleted points in the section "Key Factors in the Decision" earlier in this chapter. In particular, we invoke the second of them, namely that your home, unlike your car, is an appreciating asset. This means that you should view all the money that you shell out at closing as an *investment,* not as an *expense.* All of the down payment becomes equity in your house. The rest of the money you expend at closing should be viewed as a cost of the investment. The appreciation in the value of your house should compensate for those expenses within one to three years at most. And this brings me to another crucial point. I intimated that the biggest item in the list above of homeowner costs is *improvements.* People often spend a lot of money upgrading their kitchens and baths, adding rooms, installing wet bars or skylights, etc., and improving basic structural items. Again, all of this should be viewed as an additional investment in your property. Every improvement increases the value of your house. Whether you will eventually recover all of your investment, or make a profit, or take a loss is uncertain—although history teaches that your chances of profiting are excellent. The process is not so different from buying more stock in a company you already own. You are enhancing your investment position. There is no analog whatsoever in a rental property.

The upshot of the last paragraph is the following. To compare monthly expenditures in a home rental versus those in a purchase, you can legitimately compare only the monthly rent against the monthly mortgage payment plus the monthly real estate tax costs plus the maintenance. (If you are in a townhouse or condo and paying a fee, those funds are overwhelmingly expended on maintenance.) Improvements and closing costs are dynamic investment expenses that have no analog in a static rental property. Other typical items such as furniture, insurance, and utility bills are common to both renters and buyers.

CRUNCHING THE NUMBERS

OK, let's try to put some numbers into this exercise. A famous saying in real estate is that there are three critical factors that determine the price of a property: "Location, then location, and then location." Indeed, there is a great deal of truth, locally and globally, to the saying. You will pay a lot more for a house in New York than you will for the same house in Tulsa. And even within both of those cities, there are neighborhoods that are, for one reason or another, more desirable and in greater demand than others, and so the real estate prices are higher than for comparable properties in other neighborhoods.

Therefore, in a book such as this, giving typical real estate figures that are applicable all over the country is difficult. (It's much easier for cars.) So, I will give some sample numbers that pertain to rental properties in the Washington, D.C., metropolitan area in the year 2003. Let us consider three different types of rental properties. In the first, the neighborhood is not so desirable—the property is a bit old or run down, and the net square footage is low. Nevertheless, in the D.C. area a property meeting such a description commonly rents for something on the order of $1,000 per month. To step up to a better neighborhood, maybe with better schools, more space, newer or refurbished facilities, you are likely to pay as much as $1,500 per month. And, finally, if you take another step up in all these categories (don't mistake me, I'm not talking about a penthouse in the Watergate, just a very nice rental property), you could easily be up to $2,000 per month. In every instance, the rent is out-of-pocket cash, gone forever with no return of any kind.

Now, we want to compare these rental costs to those incurred by owners of comparable properties in the D.C. area. In order to do it properly, we bring in the first of the three key homeowner advantages mentioned on the first page of this chapter—namely, the tax laws. The point is that the interest you pay on your home mortgage is deductible from your federal and state income tax. Moreover, the real estate tax that you pay on the property is deductible from your federal income tax. The actual savings to you depends on your marginal income tax bracket. Let us take a relatively conservative approach. We'll assume that the individual renting the low-end apartment has marginal tax rates of 15% (federal) and 5% (state), the mid-end renter has rates of 25% and 7%, and the high-end renter has rates of 30% and 8% rates. (These are at best educated guesses. Brackets were changed in the 2001 tax laws, and there may be further changes soon.) Their total effective marginal rates, therefore (taking into account that state taxes are deductible on federal returns), are 19.25%, 30.25%, and 35.60%, respectively.

Next, let's compute for each of the three cases what a comparable monthly expenditure would be if these renters were homeowners. An important observation is that not all of the monthly mortgage payment goes toward interest; some of it goes to principal. In fact, at the beginning of a typical thirty-year mortgage, roughly 85% of the monthly payment is applied to interest and will be deductible from income tax. We will presume an after-tax monthly real estate tax payment of $225, $150, and $75, respectively, for the three properties. What this means is that, for example, the mid-level homeowner has a monthly real estate tax bill of $200, but his federal tax bracket of 25% leads to a deduction in federal income tax of $50, leaving a net monthly real estate tax bill of $150. The situation is similar for the other two fellows. Next we have to assess an amount for maintenance. This is highly dependent on many factors, but a reasonable set of monthly numbers would be $300, $200, and $100, respectively, for the high-, mid-, and low-level homes.

Now what is the equivalent of the three monthly rental figures of $1,000, $1,500, and $2,000 for the homeowner? In fact, the three figures are $1,116.40, $1,898.04, and $2,640.00, respectively. I will spare you the arithmetic behind all the computations, but let's double-check it for one of the levels—just so you will trust me that the numbers I supplied are correct. We'll work with the low-level property. (Stay with me now—the reasoning is a little complicated.) I claimed that the owner of the low-end property shells out $1,116.40, and that this is equivalent to the comparable renter's $1,000. How so? First, the owner pays $75 per month (after tax) for real estate levies and then $100 for maintenance costs. That leaves $1,116.40 – $175 = $986.40 for the mortgage payment. Of that figure, 15%, or $147.96, goes toward principal, and the remainder, $838.44, goes toward interest. Now, applying the overall marginal tax rate of 19.25%, we see that the interest payment of $838.44 generates an income tax savings of $161.40. Subtracting this amount from his monthly expenditure of $1,116.40, we see that the difference is $1,000, exactly what the corresponding renter lays out per month. Similar reasoning applies to the other two levels.

To reiterate, allowing $175 for monthly maintenance and (after-tax) real estate levies, then a mortgage payment of $986.40 yields a total after-tax monthly expense of $1,000—exactly what the corresponding renter is paying out per month. The analogous numbers for the mid-level homeowner are $350 for maintenance and real estate, $1,548.04 for the mortgage, and for the high-level homeowner $525 for maintenance and real estate, $2,115.00 for the mortgage. The key question now is how big a mortgage those payments will support. The answer depends of course on the interest rate. Table 8.1 gives answers for several interest rates on a thirty-year mortgage.

To ensure that you understand: the middle entry, $232,682, means that to have monthly housing expenditures for a mid-level home equivalent to the $1,500 that the renter would spend, you can have a mortgage of up to $232,682.

Table 8.1
What you can borrow at different rates corresponding to certain fixed payment amounts

	Monthly Payment Amounts		
Interest Rate	**Low-End ($986.40)**	**Mid-Level ($1,548.04)**	**High-Level ($2,115.00)**
6%	$164,523	$258,200	$352,764
7%	$148,263	$232,682	$317,901
8%	$134,430	$210,972	$288,240

Now, presuming that mortgage represents 90% of the purchase price—that is, your down payment was 10%—then this figure translates into a $258,536 purchase price. Instead of forking out $1,500 toward a nonequity-building rental property, you now own a quarter million-dollar house and, in principal, aren't laying out any more cash every month. So

 Save up that down payment and closing cost money. It's vital to get you into a home of your own.

Incidentally, note that in the financial analysis that culminated in Table 8.1, I made explicit use of the first bulleted item in the section "Key Factors in the Decision" in this chapter, but I made no use of the second and third bulleted items. Even without them, the case for ownership over tenancy is powerful. With them, the argument is irresistible.

A SURPRISING OBSERVATION

What I will conclude next is based on highly subjective reasoning; others might have a different interpretation. Look back at Table 8.1. I'll work with the 6% numbers—they are quite typical at the time of this writing. I assert that a loan of $164,523 will get you into a reasonably nice small condo, certainly better than what you might expect to be able to rent for $1,000 per month. A loan of $258,200 will finance entry into a nice, modest-size townhouse in many attractive neighborhoods in the D.C. area. It will be comparable in quality to what you could rent for $1,500. And finally, a loan of $352,764 will get you into a very nice house with four bedrooms and lots of nice amenities, but perhaps not quite as fancy as a $2,000 apartment will be. In short, what I am saying is that in all instances you can live as well, often better, for the same monthly expenditure in a home you buy as you can in a rental property. The potentially controversial conclusion I am outlining is that this assertion is even more pronounced for low-end homes than for high-end homes. Comparably speaking, you can get more for the same money in a low-end property than you can in a high-end property. So, you young folks out there, get yourself into home ownership ASAP. You'll live better, you'll have more money, and your investment will grow in value.

NONFINANCIAL CONSIDERATIONS

Next, let's do what we did in the last chapter for cars, that is, lay out some of the *nonfinancial* considerations that enter into the decision between owning and renting a home. Here goes:

Reasons to rent rather than purchase:

- A home constantly needs attention. Grass must be mowed, appliances break down and need repair, walls get dirty and wallpaper gets torn, bath tiles break and light fixtures short out. Harry Homeowner must either repair and replenish by himself or pay someone to do the work for him. Either way, it costs in time, money, and energy. The renter just contacts the landlord and lets someone else take care of the problem. If the landlord is unresponsive, the renter can always relocate to a different rental property.
- Many people like change—they grow weary of the same situation over time. Well, it is much easier to change rentals than it is to go through the enormous hassles associated with buying and selling real estate.
- Generally, but not universally, rental properties are more conveniently located to shopping, transportation, education, and entertainment. The suburban home is often quite isolated from these amenities, while the urban or quasi-urban apartment rental is often very close to them.
- A house is a lot of work. If you are elderly, have some physical limitations, or would prefer to spend your Saturdays in the park rather than tending to the needs of your house, then renting looks attractive.

Reasons to buy rather than rent:

- You value the privacy that being surrounded by only your four walls affords.
- You take pride in the things you own and love to put them into the best possible condition, either for your own satisfaction or to show them off. Except for your children (well, maybe your job, or your car, or your dog for some of you), nothing is a greater source of satisfaction and pride than your wonderful house.
- You want to leave a legacy in the form of an inheritance for your children, one they can live in rather than spend.

These are all very subjective considerations. Different people might arrive at different conclusions based on the same evidence. Moreover, I'm sure that you would add items to both lists depending on your own inclinations. In fact, I will list two more issues that touch on the decision between ownership and tenancy. They are somewhere in the gray area between financial and nonfinancial, and since they are also subjective in nature, they might swing you either way in the choice. They are:

- Repair and renovation needs that arise in a home are not only an immediate concern, but also a long-term issue. If you don't maintain a home properly, its resale value could plummet. Since your home is an investment, you need to nurture and maintain it. This requires perseverance and discipline as well as the time, money, and energy mentioned above.
- Many popular writers have said that a home is an investment but that you should not select a home primarily, or even largely, on that basis. You should choose a home because you want to live in it; the fact that it's also an investment should be secondary. Well, not everyone agrees with that opinion. I have encountered many young people, typically young couples without children, who view their homes almost totally as an investment. They research real estate markets, buy a home with the intention of trading up after a short period, and then do it again. They turn over houses like some people churn a stock portfolio. Hey, it's a free country—if that works for you, fine. Others might say that it's too much of a hassle, that they can do much better building assets in the stock market and will either buy or rent for the classic reasons.

BUY A HOME!

All the previous being said, I still believe the case for ownership over tenancy is overwhelmingly clear. The three items in the bulleted list near the start of this chapter are extremely persuasive. The first one factored prominently in the financial analysis I did, and the others are mighty compelling also. In particular, inflation works for you in ownership but against you in rental. If you rent, then, whether you move a lot or not, you can expect that your rental costs will accelerate along with the cost of living. However, if you bought your house and have a mortgage, then those mortgage payments are fixed, for *thirty years* in many cases. Now that is what I call *inflation protection.* The other expenses of your home (maintenance, taxes, etc.) will be subject to inflation, but not that old mortgage payment. To quote another well-worn real estate phrase, as we did in Chapter 7 when introducing loans, "You are paying back your debt in deflated dollars."

This book is being written at the time of a real estate boom. Real estate values have been leaping ahead all over the country, starting in late 2000 and continuing until who knows when. Nevertheless, one always has to keep in mind that the overall trend up in real estate values is a *long-term* one. There will be periods of sharp upturns, slow growth, flat prices, and modest declines. Fortunately, it has been a very long time since our country witnessed any period of rapid decay in real estate prices. Over the life of a thirty-year loan, you can expect an appreciation in your property values of something of the order of 3–5% per year. That, of course, means that you can predict nothing about what will happen in the year 2006, for example. Incidentally, I and a lot of other folks learned the same painful lesson about the stock market recently. But more on that later.

The appreciation in real estate values makes your home a convenient target for folks who want to lend you money. If the estimated value of your home has gone up $50,000 (over whatever period), then it becomes very tempting to take out the accumulated equity in the form of a home equity loan—especially if interest rates have declined. You might be able to pull out the entire sum in cash without increasing your payments too much. This can be a useful thing to do, for example, if you need to buy a new car and your monthly income is stretched to the limit already with various payments, or you want to pay for a college education, or you need to ransom your spouse. You need to keep in mind that the equity you took out will not be there for you when you eventually sell the house, and you may not be able to structure the transaction to keep your payments as low as you hoped (if interest rates are not cooperating, for example). We'll have more to say about debt, home equity lines of credit, and credit cards in general in Chapter 10.

YOUR NEW COMPUTATIONAL SKILLS

How to compare the monthly costs of a homeowner with a renter for comparable level properties, and how much mortgage a specific monthly allotment will support.

CHAPTER 9

Insurance

You have a job that provides you with a salary. Thanks to that salary you have a car, maybe more than one; you have a house, hopefully with a family in it; you have a life filled with material goods and human relationships that enrich your days. Naturally, when you contemplate your situation, you wonder, "How am I going to protect this stuff?" One component of the answer is surely the wise and judicious decisions and actions that you make and take. If you have reached a level of success in your life, then it is likely that the main reason is your own energy, ambition, and drive. Keep it up! Still, you worry, "Part of the explanation for my success is definitely good fortune. There were a few key points over the years where if things had broken differently, I might not be in such a good place. What if my luck takes a turn for the worse?" A classic solution to the dilemma is *insurance*. Resorting to insurance is a tried-and-true method for protecting oneself and one's family, home, business, and possessions.

In this chapter, we will discuss several types of insurance. A select few will be very familiar and extremely important to you: health, life, car, home. Some are less familiar, and less often deployed, but still very important: disability, umbrella, business, long-term care. Some are programs and practices, which, although they may be familiar to you, you may not think of as insurance: extended warranties, stock options, prenuptial agreements. Finally, we'll discuss some government programs that most people think of as insurance, but that I will argue are something else: Social Security, Medicare, workers' compensation, and unemployment insurance.

THE DEFINITION OF INSURANCE

In order for me to make the argument implicit in the last sentence, we need to have a clear understanding of what we mean by insurance. An *insurance* policy or contract is basically a *bet* between you and the insurer, that is, the company or organization that issues the policy. You bet that something *bad* is going to happen to you and/or yours, while the insurer bets that it won't. The "something" is confined to a specific type of bad occurrence, although the exact nature of the occurrence may be quite variable within the type. A key difficulty in administering the bet is to define as precisely as possible the bad occurrences that qualify under the policy. Once you and the insurer reach agreement on those, then the policy is almost always administered as follows. You pay a predetermined fee to the insurer. The fee may be paid completely up front or on a regular cycle. Until and unless something bad happens, the insurer is winning the bet—he is collecting and you are paying. If the policy term expires without anything bad happening, then the insurer has won the bet. If, on the other hand, something bad happens, then the insurer has to pay you—probably according to a payment structure that was also part of the original agreement. The amount disbursed may far exceed the total fees you have paid. That means you have won the bet. Of course, it also means that you may be sick, homeless, or dead—not exactly in a position to enjoy your winnings. But if you hadn't placed the bet, you'd still be sick, homeless, or dead, and without any financial compensation.

This illustrates that insurance is either a win-win or lose-lose proposition—it depends on your point of view. If you are a "glass is half-empty" kind of person, then you might reason as follows: If I lose my insurance bet, then I spent money, which, it turns out, I did not have to spend. If I win the bet, I am sick, homeless, or dead. Either way, I feel cheated. But if you are a "glass is half-full" type, then you might think: If I lose the bet, then at least I bought myself peace of mind, which relieved me of a lot of worry. And if I win the bet, then the financial compensation is a great help toward easing the pain of my loss.

Most people, regardless of their stance on the amount of liquid in glasses, believe in and purchase some insurance. And yet there are those who buy little if any. Their reasons vary: inability to afford, forgetfulness or ignorance, playing the odds, or perhaps philosophical objections. It's a free country and your choice. But, in one instance—namely, *health* insurance—the decision to forego insurance is certainly the height of folly. Only the direst financial straits should prevent you from securing health insurance. As for all the other forms of insurance available to you, there are important decisions of whether and how much that await you. Hopefully the discussion below will help you to decide on your needs. I will treat the various forms of insurance in descending order of importance, at least as I see it.

INSURANCE IS A BET

But first, a few comments:

- If insurance is a bet, then you would like to know the odds. How likely are you to wind up sick, homeless, or dead? When you bet on the ponies or place any other (legal?) sports bet, the odds are usually available to you. But, the odds are generally *not* available to most bettors in many other forms of gambling. People usually don't know the odds of winning at the bingo parlor, in their state lottery, or at the blackjack table in Vegas. Yet, this doesn't stop them from betting. That may be because aside from the desire to win, there is an ulterior motive for making the bet: entertainment, or a need to conform (being part of a crowd you're with), or a compulsion you cannot resist. Similarly, most of us buy insurance unaware of the exact odds that we will become sick, homeless, or dead. The ulterior motive, indeed the prime motive or reason behind the purchase, might be found among peace of mind, desire to conform with the expectations of society, mandatory nature of insurance (e.g., car insurance), the ease of its purchase (e.g., through payroll deduction), or the intense fear of winning the bet regardless of the odds.

- Providing exact odds is often not simple. There are so many factors that go into determining them that insurers might need to narrow the pool too much in order to specify them. Some of the factors affecting the odds (of course depending on the type of insurance) include age, gender, race, geographical location, profession, nature of dwelling, family structure, family history, psychological profile, and more. Nevertheless, statistics being the sophisticated discipline it is today, insurers could provide meaningful odds on insurance bets. But generally, the insurance industry does not specify the odds. This suits them just fine. After all, who wouldn't want to make a bet knowing the odds when the other bettor does not know the odds? Moreover, the public usually does not ask. The reason for the apparent lack of curiosity is twofold. First, as indicated, the prime motivation for the insurance purchase may not be financial. Second, the general level of math anxiety among people depresses their desire to know. So they don't ask. Well, I'll try to give some rough indications later in a few of the insurance types that I discuss.
- Even knowing the odds might not simplify your insurance shopping. The reason is that even within a specific type of insurance, the policies drawn up by different vendors may have significant differences—thereby, of course, affecting the odds and making comparisons difficult.

I think people understand, even if only subconsciously, that buying insurance is basically a bet. But their decision on whether to buy a type of insurance, in what form, at what level, and from which vendor, is not made with the notion of a bet in mind. They try to approach the purchase of insurance like they do the purchase of a commodity. Namely, they reason that insurance is something they need or want (for the reasons enumerated above)—just like they might want a stereo or need a washing machine—and they only need to figure out who is selling the best product at the most economical price and then buy it. They think of it as a purchase, not a contract or a wager. What they buy is peace of mind and/or financial compensation for specific but unpredictable future events.

Here's a personal story that impinges on both insurance and loans. As I've told you, when I was a student at City College of New York, I worked one summer in the Bowery Savings Bank. In those days there were very few summer jobs for students; I got the job by pretending to be a high school graduate who never went on to college. The bank hired me as a file clerk in the life insurance department. Most of what I filed was correspondence between policyholders and the bank, documenting all manner of excuses for why policyholders needed to skip a payment, or why they really were entitled to a payout even though they were not dead, or why they absolutely must have an interest-free loan against their policy. They rarely prevailed. When my extraordinary filing capabilities became evident to my supervisor, he decided that I should be promoted—from filing to posting. I posted payments—both policy premiums and loan payments. In order to qualify me to do so, the supervisor felt he should explain the concept of compound interest to me, for two reasons: (1) the policies were whole life and so carried cash balances that accrued interest, and (2) loan fees compounded when not paid in full on time. So he explained compound interest to me. Not wanting to reveal my true status as an "educated" college student, I listened politely and gradually acknowledged that I understood, whereupon he proceeded to explain it again. Once more, I confirmed my understanding. Nevertheless, he launched into yet a third explanation, and the process repeated itself several more times, despite the fact that I never gave him any reason to suspect that I did not understand. Finally, he drew close to me and whispered in his thickest New York accent, "You da foist guy dat ever understood dis stuff!"

My point in telling this story is not to snobbishly highlight the relatively low intellectual level of the clerks who worked in the life insurance industry in the 1960s, but rather to illustrate the fact that it was, and is, unquestioningly accepted by most people that one could not expect anyone to have even the most rudimentary understanding of a concept such as compound interest or any receptivity to gaining that knowledge. The same attitude prevails in regard to all the basic arithmetic concepts that we have encountered in these pages. Those attitudes were, and are, most unfortunate, and they supply the prime reason for this book.

HEALTH INSURANCE

You must have health insurance. Why? Because you are not going to lose the bet. Something bad *will* happen. It's almost guaranteed. You or a member of your family will get sick. It will probably be routine stuff such as flu, or an ingrown toenail, or an allergic reaction that causes a nasty rash, or some minor ache or pain that sends you to the orthopedist. Maybe you'll get a toothache, or need an eye exam, or suffer from a urinary tract infection. It is the nature of life and the less-than-perfect design that G-d has produced for the human body. It breaks down periodically. Fortunately, most of the time it is not so serious, and although we may need the ministrations and nostrums that medical professionals can supply to quickly heal our minor wounds, the vast majority of us are not so tough or pigheaded to endure the symptoms while waiting for our bodies to heal themselves. We go to the doc. The amount we collect from our health insurance policies to compensate for the medical fees we incur to treat our minor illnesses and injuries may not exceed the premiums we pay, but still I think it fair to say that the health insurance bet is worth making.

Sometimes our medical needs are more serious: broken bones or persistent aliments that are not life-threatening such as irritable bowel syndrome, a chronically bad back, asthma, gout, menopause, or an enlarged prostate that may cause repeated doctor visits and extensive medication. In these situations you will incur more than minor medical expenses, and so you clearly win the bet. And finally, you could win the bet big-time, that is, you might encounter something catastrophic such as heart disease, cancer, or a devastating injury. In that case, to not have placed the bet, that is, to be without health insurance, can lead to poverty if you pursue treatment or disability or death if you fail to treat. Regardless of the level of your medical emergency, you will find that medical costs are high and climbing steadily. Even medical expenses for injuries, conditions, and illnesses that are not life-threatening can easily exceed an uninsured person's budget.

So go get health insurance. Where do you get it? The answer is a consequence of a historical accident that may be at the heart of much of our health insurance problems in the United States. Namely, the vast majority of us obtain our health insurance through our employers. That this is so is an anomaly. Generally, we do not obtain life, car, home, and most other forms of insurance through our employer. We buy them in the open market as we would any other product. But we get health insurance through our employers. This situation arose more than fifty years ago when employers were looking for ways to provide benefits to employees other than straight salary. One motivation was to minimize taxes, both for employers and employees—yet another case of an unintended consequence of our tax laws. Well, for better or worse, the system whereby health insurance is obtained through the employer is firmly entrenched in our society. With the increasing popularity of *cafeteria plans* that embrace tax-deferred status for the premiums we pay for health insurance, I have a hard time imagining the system changing.

Why is employer-sponsored insurance a good thing for the consumer? Why is it bad? There are two main reasons for each. It is good because it is convenient and also because it is (relatively) cheap. It is convenient since you pay for it through payroll deduction and you have a limited number of choices, the research for which is all handled by your employer. It is cheap since you, together with all your coworkers, form a *group*. Group rates for health insurance are *much* lower than individual rates. This is particularly beneficial if you work for a large company or a government agency. Conversely, employer-sponsored health insurance is bad for two reasons. First, you can only select from the plans that your employer offers. A limited choice may be convenient, but it also might mean that the available plans do not meet your needs. Second, your insurance is not portable. If you or your employer severs the relationship, you lose eligibility for the employer-sponsored plan. Job changes are traumatic enough on their own; having them entail health insurance consequences makes them even more so.

Of course, you can buy health insurance on your own in the open market. If you do, you will quickly find that it will be much more expensive than the group plans offered by your employer. But at least you can select a plan more to your liking. Either way, most folks recognize the importance of health insurance, and they buy it. But not everyone. Who are the folks who don't have health insurance?

1. *Poor people.* They may not be able to afford it. Fortunately, many people in this situation find health care in emergency rooms, clinics, and other venues designed to aid the poor.
2. *Young people.* They are playing the odds. Young adults in general don't get sick very much, so they save money by not buying health insurance. Of course, the strategy could backfire big-time, but that's the nature of a bet. Sometimes these folks buy very cheap temporary policies that are limited to catastrophe coverage. Young people, as they age or get steady jobs, usually eventually buy conventional health insurance.
3. *Self-employed people.* There is no employer plan to turn to. Entrepreneurs have to buy their own policy. Some of them don't do it. That's a foolish choice, but one they are free to make.
4. *Unemployed people.* Again, no employer, so no plan to choose from. There is still the route of an individual plan. Also available are so-called COBRA (which stands for Consolidated Omnibus Budget Reconciliation Act) policies. These allow employees whose job affiliation has just ended to retain the same coverage for a limited period (six months or a year) by paying the employer's portion of the fee as well as their own.

There are many different health insurance plans. One size definitely does not fit all. Some of the components that may or may not be included are dental, vision, prescription drugs, and mental health. Whatever plan you choose, you should be sure that it covers catastrophes. That is the main reason for health coverage. In fact, many have argued that the consumer's ability to collect for noncatastrophic illness or injury is one of the prime drivers of high health care costs. Too much demand chasing too little supply. If people paid out of their pockets for minor or moderate health expenses, then they would make doctors appointments more carefully. As we will see, neither car nor home nor life insurance covers routine or preventive maintenance. Why should health insurance?

The answer is third-party payments. If I buy an item from you, I pay you. We are the two transacting parties. However, if I buy routine health care from a doctor, most of the cost is borne by the third party, that is, the insurer. There is little incentive for me not to buy the service since I am not paying for (most of) it. The situation is even more extreme when the government is the insurer (see the sections "Social Security" and "Medicare" below).

Get health insurance. Get basic catastrophic coverage. Select other components as your budget dictates. Even if you don't win the bet in a big way, you won't lose it in a big way either.

Final comments about health insurance:

- Another feature that your employer's cafeteria plan may include is health care accounts. They provide a way to switch your health costs that are not covered by health insurance—e.g., deductibles—to tax-deferred status. Basically, you set aside a fixed amount per paycheck, tax-deferred, that you can use to pay medical bills. The upshot is that the government is paying a percentage of your bill that equals your marginal tax rate. The catch is that if you withdraw more than you spend, you forfeit the surplus.
- If all else fails and you have to pay some big medical bills from your pocket, then you can take some solace from the fact that medical costs are deductible on federal and most state tax returns. Unfortunately, there are floors that limit the deduction, currently 7% of your AGI (adjusted gross income) on your federal return. The net effect of that restriction is to preclude almost any mid- or high-income taxpayer from being able to deduct very much, if anything, of their out-of-pocket medical expenses.
- There are three predominate types of employer health insurance plans available today: HMO, or health maintenance organization; PPO, or preferred provider option; and POS, or point of service. In the latter (POS), you can go to any doctor you choose. In a PPO there is a (hopefully big) list of doctors to choose from. If you use a doctor on the list (or "in the network," as they say), then you pay much less than if you go out of the network. And finally, in an HMO, you have a primary care physician who must approve any visit to a specialist or any nonroutine treatment—but, of course, only with network providers. As you go from POS to PPO to HMO, the benefits paid become more generous, and the premiums you pay are less expensive. The catch is, as the general public is well aware these days, that the quality of the medical care you receive may deteriorate significantly.
- People are so concerned about their health insurance needs that an industry in *supplemental health insurance* has grown up. A decent health insurance plan probably renders supplemental plans unnecessary, but those of you without a good plan or with *very* special health risks may want to investigate them.

AUTOMOBILE INSURANCE

You might argue that either home or life insurance is at least as important as car insurance. Why have I placed the latter in second place in my priority ranking? Because car insurance is mandatory. Indeed, an automobile insurance policy covering the cars you drive is required by law in forty-seven of the fifty states.[1] Still, some less than law-abiding citizens neglect to purchase it, but that wouldn't be you. Like health insurance, car insurance covers both minor and major expenses. Within the former are nuisances such as fender-benders, minor vandalism, and small automotive glitches. Among the major occurrences are theft, serious vandalism, crashes resulting in severe damage and/or bodily injury, and the medical expenses and liability issues that may ensue. But there are two major differences between the two types of insurance. First, routine or preventive maintenance is not covered by your auto insurance. You cannot claim expenses for an oil change, new tires, or even for a diagnostic inspection. Second, the fee structure is designed to encourage you to pay for minor expenses out of your pocket. This is accomplished by (1) offering substantial savings for policyholders who take high deductibles and (2) raising your rates after you file claims, especially claims that result from your actions or negligence. In fact, the best and most economical way to structure your auto policy is to have a very high deductible, say $1,000 or more. This will keep your premiums as low as possible and force you to pay for minor expenses out of pocket. Nevertheless, statistically, you will still save money overall. But more importantly, a higher deductible will cause you to view your auto policy basically as catastrophe insurance for major events, which is the correct way to view it.

There is another important point to be made here. Namely, the quality of the service provided by the company that issues your auto policy is as important as the price the company charges you. Are its policies and statements clear and concise? Can you reach the insurance company all the time? Does the company dispatch claims adjusters quickly? Will the company work hard for your interests in disputed and litigated cases? Does it pay promptly? Are the employees courteous, responsive, and helpful? Many consumer organizations rate insurance companies; the ratings are worth a look. I have been using Amica Mutual Insurance Company for twenty years and can vouch that in its case all the questions above have the right answer. In fact, I think the quality of your company is more important than the price of your coverage. Prices can be influenced by various factors, including your age, the category and status of your car, where you live and work, your driving record, and most importantly whether you or other drivers on the policy are teenage boys. You cannot influence the quality of the company you select.

1. The three exceptions were New Hampshire, Tennessee, and Wisconsin in March 2003.

Choose a reputable firm for your car insurance; choose a policy with high deductibles; accept the fact that car insurance is a necessity, primarily to assist you in coping with calamitous car accidents; recognize that like health insurance, car insurance is a bet you hope not to win in a big way, but you might; and move on to the next insurance decision.

HOME INSURANCE

If you own a home filled with stuff, then you need to insure it—both the home and the stuff. Even if you rent, insuring your stuff is not a bad idea. There are no laws mandating homeowner's insurance, but if you have a mortgage the lender will almost certainly require it as a condition of the loan. As with health and car insurance, home insurance will cover both minor and major expenses. Minor claims against homeowner policies are even rarer than minor claims on auto policies, but they include minor damage from storms, furniture breakage, and loss of jewelry or other valuables that you have placed on your policy through riders (see the last item in the bulleted list below in this section). Major claims usually involve destruction due to fire; major damage caused by flood, earthquake, or other environmental disaster; medical or liability costs due to an accidental injury; and theft or other criminal activity. As with auto insurance, no claims for routine or preventive maintenance will be entertained. You cannot file a claim for a new water heater or to paint the house or clean up the yard, or for any renovations, home improvements, or estimates for construction or repairs. Finally, like auto insurance, you are best served by structuring your policy to have high deductibles and to plan to pay for routine or modest expenses out of your pocket, thereby regarding the policy almost exclusively as catastrophe insurance.

Claims on homeowner policies occur with much less frequency than claims on auto policies. The chances of you losing the bet are actually pretty good. For that reason, people pay much less attention to their homeowner's insurance than to their auto or health insurance. And so sometimes they sign up with a marginal company that does not come through for them when the need arises. I have had my homeowner's insurance with Amica for a long time. Actually, I have never filed a claim, but my experience in dealing with the company in auto affairs gives me complete confidence that service on my homeowner's policy would be just as excellent.

Prices on homeowner's insurance are more predictable than they are for auto insurance. Your rates will largely be determined by the size, style, age, and structure of your house as well as its locale, what it appraises for, and any special features. Rates are generally low, again reflecting the relative paucity of claims. So the same basic principles that were stated for auto insurance apply: select a reputable firm, set your deductibles high, view the policy as catastrophe insurance, pay it, and (hopefully) forget it.

Since the rates for homeowner's insurance are relatively low, it behooves you to consider several additional features that may enhance your peace of mind:

- You usually set the policy amount on your homeowner's insurance. The insurer will not approve a ridiculously high amount but generally will write a policy for any amount you specify up to some maximum amount that the carrier deems the the house may be worth. If you allow the insurer to set the amount of coverage, the company will peg it to appraisals in your area. The insurer will also guarantee that you are covered for replacement cost if your house is destroyed, and you may save some money on your premium. Amica has a program such as this; other companies may not.
- You also may be able to get replacement cost coverage on your furniture and household belongings. If you suffer a loss and show an adjuster a receipt for an item purchased many years ago, the amount shown will be all the company will reimburse. With replacement cost coverage, the insurer is obliged to reimburse you for the cost of a replacement item at today's prices.
- The coverage amount for certain personal valuables such as jewelry, furs, silverware, and fine china may be limited on your policy. To set higher payment limits, you can write a *rider* to your policy spelling out those items and their worth. You will need to secure appraisals of the items to get the coverage. You can do this for any item—e.g., electronic equipment, cameras, memorabilia—and then those items will be covered in full; the high deductible will not apply to them.

LIFE INSURANCE

You may own or lease many cars in your lifetime. You may own several houses or rent many apartments. Your health may vary from excellent to poor. But you only have one life. You will win the life insurance bet only once. Therefore, life insurance should be a very simple and straightforward product. You live, you pay; you die, they pay. Well, leave it to the life insurance industry to make it complicated. Before I elaborate, let's state succinctly why (most) people buy life insurance. In the vast majority of cases, it is purchased by a breadwinner on behalf of his/her family members (spouse and children usually) in case the grim reaper removes him/her and the supply of money, love, and guidance that he/she normally provides to them. The life insurance proceeds won't replace the love and guidance but will ease the pain of the financial loss.

The complications arise from the fact that life insurance policies come in many flavors. The simplest is *term*. You specify a term (e.g., one year), a benefit amount, and a beneficiary. The insurance company specifies a corresponding premium amount based on your age, sex, and perhaps other factors. You pay the premium. If you survive the term, nothing further happens and no obligations are due. If you don't, then the insurer pays the benefit to the beneficiary. Simple, clean, straightforward. If you are young and trying to provide financial protection for your family, term life insurance is what you should buy. But as I said, the industry has developed alternate products, and I am tempted to say for no other reason but to confuse you. You can buy *whole life*, *universal life*, *convertible term*, and other forms of life insurance. I will not dignify them with a description except to say that most combine insurance with an investment of some type—often involving *annuities*, about which I'll have more to say in Chapter 12. In fact, you will do better on both (i.e., insurance and investment) by keeping them separate. In these vehicles, since some part of your premium goes toward an investment, the policy accumulates a face value, which, on the one hand, is growing (via compound interest and regular additions) and, on the other hand, can be borrowed against. If you read my Bowery Savings Bank story earlier in this chapter, you will appreciate the fact that the industry expects that you don't have a very good handle on what is going on. Stick to term life insurance!

This completes my discussion of the four most important forms of insurance as enumerated in the second paragraph of this chapter. Let's go on now to the next group: disability, umbrella, business, and long-term insurance. My discussion of these will be terse.

DISABILITY INSURANCE

For a young adult, the chances of being disabled easily exceed the chances of a premature death. Nevertheless, far fewer young adults purchase disability insurance than purchase life insurance. They may want to rethink their strategy. Disability insurance is a bet that you will become disabled—partially, temporarily, or permanently—with the payoff being a guarantee of some portion of your salary if you do. Premiums are generally inexpensive for healthy young adults. Both the premiums and the benefits can be tailored according to which of the three categories of disability you want to cover, the nature of the benefits, how long after the onset of the disability they should begin, etc. Many cafeteria plans include disability insurance as an option. Policies are also widely marketed by well-known insurance firms. Naturally, premiums skyrocket as your age increases. But for young folks who have a family and are making a good salary, disability insurance is an excellent idea.

UMBRELLA INSURANCE

This insurance is really an *excess liability* policy. Your home and auto policies contain liability coverage, but there are maximums—the largest amount the insurer will pay if you are successfully sued by someone you injure (or who is injured) in either your car or your home. Those maximums will typically be in the hundreds of thousands of dollars. That may not stop someone from suing you for millions. Umbrella policies give you liability coverage beginning where your home and auto policies leave off, perhaps up to a million dollars or more. You probably don't need this coverage if you don't have millions. If you do, you may want to consult with your lawyer and/or accountant about the desirability of this kind of insurance.

BUSINESS INSURANCE

If you own and operate a business, you have assets therein to protect and perhaps also potential liabilities to forestall. Insurance to do so can take many forms: property insurance on the physical structure in which your business is located as well as the infrastructure it contains; life insurance on the corporate leadership; health insurance or more broadly based cafeteria plans for the businesses employees; fleet insurance on the vehicles the business operates; and liability insurance against the possibility that your clients or customers are injured, slandered, or otherwise maltreated in their dealings with your business. The nature and desirability of different kinds of business insurance depends on the size, structure, and scope of your business. I confess that my limited experience in the business world constrains my expertise to make recommendations to you here. I strongly suggest that you consult the relevant business and insurance experts in deciding how extensively you need to insure your business.

LONG-TERM CARE INSURANCE

An increasingly popular new form of insurance is long-term care insurance. These programs reflect the fact that as people live longer and modern medicine continues to make great strides, many of us will have to spend considerable periods of time under the care of others, especially outside of hospitals. This could take the form of an extended stay in a nursing home or a rehabilitation center, or even at home but under the care of visiting medical and paramedical personnel or friends, relatives, and hired help. The expenses associated with this kind of care can be astronomical—easily beyond most budgets, especially those of elderly folks subsisting on limited funds. An increasing number and variety of policies addressed to those needs are under development by the insurance industry. Many of them are very poor investments. Exposés have been produced revealing fraud, mismanagement, and false promises in this industry. However, recent evidence seems to indicate that the quality of some of these products is improving. This is not the place for a detailed analysis of these programs. But if you are attracted by the idea, you have a lot of work cut out for you browsing the Internet, consulting with friends and your doctors, and evaluating plans. One feature that will make your deliberations painful is that if you are elderly, say in your seventies or eighties, then the premiums for these plans are, not unexpectedly, very high. If you are younger, they can be quite inexpensive. But it may be many years, if ever, before you need the services provided—during all of which time you are paying. Worse, the company may go out of business, or the design of the policy may be completely inappropriate by the time you want to invoke it because of advances in medical care or changes in the economy. Decisions on long-term health care insurance are fraught with uncertainty and inadequate information. Good luck.

OTHER INSURANCE

Now I turn my attention to other forms of insurance, namely, purchases you make and transactions you enter that you may not think of as insurance. But if they basically constitute a bet against the possibility that something bad will happen to you, entailing some form of compensation if indeed the bad something does occur, then you have bought insurance. Actually, there are many items in this category. I already mentioned a few:

- *Extended warranties.* Whenever you purchase an extended warranty, whether on a new car or electronic appliance, or on a product that you already own, you are of course buying insurance. You are betting that the gadget will break down in the period after the manufacturer's warranty expires but while you still own the product. The intended payoff is a low-cost or no-cost repair or replacement. I *never* buy extended warranties. Whoever is offering the deal knows that the odds favor them; that's why they are willing to make the bet. You are throwing away your money. Which gadgets do you insure—all of them? Better to insure none—you will pay less out of pocket on repairs than you will on all the extended warranties.
- *Stock options.* I will describe several forms of stock options in Chapter 12. At this point I will only say that the purchase of a stock option is basically a bet that the price of a stock will move (up or down depending on the nature of the option). The payoff is that you will cut your losses or enhance your gains. These are really risky bets. More later.
- *Prenuptial agreements.* Surely you now recognize these as insurance. You are betting that something bad will happen in the marriage you are about to enter, and you seek to protect your assets if that indeed transpires. You pay for these in legal fees but also in lack of trust between you and your new spouse—sometimes a high price, actually.
- *Others.* An interesting exercise is to see if you can discover other "insurance policies" in your life. Here's a silly one: when you stockpiled your basement in December 1999 because you thought the world was going to fall apart at the turn of the millennium. And a gruesome one: when you pay protection money to the mob. Can you think of others?

Next let's turn our attention to government programs that most folks think of as insurance but that to varying degrees I would like to characterize as something else. I am speaking particularly of Social Security, Medicare, workers' compensation, and unemployment insurance.

SOCIAL SECURITY

This is a highly political, extremely contentious issue that currently engages the hearts and minds of the American populace. One could write a whole book on Social Security. However, any way you slice it, Social Security is definitely not an insurance program. It is at best a retirement program, perhaps an investment program. Taxpayers pay Social Security taxes expecting to get back something at retirement age. They are not betting on anything bad happening, unless you count a long life as an unfortunate occurrence. Contribute now, collect later—sounds like a retirement program to me. But as such, it has a tremendous flaw. Namely, the money that you pay in does not get put to work for you in anticipation of your retirement. Rather, it is used immediately to pay the benefits of current retirees. The money that you might expect to "get back" will be paid from the payroll taxes that will be collected from workers at the time you are retired—if the current system doesn't collapse before then. Virtually every reputable retirement program that one encounters does not work like this. The money that individuals put in a respectable retirement account is invested for their benefit, often augmented by contributions from employers or other sponsors, and the proceeds from those investments—growing over time—constitute the funds that will be paid out to the individual upon retirement. (For additional related information, see Chapters 1, 2, and 13.)

Social Security is definitely not a retirement program in any reasonable sense—and if it is, then it is a disgrace. It is not really an investment program either—at least not a respectable one. The reason is basically the same: the money you "invest" is immediately spent. All you have in your Social Security "account" is a government IOU. But you might ask, "Since people have been paying Social Security taxes for sixty-five years and many of them have collected benefits, what kind of return have they received?" The answer is that those who entered the program at its inception, such as the people in my grandparents' generation, and those who came immediately after them, from my parents' generation, did not do badly. They got a return on their "investment" not incommensurate with what they might have earned in a classic conservative investment program. However, for my generation, current projections are indicating a likely return on the order of 2–3% at best. This is not exactly a smashing success. If Social Security participation had not been mandatory for me, I could have done better investing my money in stocks, bonds, and bank CDs. Unfortunately, the story gets worse. For my children's generation—generation Xers, and even for the baby-boomers, who are only a half generation behind me, projected returns are meager, maybe as little as 1%, perhaps less or even negative real returns.

Well, boys and girls, this sounds suspiciously like a Ponzi scheme to me. Your classic chain letter. The first folks in make out like bandits; those who come later get screwed. The reason is not hard to find. In the first wave, thirty to forty workers were paying taxes for each benefit recipient. Today the ratio is down to three workers for each benefit recipient. Soon it may be two workers for each recipient. You do not have to be a genius to see that we are headed for a political and fiscal disaster. To maintain a solvent Social Security system in the present model, either taxes will have to raised drastically or benefits will have to be cut drastically, or both. The taxes are already too high, the benefits too low. Can you say "train wreck"? That the entire American public does not understand this situation is a testament to the outrageous behavior of politicians who, pretending that we are not headed for a brick wall, make ludicrous statements about the sanctity, stability, and reliability of Social Security.

So, Social Security is not insurance, and not a legitimate retirement program, and not an investment program in any reasonable sense. What is it? It is a transference of wealth—from young working people to elderly nonworking people. In other words, it is *welfare*. Whenever I say that, it drives my mother crazy. Sometimes the truth hurts.

MEDICARE

The administration of Medicare mirrors that of Social Security. Workers pay in now, the money is used to pay Medicare benefits for America's elderly population, and the current crop of workers is left to hope that future workers will be as generous or stupid. In that sense it is a welfare program like Social Security—in this case a transference of wealth from young, healthy, working people, to old, ill, nonworking people. But in fact it is not as egregious as Social Security. In paying Medicare taxes, you are at least in principle trying to plan for a bad occurrence—illness in your old age. But it isn't really a bet in that the money you stake now is not what buys you the compensation when it's time to pay off. You are buying an implicit contract with the insurer—that is, the federal government. Unlike the private industry health insurer, the government is not investing the money and using the proceeds to pay off future claims; the government is spending the money now, assuming that it will be able to collect enough funds from future taxpayers to pay your bills when your time comes. For the same demographic reasons as enumerated in the Social Security discussion, that assumption is problematic.

There is another feature of Medicare that does make it more like an insurance program, rather than welfare—namely, there are some choices to be made that affect your premiums as well as your benefits. In Social Security, your contribution is determined solely by your income—there is nothing voluntary. Moreover, your benefits are established by federal law, and again you have no control over the amount. But Medicare has several pieces, some of which are optional, and you can choose to supplement your coverage after you are retired.

So in this sense it is more like a classic health insurance program and therefore is not as outrageous as Social Security.

WORKERS' COMPENSATION AND UNEMPLOYMENT INSURANCE

These two poorly publicized and ill-understood programs are in fact insurance programs—but not in the precise sense that I have defined insurance in the third paragraph of this chapter. As you will see, there is a key ingredient missing. First of all, these programs are mandated by federal law but administered through the states. The administration and rules vary tremendously from state to state, so I will only say the following. Workers' compensation is basically a requirement that employers meeting certain conditions (e.g., having some minimum number of employees) must carry disability insurance on their workers—policies that will pay compensation to workers who are injured on the job. Unemployment insurance, also varying greatly from state to state, is a pool that workers can draw upon if they lose their job because of downsizing or some other occurrence that is not their own fault. Both programs are funded primarily by employers with supplements from the states and sometimes also from the federal government. Workers incur no payroll deductions, nor do they receive any bills. Thus, these insurance programs are indeed bets (against bad occurrences—on-the-job injury or loss of job), but the bet is placed and financed by the employer, not the employee on whose behalf it is waged. So, although they are insurance programs, neither is anything you have to make a decision about. The coverage is there for you because your employer has no choice but to provide it. This is a classic example of an *unfunded mandate.*

Advertising. America's business community is rather adept at using the media to promote its products, sometimes in a misleading manner. The insurance industry is no exception. As you must when confronting all advertising, you should bring a healthy dose of skepticism when encountering insurance ads. The ones that particularly tick me off are the pitches to the elderly in which it is asserted that "you can't be turned down" and "you can buy peace of mind for your heirs." If you examine those products closely, you will see that the benefits are tailored so narrowly, the coverage is so meager, and the odds are so skewed against the consumer, that whether any of these products is worth your dollar is highly dubious. Purchasing life insurance is no different than any consumer activity in which you engage: you should do your own comparison shopping; read all the fine print; talk to your friends, relatives, and neighbors who have purchased similar products; and choose carefully.

The previous aside notwithstanding, I reiterate that most American business firms, including insurance companies, are generally marketing good products at fair prices. If so, then how do the insurance companies make any money? After all, when disaster strikes in the form of a hurricane, an epidemic, or an act of mass destruction (e.g., the terrorist attacks of September 11), then the payouts will be so massive as to call into question the viability of the industry. How can insurance companies afford to pay out all that money? The answer is in the odds. The occurrence of horrendous events is factored into the computation of the odds that the insurance companies are doing, so that in normal times they are making enough money to more than compensate for the days of calamity. The folks who do these computations are called *actuaries*, and they are experts in statistics and probability. Some of them make very big salaries. Many advance to become presidents of large insurance firms. You can be sure that *they* did not shrink from learning the basic arithmetic computations that I have been trying to highlight throughout this book. They mastered them and a lot more, and it is paying off big time for them. I am not promising that if you advance your arithmetic competence in dealing with life's financial quandaries, then you will ascend to the head of a large corporation. But if you don't, you won't.

BASIC PRINCIPLES OF THE INSURANCE GAME

Let's conclude by stating a few general principles that will sum up the overall discussion in this chapter. There has been little computation in this chapter, for two reasons: first, as I explained, most insurance is purchased for other than financial reasons; and second, the description of the actuarial computations behind insurance odds are too complex for this book. Here are the principles that I recommend to you:

- Buy your insurance from reputable companies, not from fly-by-night firms that you find on the Internet or through infomercials.
- Maintain high deductibles.
- Use your policies purely for insurance—don't borrow against them or combine them with annuity or investment programs.
- Try to take advantage of insurance programs offered through your employer's tax-deferred cafeteria plan.
- Understand that insurance is a bet in which you are wagering against your own welfare. Enjoy the peace of mind it brings, and appreciate the financial compensation it affords to cope with the disasters associated with a "winning" bet.

YOUR NEW COMPUTATIONAL SKILLS

None in this chapter.

CHAPTER 10

Cut Up Those #$%^ Credit Cards

"Born to shop!" "Shop till you drop!" "Shopaholic!" Familiar T-shirt slogans in any resort area in the USA. Do they describe you? They certainly apply to many Americans, as shopping is indeed an avidly pursued activity by many in our fair land, encouraged by the economists who bemoan the state of the economy if consumer spending dips and by politicians who covet the sales tax revenue it generates, not to mention the merchants, financiers, and industrialists who exhort us on to greater and greater levels of consumerism. Now, I don't think this is necessarily such a terrible thing. Our consumer economy is deemed by many to be the backbone of the great material prosperity that our society enjoys. But clearly, the consumer mind-set, when taken to extreme, has landed a more than negligible percentage of our population in financial difficulty. Easy credit—too easy credit—especially in the form of credit cards, has often played a significant role in that process.

WHY WE USE CREDIT CARDS

Before we examine this predicament, let us recall the path you have already tread in these pages: Your education is secured; you have a job and a salary; you've bought a house and a car (especially if you have a family); you have taken care of the basic necessities of life such as food, clothing, transportation, communication, etc.; your various insurance policies are all paid up; and, most important, you have embarked on a regular program of investment. Now you want to have some fun. That stereo system you saw in the local appliance mart looks pretty enticing; a nice vacation at Disney World with the family would be welcome; season tickets for the local football team have just become available; your spouse wants to join the nearby country club; and you always promised yourself that you would take flying lessons before your fortieth birthday. The only problem is that there isn't much left over from your salary after all the basics are accounted for. What to do? Unfortunately, for too many Americans, the answer has been to indulge their desires and to finance them by going into debt. The form of the debt may vary: a home equity line of credit, a loan against your life insurance policy, or even worse, a loan against your retirement pension. But perhaps the most common method is to run up the balances on your credit cards. Credit card debt has become a serious problem in our country. Recent estimates indicate that the *average* credit card debt of an American family is approaching $10,000. For too many people, this is a calamity that will eventually lead to financial ruin. Hopefully, you are not one of these people. But if you are, or if you might be, let's step back and look at how credit cards work, how you may have arrived at the unfortunate situation of out-of-control credit card debt, and then what might be done to escape from it.

HISTORY OF CREDIT CARDS

Credit cards have been around for many years. Diners Club cards and American Express cards have been available at least since I can remember. But they were not credit cards in today's sense. They were called *charge cards* and were intended as a convenience for upper-income individuals. You were not allowed to maintain an outstanding balance. Namely, whatever you charged during the month was payable at the end of the month when you received your bill. This allowed the user to limit the amount of cash in pocket, afforded spontaneous purchases, and enabled a certain amount of categorizing and tracking of expenses. In fact, these motivations for the use of credit cards remain valid today. Merchants paid the issuing company a fee based on purchases. They felt it was in their interest to do so, as the customer might not make the purchase if the opportunity to charge the item was not available. This feature of the credit card industry also remains in force today. But, I reiterate, all charges were payable in full upon receipt of the monthly bill.

Credit cards as we know them now are about thirty-five to forty years old. Here's how they work. Everything I said above remains true concerning the reasons that customers use credit cards and merchants accept them. The main difference is that the user no longer has to pay the bill in full when it arrives monthly. Oh, some cards still work the old way (for example, the two mentioned above), but your garden variety credit card, issued by VISA, MasterCard, Discover, or your local department store, allows you to pay some minimum amount each month, an amount that is usually a small fraction of the amount that you actually owe. When you do that, you are automatically taking a loan for the outstanding balance. But as we shall see, this loan is structured very differently from those we discussed in Chapters 6–8.

HOW CREDIT CARDS WORK

To illustrate, let's look at some numbers. For a standard user, a typical month might unfold as follows. You purchase twelve to fifteen items in various department stores, restaurants, and gas stations and from direct mail catalogs that add up to $425. Within five to ten days from the end of your monthly period, you receive a bill for $425 from your credit card company. However, the statement says that your minimum payment is $8.50. You have ten to fifteen days to pay that amount or you will be assessed a late charge, which could be considerably more than the minimum payment. Note that the minimum payment amount is 2% of the total amount due. Indeed, 8.50/425 = 0.02. Now let's assume you pay the $8.50 in a timely fashion, and during the second month you charge another $250 worth of merchandise. Then when your next bill arrives, it shows a balance of $672.75. "Where in heaven's name did that come from?" you wonder. Here's where. You paid $8.50 of the original outstanding bill of $425, leaving a balance of $416.50 that you still owe the credit card company. You have now taken out a loan for that amount. The annual interest rate on the loan is 18%. (Many credit card rates are lower at the time of this writing because the Federal Reserve has been lowering short-term interest rates, but I remember days when the rates were as high as 21% and more.) That translates into a monthly rate of 18%/12 = 1.5%. Therefore, the balance due on the loan is $416.50 × 1.015 = $422.75. Now add to that the second month's charges—that is, $250—and your bill is $422.75 + $250 = $672.75. Moreover, the credit card company is indicating that the minimum payment is now $13.46, which is 2% of $672.75. So, if you make the minimum payment and then charge nothing at all in the third month, the bill that arrives at the end of that month will be for $669.18. That figure appears because you had an outstanding loan balance of $672.75 – $13.46 = $659.29, on which you are assessed an interest charge of 1.5%, which is $9.89. Adding that to the loan balance yields the amount due of $669.18. The minimum payment will now be $13.38. Clearly, even if you never charge another item, you will never pay off the outstanding balance if you only pay the minimum amount due each month. And if you keep charging items and pay only the minimum due, you are going to hit your credit limit surprisingly soon.

The credit limit is the maximum outstanding balance that the credit card company will allow you to carry. Limits of $5,000 or $10,000 are common—even for people with poor credit ratings. Limits of $20,000 and more are increasingly available. When your outstanding balance reaches your credit limit, this is referred to as maxing out your credit card. Unknowingly presenting a maxed-out credit card and having a merchant inform you that your card is no good is one of life's least pleasant moments. If you max out several cards with five-figure credit limits, you may find yourself with a total minimum payment in excess of a thousand dollars. Paying that amount doesn't get you out of the quicksand; it only keeps your head from slipping under. And the same disaster is looming next month.

FEATURES AND DANGERS OF CREDIT CARDS

The scenario described in the previous paragraph depicts a typical credit card account and its hazards. Details may vary according to issuer. Here are some additional comments:

- Credit card companies may (temporarily) set their minimum payments at even less than 2% of the outstanding balance, thereby encouraging larger loans. On the other hand, most companies have a dollar amount minimum payment, currently typically $20, so that the 2% figure does not become applicable until your balance exceeds $1,000.
- The interest due on many credit cards is computed on a daily, rather than a monthly, basis. That may change the arithmetic slightly—in your favor or not, depending on when in the month you did the heaviest charging—but the basic mechanism described above is unchanged.
- When you take a loan from your credit card company by not paying the full balance due, you are basically taking out an unsecured loan. There is no collateral as there is in the case of a car or home loan. That is one of the reasons that the interest rate is so high; the credit card company needs some protection against your defaulting on the loan. Namely, when you literally don't have the money to cover even the minimum payment, you are then in default. An unfortunate consequence of default, especially when multiple cards are maxed out, may be personal bankruptcy. This is an exceedingly unpleasant topic that I will avoid discussing in this book, although the number of Americans declaring personal bankruptcy has increased dramatically in recent years. There is no doubt that the ready availability of unsecured loans on credit cards is one of the prime reasons for this development. I shall discuss momentarily how the effective and careful use of credit cards can be a great convenience to the consumer. But, as with so many of the other aspects of your financial affairs (as we have seen), this requires diligence, self-discipline, and responsible behavior. Sans those, the wanton and careless use of credit cards is indeed a one-way path to financial hell.
- Another dangerous temptation that your credit card company entices you with is the ability to go straight for a loan without any intervening retail sales purchase. That is, you can borrow cash with your credit card. This can be done by going to the bank if you have a bank-issued card. But more simply, many issuers provide cardholders with "checks" that they can use to write themselves a loan, which then appears in the outstanding balance on their credit card bill. A particularly nasty feature of this arrangement is that many issuers charge higher rates of interest on *cash advances*—as they are called—than they do on balances from normal charges.
- The actual interest rate that you pay on your outstanding balance may vary tremendously from company to company. Some charge a specified percentage rate over some fixed consumer indicator (such as the federal *prime rate*). Others have more opaque procedures. When you sign up, you receive some literature detailing the way interest charges are computed. You may also receive that information monthly with your bill—usually printed in tiny type on the back of the bill. Working your way through the fine print takes patience and perseverance, but if you really want to know the exact charges you are paying and how they are computed, it is your only option.

- Here are some other nasty practices that credit card companies have occasionally instituted:

 1. You don't get the twenty-five-day float. That is, twenty-five days is the normal time from the date on which your billing cycle closes until the day your payment is due. If you pay your bill in full within the float period, then you don't incur *any* interest charges. But some companies allow fewer days, and some don't provide it at all—that is, you pay interest charges from the day of the charge. Fortunately the latter practice is not very common.
 2. Even if you get the float, the issuer may have the policy that if you do not pay the full prior balance, then you are charged interest on all outstanding balances, including the charges you made during the month for which you are receiving the bill.
 3. There is a minimum finance charge on outstanding balances, so even if your outstanding balance is very low and the computed interest is small, you still must pay the minimum finance charge.
 4. The credit card company charges you an annual fee for the "privilege" of using its card. The fee may be $25, $50, or even $100. This practice used to be common. Then, as part of promotional efforts, most companies did away with it. However, recently, as "specialty" cards have become popular, annual fees have made a comeback.
 5. If you don't pay assessed late charges, they are tacked onto your outstanding balance and you wind up paying interest on your late charges.
 6. Speaking of interest on money you didn't really have available, when you continually carry an outstanding balance, you are essentially paying interest on your interest. What an incredible waste of money!

In light of the previous discussion, if you ask the basic question

How much credit card debt should I carry?

then the obvious answer is

Zero. Under normal conditions, you should not have any outstanding balances on your credit cards. Pay off the outstanding balance every month.

When you carry credit card debt, you are basically floating yourself a loan at interest rates that may be double or even triple what the prevailing rate is on, say, a car loan or a mortgage, or certainly what it would be on what used to be called a passbook loan. That's a secured loan where the collateral is the money you maintain in a savings or investment account at the same institution that gave you the loan. Loans such as these are mostly confined to credit unions these days.

Why would you knowingly arrange for a loan at an exorbitant interest rate? That's what you are doing when you don't pay off the balance on your credit card bill. Not paying off the balance is bad enough when you are strapped for cash and you feel that you have no choice. But many people with substantial assets carry large credit card balances. The interest rates they pay to their credit card company far exceed the return they are getting on their assets. This is lunacy. Using some of your assets to pay off your credit card debt is a much wiser choice. The net income you lose on the spent assets is much less than the income you gain in avoiding those credit card interest payments. An alternate strategy is to consolidate your credit card debt and arrange for a single loan at a lower interest rate than you are paying on any of your credit cards. Your ability to do this may depend on your income level and/or what collateral you may be able to specify in order to secure a low rate. And, of course, this strategy will only be successful if you have the self-discipline to cut up those #$%^ credit cards and not take out any new ones.

THE POSITIVE SIDE OF CREDIT CARDS

Whew. That was a pretty strong tirade against credit cards. Are there any redeeming values to those gadgets? In fact, there are. Credit cards are most effectively and safely used if you only charge what you can afford to pay off at the end of each month. If you do so, then you will discover the following advantages in the use of credit cards.

- They allow you to limit the amount of cash you carry. This is particularly helpful when traveling, or purely from a security point of view in certain situations.
- They give you the freedom to engage in spontaneous purchases. Of course, you must have the self-discipline not to indulge unless you know the cash will be there at the end of the month when the bill arrives.
- They provide you with the ability to elaborately track and monitor your expenses, especially today with the fantastic software that is available. If you desire, you can keep score of how much you spend on various categories of expenditures on a monthly basis. This may only be for the finicky, but if you are so inclined, it is a useful feature of regular credit card use. Actually, there are other software products that may enable you to do similar bookkeeping with your checking account. If so, fine. But I find that the person in line behind me at the checkout counter in the supermarket is more impatient with the lengthy check-writing process than with the relatively speedy credit card swipe that completes a transaction.
- I also find credit cards very convenient in that I don't have to worry about how much cash I have or who's going to accept my check with what identification. That handy piece of plastic gives me lots of purchasing power almost any-

where I go. Of course, one has to have in mind one's monthly income and budget so as to be aware of how far one can go in charging and still be able to easily cover the freight at the end of the month when the bill arrives. Getting into good habits when you are young and maintaining them over the years goes a long way toward reasonable use of credit cards.

- Let's not forget that you get an interest-free twenty-five-day loan. This may seem trivial and unimportant, but it adds up over the years. And it's convenient. The sale on that 45" high-definition TV you covet runs only through Sunday, and you don't get paid until next Friday. That twenty-five-day interest-free loan enables you to buy now at the sale price.
- Finally, there are lots of specialty cards these days that carry bonuses of various sorts. Every charge gets you frequent flyer miles, or a reduced-rate hotel room, or merchandise at your local sports team store, or a cash rebate, or various other bonuses. If you are going to spend the money anyway, and you are going to pay off the balance monthly, then the extra bonus is found money—provided the bonus exceeds the annual fee, if there is one.

All of these advantages are predicated on the responsible use of your credit cards. Pay off the balances every month; avoid cash advances; always be aware of your internal limit rather than the card's limit; and don't carry a slew of cards—two to three are more than enough.

I have been using credit cards for about thirty years. In that time I have *never* not paid the full balance that appeared on my monthly bill. Alright, I know that sounds like I am bragging. Maybe my father has had a greater influence on me than I think. But when I got my first credit card and figured out the rules, I decided that there could scarcely ever be any justification for taking out a loan at the rates they were charging. And I never have. I think it's a matter of setting good habits when you start the process. Maintaining good habits is much easier than overturning bad ones.

Speaking of getting into good habits, most folks are very young when they get their first credit card these days. If their parents don't get one for them, then college students can count on receiving an unsolicited approach from credit card companies in their dormitory mail. The companies are not fools. They want to sign up clientele as soon as possible, counting on consumer loyalty to maintain the business in future years. Clearly there are risks to the companies in putting out unsecured loans to youngsters with limited income. But the risks are outweighed by the volume of customers. Unfortunately, experience has shown that just as a sixteen-year-old person is frequently too young to be entrusted with a vehicle, college-age youngsters are often too young to be entrusted with a credit card. Even worse, companies entice young people with appealing entry rates, that is, the loan rate may be only 5% or less during the first six months the card is in play. This accomplishes two bad outcomes: first, it entices them to sign up, and second, since the introductory rate is so low, it encourages them to *not* pay the full balance at the end of the month. Talk about getting into bad habits right out of the batter's box.

Here is another way that customers wind up incurring debt on their credit cards without necessarily meaning to do so. Occasionally, you will enter into a dispute with your credit card company. An item will appear on your bill that you don't recognize; or there will be an arithmetic mistake, perhaps because a clerk scribbled a number unintelligibly at the point of sale; or the merchandise is so defective that you decide to return it, but your charge shows up on the bill while your credit is delayed. There are many reasons that you might want to contact your credit card company and ask to be excused from paying a certain amount on your bill. And believe it or not, credit card companies will usually handle these requests politely and fairly. They will commonly grant you a delay in paying for the disputed item while they investigate your complaint, and then they'll remove the charge if the circumstances warrant—*provided you follow the rules.* This usually requires that you submit *in writing* the exact nature of the dispute, the relevant details of the transaction, and the amount in dispute. If you do so, you can then subtract that amount from your payment. You should then not incur any interest charges. But two things can go wrong. If you don't follow the instructions precisely, the outstanding balance will incur interest charges. Even if you do follow the rules, your request may be processed by an incompetent who nevertheless places the interest charges on the account. Alas, then you are in for many months of phone calls, letters of explanation, and other exhortations to get them to eventually remove all illegitimate interest charges from your balance. I know—I have played this game too many times. Incidentally, it is the prime reason for having two credit cards. As soon as I enter into a dispute with a credit card company, I cease using the card in question and turn to one of my backups.

Here's another suggestion that only a kook such as me would think of. I explained earlier, in Chapter 5, the twenty-four-paycheck monthly bill-paying system and the implication for two freebie paychecks during the year. In order to successfully implement this system, you need to have your monthly bills arriving at your home in roughly two equal stacks. That's because you are getting two paychecks per month to pay off all your monthly bills. You probably can't adjust the due dates on your mortgage, tax bills, utility bills, or insurance bills. But you can adjust the due dates on your credit card bills. You just need to ask the credit card company. There may be a period of adjustment until your due dates are exactly where you want them, but my experience has been that credit card companies are usually cooperative and willing to work with you on this score. Remember, they want your business, and there are plenty of competitors out there.

GETTING OUT OF CREDIT CARD DEBT

I would like to add another word about escaping from credit card debt. Previously, I indicated two strategies for doing so—either using your assets to pay off your debt or coalescing the debt under one roof and paying it off via a lower-cost loan. If neither is possible and you have the laudable goal of avoiding personal bankruptcy, then the only choice you have is to *slowly* pay off the debt. You may be able to work with the companies to arrange for a payment schedule that your income will allow. It may take a while. And, of course, it will require you to pinch your pennies for some time and to exercise self-discipline, and naturally you'll have to cut up those #$%^ credit cards. An encouraging remark I can make here is similar to one made earlier—hopefully, your job situation is advancing, your salary is increasing, and what looks like a formidable payment schedule today may look less so in a year or two.

CREDIT CARD LOOK-ALIKES

The last order of business in this chapter is to discuss the "cousins" of the credit card. I have in mind here debit cards, ATM cards, and lines of credit. Before we do so, let's run through the means you have at your disposal to pay for stuff. The most basic is *cash*—the merchant tells you the price, you pull out the requisite greenbacks from your wallet, the merchant hands you the merchandise, and you go on your merry way. Next in the historical order of evolution is the *check*. (Actually, if I were going to be historically correct, I would place *barter* before cash, but let's not go overboard.) Governments print and mint cash; banks make checks possible. When you write the merchant a check instead of forking over cash, the merchant may simply accept your check, trusting that the funds will be in your account when his bank presents the check to your bank for payment. Or he may take some information, such as your driver's license number, a credit card number, or your passport number (if you are overseas) in case the check bounces and he needs to "reach out to you." Or he may employ a check verification service that will give him an assessment of the trustworthiness of your check. None of these are particularly great for the merchant, and their inadequacy has fueled the increasing popularity of credit cards. You hand over the plastic, the merchant swipes it through a handy-dandy electronic device that ascertains whether you are still under your credit limit, and he hands you the merchandise, secure in the knowledge that the credit card company will reimburse him and that any future monetary difficulties will be between the credit card company and you—he is blissfully removed from the process, with funds in hand. (For the reasons enumerated above, it's also a good deal for you—or not, as the case may be depending on your habits.) Now what are some of the other possibilities for payment?

1. *Debit cards.* These look like credit cards but work like checks. The merchant swipes the card, and this arranges for the transfer of funds directly from your checking account. The merchant is paid, you have not charged anything, and no bill is coming to your home. Of course, like a check, the presumption is that the funds are in your account. Debit cards are more convenient for both of you because the transaction goes quicker than a check payment transaction, and you don't need to carry around blank checks. For those of you who have had to cut up your #$%^ credit cards, debit cards are a convenient and safe alternative.
2. *ATM cards.* These cards are issued by banks in which you have accounts. They allow you to access the money in your accounts remotely at the site of any banking machine that the bank maintains. ATM cards are very convenient when you need some cash to buy fast food or beer at midnight and the wallet is bare. You can also use the bank machines of other banks, but then you will pay a fee, perhaps a hefty one—like maybe a couple of bucks even if you only take out $5. ATM cards are like virtually every other financial vehicle that I have examined in this book. Used properly, they are a wonderful addition to your repertoire of financial tricks: you can get cash at inconvenient times or inaccessible places; you can make deposits and transfers at a time and place of your choosing; you can access your accounts if you need information. But poorly used, they are also a danger. They give folks too-easy access to their money. One of the old advantages to banks (as explained in Chapter 1) was that their imposing stature gave you pause about withdrawing your money. You thought twice before making a withdrawal: "My money is so safe here, do I really need it?" No ATM machine has ever engendered any such feeling in any customer. Withdrawing your money with an ATM card is just too easy—even from accounts in which you are saving for a down payment on a home, for a car, or for a college education. You have to be judicious.
3. *Lines of credit.* A line of credit can take various forms, but basically it is an open line of credit provided to you by a creditor. It may be secured or unsecured. An example of the former is a home equity line of credit. In that case, your home is the collateral and there will be some maximum amount that you can float for yourself at an agreed-upon interest rate. The advantage to a home equity line is that since the interest payments go toward a loan for which your home is the collateral, they are tax deductible. The disadvantage is that you are robbing equity from your home. Unsecured lines of credit are available through credit

card companies and other creditors. They do not differ very much from the checks that your credit card company provides. You write yourself a check, and you now have a loan at a high rate of interest. Don't do it.

YOUR NEW COMPUTATIONAL SKILLS

How to understand your credit card bill by being able to compute the monthly interest charges and minimum payment due.

Part III

Accumulating Wealth

CHAPTER 11

Gambling: Can I Win the Lottery?

In the first two parts of this book, we dealt with the basics of your financial life: financing a college education, coping with inflation and taxes, managing your salary, buying or renting houses, buying or leasing cars, purchasing insurance, controlling your debt. How are you doing? Whether the answer is "well," "poorly," or "some of both," I am certain that the following thought has occurred to you—especially after a long, frustrating bill-paying session: "Geez, I wish I was rich!" If things are not going so well, then the thought is not surprising. But even if things are going well—you have the house, the cars, some money in the bank—the desire for wealth still wells up in our breast on occasion. After all, if you are rich, you do not have to sweat the details of covering your normal expenses, and, even better, there are ample resources to indulge your taste for luxury: elaborate travel, fancy homes and cars (not to mention planes and boats), fine dining and clothing, tickets to the Super Bowl, and whatever else tickles your fantasy. Fantasizing about wealth is pleasant; achieving it would be even more satisfying.

HOW TO GET RICH

I would venture that there are three standard methods that one might employ to "become rich." The first one is potentially quick, the second is unpredictable with regard to time, and the last is slow and painstaking. Not surprisingly, the chance of the first method succeeding is exceedingly small. The odds improve in the second method, although they are still not terribly favorable, while the last method has the greatest likelihood of success. The three methods are: gambling, starting your own business, and investing for growth. In this chapter we will explore gambling, and in the next chapter we will consider investing. I won't take up entrepreneurship in this book, partly because there are relatively few simple arithmetic tidbits I could teach you in this regard, and partly because it is a subject that demands a full book of its own. Actually, there is a fourth method for achieving wealth—namely, inheritance. If you have inherited wealth, you are probably not reading this book.

Before I discuss gambling, I want to state an important disclaimer. In the introductory paragraph, I clearly meant "rich" in the sense of having a lot of money. There are other ways to be rich: enjoying the love and loyalty of family and friends; taking pride in the achievements of one's children and grandchildren; deriving great pleasure and satisfaction from one's job, profession, or avocation; pursuing spirituality, whether through organized religion or other informal routes; or finally, tasting the natural beauty of our country. These are rich pursuits and experiences that are within the reach of most of us, regardless of one's financial assets. Nevertheless, there is a natural human inclination to want to accumulate monetary wealth. Gambling is a tempting and readily available avenue for indulging that desire. Is it a good idea?

GAMBLING SCENARIOS

So, as we did with insurance, we need to start off with a definition. Let's consult our old friend Webster, which says that *to gamble* is "to play a game for money or other stakes; to bet on an uncertain outcome; to stake something on a contingency"; the synonyms listed are "speculate, wager, venture, hazard." In short, a good old-fashioned *bet.* I lay down some money asserting that something will happen. The individual, group, or organization at whose dais I lay down the money asserts that it won't happen. If the something does happen, then they pay me an agreed-upon amount of money—maybe many times what I laid down. If the something does not happen, then they keep what I gambled. There are an infinite variety of forms to the exercise. Let's list some of the most common:

- Wagers on the ponies at the track; similarly, dog races, jai alai, and other pari-mutuel venues.
- Blackjack, roulette, one-arm bandits, and all the other games that you find in a gambling casino in Las Vegas, Atlantic City, or comparable establishments.
- Bingo and other parlor games that you might encounter at your local neighborhood association or social club.
- Sports betting, including football and basketball games, but also baseball, hockey, and golf.
- Numbers, as run by state lotteries or your neighborhood bookie, who may very well be acting on behalf of an illegal organization.

This is really just a small and relatively unimaginative sample. Gambling goes back to the dawn of civilization. It has been, and continues to be, all around us—from wagering on the sex of the fetus of a pregnant woman, to purchasing magazines that you don't read in the hope of winning the Publishers Clearinghouse Sweepstakes, to the innocent but fervent locking of pinky fingers that children do when they seal a bet. Aside from the desire to accumulate riches, there is obviously a human need that is fulfilled by gambling. I mentioned some plausible reasons in Chapter 9: entertainment, addiction, or need to conform. Those are not our concern here. The question before us is,

 Can you get rich gambling?

In order for me to answer the question, you have to understand *odds* and how they affect the outcome of an event on which you have wagered. So, in this chapter, I am going to teach you a little probability theory.

Before I do, I will state up front the answer to the question posed above.

 Gambling is a losing proposition.

The odds are against you. The overwhelming majority of people who gamble lose money. Many don't admit that they do, but in fact they do. My object here is to use very elementary probability theory to explain why this is the case, and hopefully to convince you that you shouldn't gamble. If you are not a gambler, please don't be tempted to try; if you are a gambler, you should seriously attempt to cut it out.

PROBABILITY

Now let's learn a little elementary probability theory. To start, we recall how odds are usually quoted. We commonly see phrases such as "The odds are 3–1 against that." The "that" might refer to a certain horse winning a specific race, or three red cherries coming up on a single pull of a one-arm bandit, or your getting bingo on the card you are playing. The odds quotation means that if you could stage the event over and over and over again, with the same conditions prevailing each time, then you would lose *on average* three times for each time you win—that is, on average, you would lose three out of every four times. In probability theory, we speak of trials or events to describe the simple "play of a game"—i.e., the horse race, the spin of the slot machine's wheel, or the bingo game. We postulate that there are only a finite number of outcomes of the trial that can occur—often only two. (In all the cases we will look at, there will be no more than a few.) To each outcome we associate a probability, the likelihood of that outcome occurring. The probability is a number between 0 and 1. Think of it as a decimal form for the percentage likelihood of that outcome. Thus, if the chance of my horse winning the race is only one out of four, or 25%, we say that the probability of that outcome is $\frac{1}{4}$. The probability of my horse losing the race is therefore $\frac{3}{4}$. This simple example illustrates the general fact that the probabilities of all the possible outcomes of a trial must add up to 1.

Let's give another very basic example, the classic coin flip. The probability of a *head* is clearly $\frac{1}{2}$. Just as clearly, the probability of a *tail* is also $\frac{1}{2}$. This does not preclude the possibility that, in two successive flips, you might see two successive heads. What the fundamental laws of probability say is that if you flip the coin hundreds of times, the percentage of those flips for which it lands on heads will be very close to 50%, and if you flip it thousands of times, that percentage will be *very, very* close to 50%. Let me reiterate, because your understanding of this point is crucial. If I flip the coin, I cannot say with certainty which side it will land on. Moreover, I cannot rule out the possibility that, say, five successive flips won't result in five successive tails—although, a probabilist will tell you that the chance of that happening is 1 in $2^5 = 32$, a little better than 3%. What I can say with certainty is that if I flip the coin a *large* number of times, the percentage of occurrences of tails will be *extremely close* to 50%.

Another classic example is the roll of a fair die that displays the numbers 1, 2, 3, 4, 5, 6. The probability that you "roll a 1" is obviously $\frac{1}{6}$, as it is for any of the numbers. This means that although I don't know what your next roll will reveal, I do know that if you roll the die a thousand times, you are very likely to see a "5" about $1{,}000 \times \frac{1}{6} \approx 167$ times.

Here is a somewhat more complicated example. If I randomly turn over a card from a normal deck of fifty-two cards, what is the probability that I see a face card—that is, a jack, queen, or king? Well, since there are fifty-two cards, and twelve of them are face cards, the probability is $\frac{12}{52} = \frac{3}{13}$. This means that if I shuffle the deck, pick a card, then replace it and shuffle again, then pick a card, and repeat the process over and over, on average I will see a face card about every three out of thirteen trials. Since $\frac{3}{13} = 0.2308$, we can be sure that if we do this hundreds of times, we will see a face card about 23% of the time—and according to the aforementioned laws of probability, the more we do it the closer to 23.08% the result will be.

Here is one you can work out yourself: roll a pair of fair dice simultaneously. For clarity, assume one is red and the other is blue. Convince yourself that there are thirty-six possible outcomes to this experiment. Then answer the following question: What is the probability of an instant *craps* winning roll, that is, either a "7" or an "11"? Can you see that of the thirty-six possible outcomes, there are eight in which the values of the two dice add up to 7 or 11? Hence, the answer is

$$\frac{8}{36} = \frac{2}{9} \approx 0.22.$$

We can apply what we just learned to explain the success of insurance companies. Indeed, suppose that the probability of my smacking up my car in a year is $\frac{1}{50}$. Despite this small likelihood, I still might do it and the insurance company would lose that particular bet. But if all drivers, millions of them, have the same probability of a smack-up, then we can be certain that almost exactly 2% will do so in a given year. If the average payoff is $10,000 and fifty million drivers have one million smack-ups, then the insurance industry will pay out

$$\$10{,}000 \times 1{,}000{,}000 = \$10 \text{ billion}.$$

But if insurance companies charge each driver $1,000 for insurance, then their annual income is

$$\$1{,}000 \times 50{,}000{,}000 = \$50 \text{ billion}.$$

Not a bad deal for them! These numbers represent a simplified (and purposefully exaggerated) version of the actual numbers, but the basic principle is accurately reflected.

EXPECTED VALUE

Now to understand how the odds work in gambling, you only need to learn one more notion: *expected value.* Consider a coin-toss game. Suppose I flip two coins simultaneously, say a penny and a dime. If two heads comes up, then you give me $5. If anything else happens, then I have to give you $1. What is the projected outcome or, said otherwise, the expected value of my playing this game? Of course you cannot know for certain—it depends on whether the coins come up heads or tails. Instead, you should reason from a probabilistic point of view. First of all, on any simultaneous flip, only four outcomes are possible: (1) both coins are heads, (2) both coins are tails, (3) the penny is heads and the dime is tails, (4) the penny is tails and the dime is heads. Each occurs with the probability $\frac{1}{4}$. So, for any game, the probability that I will win is $\frac{1}{4}$ and the probability that I will lose is $\frac{3}{4}$. Therefore, my expected winnings are computed as follows. On average, every four times that I play the game, I can expect to win once. In so doing, I collect $5. Each of the three times that I lose, I forfeit $1, for a total loss of $3. Therefore, on average, after four games, I can expect to have net winnings of $2. Furthermore, my average winnings for each of the four games is $2/4 = $0.50. The expected value of this game is +0.50. Of course, there is no single game that can result in my winning half a buck—either I win $5 or I lose $1 in each game. But if I play for a long time, I will amass winnings that average 50¢ per play.

Another way of computing the expected value (E)—and it really amounts to the same computation—is to multiply, for each outcome, the probability of that outcome by the financial gain (or loss) associated with that outcome, and then add up all the products. So,

$$E = \frac{1}{4} \times \$5 + \frac{3}{4} \times \$(-1) = \$1.25 - \$0.75 - \$0.50.$$

To reiterate, on average, over a long period, I can expect my winnings to be at the rate of 50¢ per game. If I play one hundred games, I can expect to win $50. If I play five hundred games, I can expect to win $250. Nice game—for me, not for you.

Next, let's build a card game on the selection of face cards as before. This time we'll assume that if I pick a face card, you give me $3, but if I don't, then I have to give you $1. Let's compute the expected value. Well, we already know the probabilities. We saw earlier that the probability of success was $\frac{3}{13}$. Hence, the probability of failure is $\frac{10}{13}$, and the expected value is

$$E = \frac{3}{13} \times \$3 + \frac{10}{13} \times \$(-1) = \$0.6923 - \$0.7692 = -\$0.0769.$$

In this game, I can expect to lose nearly 8¢ each time that I play, on average.

To compute the expected value of a game, you multiply the probability of each outcome by the monetary result of that outcome and then add up those values. Generally, some of the numbers will be positive, some will be negative. The game is favorable if the sum is positive, unfavorable if the sum is negative. On average, you can expect to win (if positive) or lose (if negative) that sum each time you play the game.

This concludes our lesson in elementary probability theory. All of the gambling you do is governed by these fundamental rules. You just need to know the probabilities of each of the possible outcomes of your game and the monetary result associated with each. Now here comes a major flash. You will be hard-pressed to find a single example of a game, legal or not, in which your expected value is positive. Thus the truth of my previous statement: *Gambling is a losing proposition.* The odds are stacked against you; get away from the gaming table.

The simplified face card game above is typical of the way things are rigged in Vegas and other gaming establishments. Namely, your expected value is a *small* negative number. You can expect to not lose very much on any single play of a game. Of course, this keeps you playing. And over the long haul, you are going to be a loser.

But, you squawk, "My Aunt Nellie won $5,000 in Atlantic City last week. Your theory must be wrong." Unfortunately, it is not. She just got lucky. Remember that even if your expected value is negative, you may win some at the beginning of your gambling session before the laws of probability catch up with you. But if you quit quickly enough, you may defy the laws of probability. All it means is that you didn't play long enough. And indeed if you continue to play long enough, you *will* lose. Incidentally, it may be that Aunt Nellie actually did play long enough. If she is a veteran gambler, she has likely lost far more than $5,000 over the years—not something she brags about generally. That is, in spite of her recent winnings, her overall balance sheet is decidedly negative. So then you might ask, "How long is long enough?" The precise answer to that question is somewhat sophisticated, too sophisticated for this book. Let's just say that you'll know it when you experience it.

SETTING THE ODDS

Next, I want to point out an interesting distinction between sports betting and casino gambling. It has to do with how the odds are set. When it comes to the roll of the dice, or the spin of a roulette wheel, or the turn of a card, the odds are completely determined by the laws of nature—assuming the equipment is fair and the management is honest. Nothing subjective is involved. On the other hand, in computing the odds on whether the Yankees are likely to defeat the Mets on a given day, there is definitely something subjective going on. The odds are set by professional sports gambling experts, who have many years of experience evaluating rosters of player personnel and the other critical aspects of sports competition that they need to understand in order to predict the likely outcome of a sporting event. However, this is an art, not a science. If they do a bad job (for example, failing to appreciate the worth of a certain player), or if they are unlucky (for example, not anticipating the impact of an unexpected weather change), then the odds they set may be inaccurate. Don't get your hopes up, though. They are very good at what they do—certainly far better than a rank amateur such as you.

Now that we understand the relevant rules of probability theory and how they affect your gambling endeavors, let's return to the bulleted list of different types of gambling formats outlined early in this chapter and say something more specific about each.

PARI-MUTUEL BETTING

The odds at the track are usually quoted, as we stated at the outset of this chapter, in the form 3–1. This suggests that the likelihood of that horse winning the race, according to some equine expert who is estimating the odds, is 25%. In fact, according to the usual pari-mutuel rules, it means that for $1 you bet, you get back $3 if the horse wins. So what is your expected value of this game, that is, the running of the race? We know how to compute that—it's the product of the probability the horse wins times the net winnings added to the product of the probability the horse loses times the net loss. That is,

$$E = \frac{1}{4} \times \$3 + \frac{3}{4} \times \$(-1) = \$0.75 - \$0.75 = \$0.$$

Whoa! The track is not going to let that happen. Well, in fact, the probability of your horse winning is actually slightly less than $\frac{1}{4}$, so that your expected value is, as I predicted earlier, a small negative number. So when the racing form says the odds are 3–1, it is referring to the betting rules and understates slightly the odds against you.

To illustrate further, suppose the racing form says the odds are 8–5. That means that for every $5 you bet, you receive $8 if your horse wins. This suggests a probability of

$$\frac{5}{13} = 0.3846.$$

In fact, the actual probability is somewhat smaller. When there is a prohibitive favorite, you may see odds such as 1–2. That means that you get $1 for every $2 you bet when your horse wins. This time the probability of success is just under $\frac{2}{3}$.

If you can't resist the ponies, at least now you have some idea of exactly how the track is taking your money. Note, incidentally, that this is one game that you cannot repeat over and over. The race happens only once. How can the track be assured of a profit? The answer is twofold. First, the track has the odds slightly on its side for every horse in the race—provided the oddsmakers have done a good job of estimating the probabilities. If so, the betting tends to match the odds. If the oddsmakers have done a bad job or the betting audience just doesn't agree with them, then since they watch the betting very closely, they can and do adjust the odds to reflect the betting as it proceeds. You just can't win. The second explanation is that as far as they are concerned, each race, even with different horses and jockeys, is really just another trial of essentially the same game. The participants may change, but the odds are still cooked more or less in the same way in the track's favor.

SPORTS BETTING

In nonpari-mutuel betting on sports, the odds are given in a different format. In the newspaper listing of the odds on the Yankees-Mets game, you will see, for example, Yankees (–2) quoted as the favorite. What this means is that if you bet $1 on the Yankees, you get back exactly $2 (i.e., you win $1) if the Yankees win by more than two runs—that is, the Yankees *beat the point spread.* If the Yankees win by less than two runs, or lose, then you lose the bet. If they win by exactly two runs, you get $1 back—no win, no loss. The number in parentheses is referred to as the *points* or point differential. The experts set the point differential so that about half the money bet will go on the Yankees and the other half on the Mets. In other words, the probability that the Yankees beat the point spread is the same as the probability that they don't. Therefore, your expected value for playing this game would clearly be zero. Since that is a luxury the bookmakers cannot afford, they compensate by charging you a fee for placing your bet. That fee, even in legal establishments, can be 10% or higher. What it does, of course, is convert your expected value into—you guessed it—a small negative number. Are you getting the point yet?

CASINO GAMES

The roulette wheel supplies a simple illustration of what you are up against. The wheel has slots labeled with the numbers 1–36. The wheel is spun, and a small ball is released into the spinning wheel. Eventually, as the wheel slows, the ball comes to rest in a slot. You can bet, say, $1 that the slot in which the ball stops contains an even number. If the wheel had exactly thirty-six slots, then the odds would be 50–50—you would win as often as you lose (on average, of course)—and your expected value of playing the game would be zero. Ah, but the wheel has two extra slots labeled "0" and "00." These are considered neither odd nor even numbers for the purpose of the game. Therefore, the actual probability of your winning the game is $\frac{18}{38} = \frac{9}{19} = 0.4737$, and the probability of losing is therefore $\frac{20}{38} = \frac{10}{19} = 0.5263$. Furthermore, the expected value of playing the game on a $1 bet is

$$E = 0.4737 \times \$1 + 0.5263 \times \$(-1) = \$0.4737 - \$0.5263 = -\$0.0526.$$

You can expect to lose about 5¼¢ per game. Classic! A small negative expected value. You can play for quite some time before your losses amount to anything significant. But, at the risk of repeating myself: This does not say that you definitely will not experience a period in which you win many times in succession or you lose many times consecutively; it says that in the long run, if you continue to play the game, your eventual average result will be the loss of money at the rate of 5.26¢ per game.

The story is the same for the other games you find in the casino: blackjack, craps, and slot machines. Blackjack is a little different from the others in that you have some control over events other than deciding how much to bet. In craps and slot machines, as in roulette, your fate is determined by the random roll of the dice or the spin of the wheel. But in blackjack, you can use your intelligence to influence the odds—slightly—by keeping track of the cards that have been played. There are many famous stories of gamblers with incredible memories who have actually changed the odds, sometimes even tipping them in their favor, by clever and seemingly almost superhuman counting and recall of cards. Such folks are not terribly welcome in the casinos, and although it seems unconstitutional to me, the gambling industry has managed to find legal ways to bar these gamblers from their establishments—when they are identified. The people with the mental agility to count the cards are few and far between. You are likely not one of them—yet another reason for you to abandon the casino.

PARLOR GAMES

What I have in mind here is church bingo, a large office sports pool, or maybe a keno-type game at your social or community club. What these gambling venues have in common is that they are run by amateurs (e.g., a community, social, or religious organization or group), they involve a game with a large number of players, and the payoff is arranged as follows: For each game that is played, the total waged by the players is collected by the "house"; a small percentage is skimmed off and kept by the house, and the rest is returned to the winner or winners. By now it should come as no surprise to you that the expected value in such a game will be negative—because of the rake-off. But there is an even more pernicious trap awaiting you that I will now explain.

Suppose you are playing bingo at your local church or social club. To simplify, let's assume that there is an agreed-upon tiebreaker, that is, some predetermined method to anoint a single winner if two or more people get bingo at the same time. For example, one method would be to look at the completed row or column on each winning card and assign the winner as the one for whom that row or column adds to the largest amount—thereby devaluing the free spot in the middle. (Analysis, analogous to the forthcoming, for games in which ties are allowed is more complicated, but the conclusion is the same.) Now, for the sake of simplicity, assume ten people are playing. Each of the players puts up \$5 for a game, meaning that the house collects a total of \$50. The house keeps \$5 per game and gives \$45 to the winner. What is your expected value for playing this game? Because of our simplifying assumption about tiebreakers, there are only two possible outcomes as far as you are concerned—you win or you lose. Presuming the cards are selected randomly and the management plays fairly, then the probability of winning is $\frac{1}{10}$, while that of losing is $\frac{9}{10}$. If you lose, you lose your entry fee of \$5; if you win, your net profit is \$40, the \$45 the house gives you minus the \$5 entry fee. Therefore, your expected value is

$$E = \frac{1}{10} \times \$40 + \frac{9}{10} \times \$(-5) = \$4 - \$4.50 = -\$0.50.$$

You can expect to lose 50¢ per game.

Now here's the lurking trap. It is tempting to "buy" and play with more cards in the expectation that doing so will increase your chances of winning. In fact it does, but at the same time it *decreases* your expected value. Here's why. Suppose you buy a second card and everyone else stays pat. Now there are eleven cards in play, your probability of winning increases to $\frac{2}{11} = 0.1818$, and your probability of losing is now $\frac{9}{11} = 0.8182$. But, in this instance, the house collects \$55, namely, \$5 from each of the other nine players and \$10 from you because of your two cards. It skims off its \$5 and returns \$50 to the winner. Therefore, if you win, your net profit is still \$40, namely the \$50 returned by the house minus the \$10 entry fee you paid; but if you lose, your loss has increased to \$10. Your expected value is now

$$E = \frac{2}{11} \times \$40 + \frac{9}{11} \times \$(-10) = 0.1818 \times \$40 - 0.8182 \times \$10 = -\$0.91.$$

Your new strategy has ensured that instead of losing 50¢ per game, you can now expect to lose 91¢ per game on average. I will leave it to you to figure out how buying three cards (again assuming everyone else stays pat) increases your expected losses to $1.25 per game. The moral of the story: Get your favorite card and stick with it throughout the evening. Buying more cards will only increase the amount you lose.

NUMBERS

Finally, we come to the most insidious of the gambling scenarios—the *numbers* game. The numbers are played either through lotteries, which are run now by a majority of the states, or through a (likely illegal) local gambling syndicate. On a given day, people buy numbers, after which the winning number is selected as follows: In state lotteries, the winning number is selected in a random drawing, often in televised events where numbered ping-pong balls pop out of pressurized tubes, while the gangsters choose their numbers based on ball scores or racing results. Let's concentrate on the state lotteries and the ping-pong balls.

In their attempts to market these games, the states have devised many betting schemes, but they all basically come down to this. You pick a set of numbers, say three numbers. That is, you go into the local beer, wine, and deli shop that sells lottery tickets and you sing out three numbers between 1 and 100 to the clerk. You buy one ticket for the specified amount, on which is printed the date and your three numbers. That night three ping-pong balls pop out of the tube. If the numbers match yours, you win. If not, you lose. Well, in fact, some states have refined the game a little whereby if you match just two numbers you also win, albeit a *much* smaller prize. These little subgames have some influence on the odds but, because of the smaller payoffs, very little influence on your expected value. (These subgames are a little like betting on *place* or *show* at the track—they make it easier to win, but you can't win very much.) For the purposes of simplification, I will pretend these subgames don't exist in computing lottery odds. Now, let's suppose your ticket costs $1. And let's suppose that if you win, you collect $10,000. If you don't win, your $1 ticket is worthless. We need to figure out two things: the probability of winning and the expected value of playing the game. In order to do that, we need to learn a little more probability theory.

When the three balls pop, because of our simplification, there is only one way to win—the three balls have to match your three numbers exactly. The probability of that happening is equal to 1 divided by the total *number* of numerical combinations that can result from choosing three numbers between 1 and 100. We have to compute that *number*. Mathematicians figured it out a long time ago. My task now is to explain the computation to you. OK, here goes. Well, like I have done many times in the book, I will simplify the numbers first, compute the simpler example, and then generalize back to the original case. So assume there are only ten balls, numbered 1–10. How many different numerical combinations are possible when we choose three? Start with the first ball that pops out; there are ten possibilities. We place that ball in a spot on a table marked "first ball." That ball having been selected, now how many possibilities are there for the second ball? Of course, only nine. Clearly, the number on the first ball has no influence on the number on the second ball other than the second cannot replicate the first. So we pick a second ball and place it in a spot on the table marked "second ball." Now, as should be evident, when I look at the two spots there are $10 \times 9 = 90$ different numerical combinations that I can see: 10&1, 10&2, . . . , 10&9; 9&1, 9&2, . . . , 9&8, 9&10, etc.

💣 Please don't read the next sentence until the preceding one is clear.

Next the third ball is chosen and there are eight possibilities for it. Lining up the three balls, I count $10 \times 9 \times 8 = 720$ possibilities. But here is an important point. I have overcounted. From the point of view of my winning the game, if my three numbers are, say, 3, 7, 9, then I don't care in which order the balls are picked. For example, either order—3, 7, 9 or 7, 9, 3—makes me a winner. In how many different orders can the three numbers be picked? That's basically the same question again; the answer is $3 \times 2 \times 1 = 6$. And so the total number of ways of choosing three balls out of ten, when the order is immaterial, is $720/6 = 120$. The exact same reasoning applies for one hundred balls, so the total number of numerical combinations possible when choosing three balls from one hundred is

$$(100 \times 99 \times 98)/(3 \times 2 \times 1) = 970{,}200/6 = 161{,}700.$$

Finally, there is nothing special about one hundred balls or three balls. If you have a set of n balls, numbered 1 to n, and you choose k of them, then the total number of numerical combinations you can obtain, when order is immaterial, is

$$(n \times n - 1 \times n - 2 \times \ldots \times n - k + 1)/(k \times k - 1 \times \ldots \times 3 \times 2 \times 1)$$

All right, that's getting a little too fancy. Mathematicians call this number "*n*CHOOSE*k*." In fact, in what follows we will only need to know the value of *n*CHOOSE*k*, when n is 100 and k is one of 3, 4, 5, 6, or 7.

Now let's return to our computation of the probability of winning and the expected value. Resume the game of choosing three balls out of one hundred, with a \$1 bet and a \$10,000 payoff. We need to know the value of 100CHOOSE3. It was given above, namely 161,700. So the probability of winning is $1/161{,}7000 = 0.0000061843$, a pretty small number. Subtracting it from 1, we see that the probability of losing is 0.9999938157, a near certainty. And your expected value is:

$$0.0000061843 \times \$10{,}000 + 0.9999938157 \times \$(-1) =$$
$$\$0.068143 - 0.9999938157 = -\$0.93815.$$

You can expect to lose 94¢ on average. But let's be careful now; this does not say you will lose 94% of the time. The probability says that you will lose 99.99938157% of the time. The winnings are sufficiently large to make the expected value noticeably less than your entire bet.

The trap that I described in bingo operates here, too. I won't go through the arithmetic, but I assure you that buying a second set of numbers for another dollar doubles your feeble chances of winning (still feeble), but also doubles your expected loss.

Actual lottery payoffs vary from state to state. But the set of payoffs for different numbers of balls in Table 11.1 is not unlike what you might see in some states.

Note that the payoffs go up by a factor of 10 for each additional ball. Actual payoffs are usually not so regular, but in some games of national scope, prizes of $100 million on a seven-ball game, commonly called *powerball*, have been publicized in the media in recent years.

Table 11.2 gives three pieces of data for the games postulated in Table 11.1: 100CHOOSEk, the probability of winning, and the expected value of playing the game. Note that the entries in the table correspond to $k = 3, 4, 5, 6$, and 7, respectively.

Are you impressed by these numbers? I hope you are. They say in particular that your chances of winning at powerball are one in sixteen billion, and that your expected value is a loss of all that you bet except for less than a penny. You should realize that your chances of being hit by lightning, swallowed up in an earthquake, and certainly of dying on an interstate highway far exceed your chances of hitting the powerball jackpot. I imagine your chance of being abducted by aliens also exceeds your likelihood of winning at powerball. Do I have to say more?

Maybe I do. Indeed, you might be inclined to formulate two rational objections to my staunch opposition to betting on the numbers. First, you might say that since your expected value is essentially –$1, there is little harm in your continually playing. After all, I have said that one should pay more attention to the

Table 11.1
Numbers payoffs

Number of Balls	Payoff
3	$10,000
4	$100,000
5	$1,000,000
6	$10,000,000
7	$100,000,000

Table 11.2
Numbers data

Number of Balls	100CHOOSE*k*	Probability of Winning	Expected Value
3	161,700	0.0000061843	-$0.93815
4	3,921,225	0.00000025502	-$0.97450
5	75,287,520	0.000000013282	-$0.98672
6	1,192,052,400	0.00000000083889	-$0.99161
7	16,007,560,800	0.000000000062470	-$0.99375

expected value than to the probability of winning. Ah, but that comment only applies when the number of trials undergirding the computation is more modest in size, no more than hundreds, at worst thousands. The expected value or average outcome has little meaning when the number of trials necessary for it to assert itself is in the billions. The key feature here is the near certainty that you will lose, which leads to your second objection—*someone* has to eventually win. That's true. But tens of millions of people are wagering each time, and it may take hundreds of millions of wagers before someone finally does win. The odds are better that there is an undiscovered birth certificate in your attic proving that you are a close relative of Bill Gates than they are that you will win at powerball.

What about the fact that you could be one of multiple winners? Does that help? Not really. If you win simultaneously with other bettors, then you have to *share* the prize money. So your odds of winning remain unchanged, as does your expected value.

STATE-SPONSORED GAMBLING IS A TAX

Here's my final point on state lotteries—one that I believe is particularly damning. Government-sponsored gambling is essentially a tax. "How so?" you ask. Well, the government is collecting money from certain individuals (the bettors) and returning *some* of it to other individuals (the few winners). That is what government does by means of its taxes and fees. It collects income taxes, Social Security and Medicare taxes, sales taxes, excise taxes, real estate taxes, licensing fees, import-export fees, airport security fees, and on and on. What does the government do with that money? It distributes the money to elderly people (Social Security), ill elderly or disabled people (Medicare), poor people (Medicaid and other welfare programs), farmers (agricultural subsidies), scientists (research grants), artists (endowments for the arts and humanities), businesses (corporate welfare), and so on. Government takes the revenue from gambling and distributes it to whoever is named in the enabling legislation. Often the state's education establishment is the targeted recipient, although that noble purpose is routinely defeated by legislative skullduggery and political legerdemain. Wherever the revenue goes, government-sponsored gambling is still wealth redistribution, facilitated by a government tax. But that is not my main point. My point arises with this question: Who primarily shoulders the burden of this tax? Studies have shown that the gambling tax falls disproportionately on the backs of the poor and the ill-educated—that is, the folks who feel the greatest need for an infusion of cash and those who have the poorest understanding of the odds they are battling. That spells *insidious* to me.

PRIVATE GAMES

There is one major category of game that does not appear in my bulleted list at the outset of the chapter—what I would call *private games.* That is a game in which there is basically no *house.* A private game is when you and some friends, or acquaintances, or strangers for that matter get together to play cards, for example. The simplest private game would be you betting with a friend on the outcome of a fair coin toss or some other random event over which neither of you had any control. Not surprisingly, both of you will have equal probability of winning and expected values of zero. You could play for a long time with very little money changing hands. On the other hand, in cards or another game of skill—for example, shooting foul shots—if you are the more skillful player, your probability of winning exceeds that of your opponent and you will have a positive expected value. Of course, unless your friend is really dense, you cannot expect this situation to last too long—your friend will tire of losing and the game will peter out. If instead you hang out in dark corners, seeking games with changing strangers who are less skillful than you, you might be able to maintain a positive expected value for a while. You might also wind up with broken kneecaps, so there are disadvantages to that strategy also.

Why isn't buying insurance a form of gambling? It's true that I characterized the purchase of an insurance policy as a bet. But it isn't gambling because of one key distinction. When you buy insurance, you are placing a bet that you dearly hope to lose. That is never the case with a gambling bet. So the simple criterion that distinguishes between the two: If you are betting to win, you are gambling; if you are betting hoping to lose, you are buying insurance.

Here's a sobering story. I grew up in a pinochle-playing family. I learned the game from my father, and even at the age of ten or eleven I was pretty good. I recall a summer day at that time when I convinced several friends that teaching them how to play and then playing for money would be a

> good idea. They caught on quickly, and so we started playing for money. Inexplicably, I got taken to the cleaners. To this day, I am not really sure what happened. Perhaps my skill was not as great as I had thought. Perhaps I was subconsciously nervous and ashamed of what I was doing and made uncharacteristic mistakes (accidentally on purpose). Perhaps we didn't play long enough for the *law of averages* to kick in. Whatever, I was so distraught from the experience that I swore off gambling forever—long before I understood the excellent statistical reasons for doing so that I have conveyed to you in this chapter. It was an oath that, I am happy to report, I have kept.

But I am not a total fuddy-duddy. I have been to Vegas, Atlantic City, and the track with friends maybe eight or ten times over the decades. It is never my choice, but I sometimes find myself with friends who want to go. I treat it as an outing for entertainment. Once there, I bet on show at the track, play a little blackjack at a low-stakes table, pull on the low-priced one-armed bandits, or bet on red-black at the roulette wheel. I expect to lose, but not a lot. I try to watch the other gamblers and guess what their real stories are. I limit myself to an hour or at most ninety minutes. And I try to have fun, secure in the knowledge that my minimalist strategy will allow me to play for a while and limit my losses. I never give in to the temptation to place a large or risky bet. In this way, it costs me no more than a family outing to the ballpark or an evening at the symphony. I strongly recommend this strategy to you if you find yourself in a casino. But more important, I urge you:

Do not gamble. You have worked very hard for your money. There are so many useful purposes toward which your money should be directed. You are cheating yourself and your family when you fritter it away on gambling losses and debts.

The odds of getting rich quick by gambling are minuscule. In the next chapter, we will look at a scenario that is much more favorable.

YOUR NEW COMPUTATIONAL SKILLS

How to compute the expected value of a game provided that you know all the possible outcomes of the game, the probability that each outcome occurs, and the monetary value assigned to each outcome.

CHAPTER 12

The Stock Market and Other Investments

Next we discuss a more reliable way (other than gambling) to accumulate wealth—a consistent and persistent investment program in the country's financial markets. At its simplest, that means the steady purchase of stocks, bonds, and mutual funds. Based on the financial history of our country, I can almost guarantee you that if you start young and pursue a steady program of equity acquisition, you will surely retire a rich person. That's a bold statement. In order to justify it, let's associate some definite numbers to the phrase "a rich person." Any such association will involve a subjective assessment. In Ric Edelman's last book, *Ordinary People, Extraordinary Wealth*, he defines a rich person as someone who has a house worth $250,000, financial assets of $500,000, and an annual income of $120,000. Maybe that's too conservative for you. You believe that rich entails bigger numbers. Of course I have already discussed how some people measure their wealth by parameters that are independent of how much money they have. But in this chapter, we are talking about financial wealth. In fact, I think Ric has set the bar a little too low. I would require assets of at least $1 million before I would consider someone rich. And I'm sure that many of you would say that is still not nearly enough. Maybe $5 million or $10 million is required to qualify. I don't know. Why don't we just examine the parameters of an investment program, and then I will show you a computation that you can do to see what you can expect to accumulate over time in a regular investment program. Then you can decide if there is a pot of gold awaiting you. As usual, the computation will depend on some variables such as the amount you invest annually and the expected rate of return, as well as some assumptions on taxes.

Why do people want to accumulate wealth? In fact, there are four general reasons:

- They want to use the money to buy things.
- They want to use the money for noble causes.
- They want to use the money to replace their income when they retire.
- They just want to.

All of these are excellent reasons. The things we desire—houses, cars, college educations, trips to Europe—cost money. The accumulation and expenditure of the money for those things teaches us self-discipline and forward planning; stimulates the economy in many, many ways; and helps us to enjoy our brief sojourn on Earth. Additionally, if we can accumulate a great deal of money, then we can indulge an impulse to do great things: start a foundation; build a hospital, opera house, or football stadium; or give large sums to charity. No less noble is the desire to accumulate enough wealth to allow us to live our senior years free from financial worry. I will have a lot more to say about this in the final chapter in the book; suffice it to say here that all those who fulfill this goal present less of a burden to society and thus do all working people a big favor.

The point of the previous observations is that the accumulation of wealth by individuals is generally a good thing for society—despite the misgivings of those of our countrymen whose egalitarian impulses exceed their common sense. But, you might object, "What about the people who have no overarching goal other than to just be rich?" Often such people are misers and not very pleasant to be around. But, presuming they accumulated their wealth legally and fairly, then they are definitely less harmful to society than those who squander their resources and end up a burden on those who behave responsibly. The money that misers stash in the mattress may not be as helpful to society as the money that's devoted to the consumer economy, the opera houses, investments in American business, or IRAs, but at least these folks are not acting as an economic drag on the system. And someday their money will reenter circulation when a descendant or inheritor gets access to it. Overall that's a positive.

I assume that you will, if you have not started already, embark on a regular, aggressive investment program. I don't really care what your ultimate goal is. (See the four possibilities above.) For the sake of argument, I will tacitly assume the goal is retirement income. The governing investment principles apply just as well if you are pursuing one of the other goals. For example, if you are investing in order to eventually buy something big—such as a college education—your time frame may not be as long. But your investment methods should be the same. If your goal is to do great things with your money (a foundation, a stadium, or an opera house), once again, the same methods apply, but you may need to be very patient or very aggressive to amass the great wealth that is needed. On the other hand, despite what I said above, I'm not really a big proponent of miserliness. You ought to have some worthwhile plan in mind for the money you amass. So I will assume that you have a long-term investment program aimed at something such as retirement funds or your children's or grandchildren's education, or maybe just to leave to your heirs or your foundation after your time on the planet is done.

THE AXIOMS OF AN INVESTMENT PROGRAM

I will take the following as axiomatic:

- You will start your program *now*, if you haven't started already.
- You intend to invest some minimum amount each year toward the program.
- You intend to increase the amount invested each year, preferably by an increment that at least matches the inflation rate.
- You will pursue this program in a tax-deferred account.
- If that is not possible, then you will plan to pay the annual taxes due on your investment program out of your regular salary and income.
- You will stick with the program through financial thick and thin. In particular, a couple of bad years in the market will not spook you to run for cover.
- You will not engage in any attempt to "time the market"; rather, the program will consist of regular investments on a steady, unchanging basis.
- You may engage in periodic alterations and adjustments to your portfolio, but not net subtractions.

STOCKS

Now that you have summoned the will to get started, you have to decide where to start. What do you invest in? In truth, the choices appear rather intimidating. There are thousands of stocks, almost as many bonds, scores of mutual funds, and myriad other investment vehicles to consider. What is one to do? Before we answer that question, let us make sure that we understand, in a rudimentary way, what these investment vehicles are. *Stocks* are ownership shares in publicly traded companies. At some point a company decides to *go public*. It offers for sale shares in itself. Anyone can buy them. The company may offer a million shares, let us say, at $10 a share. In this way, the company raises $10 million to operate, further develop, and improve the company. What it gives up potentially is control. You are free to sell your shares to someone else. There are complicated rules issued by the stock exchange on which the shares are traded as well as regulations promulgated by the states and the federal government that govern the operation and management of publicly traded companies. But, in principle, shareholders have a say in the management of the company—of course, only in proportion to the percentage of shares that they own. Typically, the control of the company remains with the people who controlled it when the shares were issued. But as time progresses, some individual or group may accumulate enough shares to take control of the company. We need not be concerned with this process here, but rather with why it's potentially profitable to buy shares.

The answer is that you are betting the company will succeed and make money for you in one of two ways: either the company will pay handsome dividends to its shareholders and/or the price of the stock will increase.

Stock dividends are a classic way for companies to reward their investors, that is, the shareholders. Just as with the interest on a bank account, the stock's *yield* is computed as the percentage that corresponds to the quotient of the dividend amount per share divided by the price of the stock. It's a more interesting number than a bank account yield, since not only the numerator but also the denominator will vary with time. Dividends are paid out of the profits earned by the company. Investors like them, and a good track record of dividend payouts is likely to make investors receptive to more public offerings (of stock) by the company, leading to more capital for the company, greater profits, higher dividends, etc. On the other hand, the company may decide to reinvest its profits (in the company, of course) in the hope of improving its earnings and profits. This will drive the price of the stock up as investors perceive the company's improved position. The reward to the investor is an increased value of his holdings, which he may choose to realize by selling the stock or by holding onto it in the hope of even more gains in the future. This increased profitability is also measured by a well-known indicator (analogous to yield for dividends), namely, the so-called P/E, which stands for *price/earnings*. The company has to report its gross and net income for the year. P/E is the ratio of the price per share to the net earnings per share. Traditionally, the P/E ratio for most stocks has hovered around eighteen to twenty. If the P/E ratio is lower, then in principle the stock is undervalued and one expects the stock price to rise. If the ratio is much higher than twenty, then the stock is overvalued and the price should decline. Unfortunately, it's not that simple, as many factors govern the price of a stock. If you want to learn more about selecting stocks using different schemes or indicators, there are dozens of resources available.

BONDS

Now what about bonds? A *bond* is basically a loan you make to the company that issues it. Or, another way of thinking of a bond is as a corporate certificate of deposit. You purchase a corporate bond in the amount of, say, $10,000. The terms of the bond are that you will receive $500 every year for ten years (from the company), after which you will receive your $10,000 back. It's just like depositing $10,000 in a bank account paying 5% simple annual interest. The difference is that the bond is not insured like your bank account is: if the company folds, you could lose your money. Also, unlike bank accounts, there is a secondary market for the bond. If interest rates go down, rendering your bond more valuable, someone might be willing to pay you more than $10,000 to buy it from you. And if rates go up, the value of your bond will go down, but only in the interim—if you can hold out for the full ten years, you will recoup all your money. Bonds are viewed as safer and more predictable than stocks, but the chances for substantial price appreciation (or depreciation for that matter) are much smaller than they are for stocks.

There is a caveat to the last claim. Bonds come with ratings. The ratings are set by established clearinghouses with long experience at evaluating the solidity of bonds. The higher the rating, typically the safer the bond, and the interest rate then is likely to be modest. You can get higher returns by buying lower-rated bonds, but your risk is then greater. The lowest-rated bonds are commonly called *junk bonds*. I've had a few of those and actually prospered, but if you lie awake at night thinking about your portfolio, I don't recommend them.

MUTUAL FUNDS

Now as you know, there are thousands of stocks and bonds from which to choose. Which to buy? And if you only have $10,000 to invest, do you buy just one stock or one bond? That seems so risky—putting all your eggs in one basket, so to speak. The solution is *mutual funds*. When you buy a stock mutual fund, you are buying shares in a company that does nothing but buy and sell stocks. You are pooling your money with thousands of other investors who are doing the same thing. In this way, the mutual fund manager has millions of dollars to work with, and she can buy dozens of different stocks. This diversifies the portfolio, minimizes risk, and increases chances for profit. Usually a mutual fund has some underlying theme, such as it only buys stock in the pharmaceutical industry; or it is a small-cap fund, that is, it only trades stocks of companies with small capitalization (small businesses with modest assets); or it only buys bonds issued by Fortune 500 companies, etc.

The value of the fund is determined by the average value of the total number of stocks or bonds that it holds. In this way, it reflects the value of a large number of investments—usually in one or at most a few sectors of the market. There are mutual funds today that are tailored to almost any portion of the market you can imagine—for example, funds that track the major indices, funds that attempt to minimize capital gains that you will incur, funds that only invest in environmentally friendly companies, municipal bonds, precious metals, you name it. There are also so-called money market funds. These are virtually as safe as bank accounts; their share value remains constant, and they pay dividends that reflect the current short-term national interest rate.

OTHER INVESTMENT VEHICLES

Now that you have a rudimentary understanding of the basic types of financial vehicles around which your investment program should revolve—namely, stocks, bonds, and mutual funds—I will digress and present a brief list of other types of investments. These are not for the fainthearted, as the risks involved can be much greater than with stocks, bonds, or mutual funds. If you are tempted to play in any of these playgrounds, you need to learn a great deal about these toys before you plunge in.

- *Treasury instruments.* These come in several flavors, the two most common being T-bills and T-bonds. They are essentially bonds that you can buy directly from the U.S. Treasury Department. They vary in term from very short to very long. These transactions used to be quite inconvenient to engage in, but in recent years the government has made it easier for individual investors to buy these instruments. You usually can beat the interest rates on treasury instruments, but some folks like the security associated with the phrase "backed by the full faith and credit of the United States Government" that appears on the paperwork. If Uncle Sam goes under, our worries are likely much greater than whether we are getting the best rate on our investment vehicles. One friendly fact—interest on U.S. government bonds is exempt from state income taxes.
- *Municipal or muni bonds.* These are bonds issued by states, counties, cities, and other municipalities that have taxing authority. Their main advantage is that the interest earned is exempt from U.S. income tax. It is also exempt from state or local income tax in the jurisdiction where issued. You can buy muni bonds through your broker. The interest rate will be considerably lower than rates on corporate bonds, which are fully taxable. Roughly speaking, if you are in a high-income tax bracket, municipal bonds make a good investment; if you are in a low-income tax bracket, they make a poor investment. A single municipal bond might have a 4% yield, but its term could be twenty-five years. There is a secondary market, but you could take a bath if interest rates are high when you sell. Alternatively, you can buy lots of bonds by investing in a mutual fund that specializes in tax-free munis.
- *Limited partnerships.* This is a more esoteric investment vehicle, not for the casual investor. A company or a group of investors establishes a limited partnership, usually as a unique entity formed solely for the specific venture to which the partnership will be devoted. The partnership sells shares to the public; the purchasers become the *limited partners.* These gadgets were very popular in the 1980s. They took many forms: oil and gas exploration, large transit vehicle rentals (boxcars, semis, even planes), real estate ventures, movie production outfits. There would be a general partner, usually linked to the outfit underwriting the venture, and then hundreds (on occasion thousands) of limited partners. Limited partnerships were typically expected to last only for a limited time frame—the time to find the gas or produce the movie, for example. Your investment was expected to pay off in at least one of three ways. The simplest was dividends paid during the life of the partnership. More complicated were the phantom tax losses. The venture would "lose" money as it went along, and you got to deduct those losses on your income tax return. Finally, the third benefit would be a final payout at the end

of the time frame (e.g., based on the oil wells the company or group developed or the property it sold). The marketers would trumpet the possibility of a payout many times the amount of the original investment. This sounded good, but it rarely turned out that way. (I know, I had a few of these.) The problems were that the dividends never matched the promises; the phantom losses were nice, but then when you got a payout you had to deduct the phantom losses from your cost basis, magnifying your tax bill at that point; or it took so many years for the final payout to occur that you could have earned a better return with a conservative investment of the original money. The annual tax records (K-1 forms) that you had to digest and manipulate also made filling out your income tax return a nightmare every year. Limited partnerships are still around and, as far as I know, just as wretched for the small investor.

- *Commodities.* You've heard of them: pork bellies, September corn. There is even an exchange in Chicago that handles them. Unless you are totally at ease with and completely in control of your affairs in the financial markets on Wall Street, you shouldn't even think about getting involved with the commodities exchange.
- *Options.* These are legal bets on the movement of a stock price. They come in two forms: calls and puts. You sell a *call* on a stock as follows. You sell someone the right to buy from you IBM shares for, say, $85 per share on May 15. When you do this on January 5, the stock price is $80 per share. The option sells for $1.75 per share,[1] and let's say you sell one hundred of these. You earn $175 immediately. The only way you "lose" on this deal is if the stock climbs to a higher price than $85 per share on May 15. If it does, the person who bought the call will exercise it and demand his one hundred shares at $85 per share. You had better have the shares. If you don't, then you will have to buy them at whatever the price is on May 15 (even if it's $105) and immediately sell them to the caller for $85 per share. So you wouldn't do this unless you had the one hundred shares to begin with. If the price doesn't climb as high as $85 or even if it declines, the option will not be exercised; you may not be so happy about the stock price on May 15, but you did earn $175 back in January for selling the call. The buyer is basically betting that the stock will climb rapidly over the life of the call. You are hedging your bets. You are hoping the price will go up, but you don't expect it to rise very much. And you have built in a bit of a cushion if it goes down. You could also buy calls as well as sell them, using the same rules. Does this seem like gambling instead of investing to you? It does to me.

  The opposite of a call is a *put.* In this transaction, you buy from another investor the right to sell him your IBM shares at, say, $75 per share on May 15. Again let's assume the price of the put is $1.75 per share and the amount

1. The determination of an option price is rather complicated. It depends on many factors including the length of time between the sale and the strike date.

in question is one hundred shares. Now you are trying to minimize your losses instead of locking in gains. If the stock stays above $75, then the put expires and you have lost $175. But if the stock drops below $75, you have the right to sell the shares for $75 per share, even if the price is $50. The seller of the put is betting that the price will not fall much. You are not betting that it will as much as you are taking out insurance against the possibility that it might.

- *Precious metals.* Gold, silver, platinum. You can buy them in bullion, or more likely as certificates certifying that you own them. Some people think it's a good idea. Whenever the stock market tanks, precious metals go up. So it's a hedge against a bear market. Invest with extreme caution.
- *Real estate.* There are many ways to invest in real estate. You can buy property and rent it out; buy property, fix it up, and resell it; or buy shares in real estate investment trusts. These are companies that own and manage real estate—commercial and/or residential. Note that real estate often tracks against the market, so this kind of investment can be another hedge against a falling stock market. Real estate investment demands a level of personal energy and time not required in monetary investments.
- *Collectibles.* Art, antiques, coins, stamps, quilts, etc. Unless you know what you are doing, you should only do this for fun as an avocation; trying to make money in collectibles may land you in the poorhouse.

MATHEMATICAL MODEL OF A LONG-TERM INVESTMENT PROGRAM

Now let's go back to our standard investments and address more quantitatively your expectations for accumulating wealth through a regular investment program. Let's assume you have a balanced portfolio of stocks, bonds, and mutual funds. I will address later what I mean by balanced, and also I will say something about the selection of the elements of such a portfolio. But first I want to outline for you how you can compute what kind of long-term return you might expect on the portfolio. I recall the axioms laid out at the beginning of the chapter and reiterate that you should be practicing them. In particular, I assume that you are in this game for the long haul: ten, twenty, thirty, or even forty years or more. What I am about to say has much less validity if your investment window is less than a decade. Conversely, the longer the window, the more accurate the assertions. Over the years, stocks have typically returned in the neighborhood of 10% annually. Bond returns have been more like 5% annually. And a balanced portfolio of both has returned, over the long haul, something of the order of 7% per year. This kind of return assumes the reinvestment of all dividends. Moreover, it presumes no attempt to time the market. For the most part, you buy equities and hang onto them. This strategy is commonly called *buy and hold*, a phrase that, if not coined by Warren Buffet, America's most famous investor, was at least made popular by him. It allows for a modest amount of portfolio retooling over the years, but certainly no churning of your portfolio. (Churning is a popular term that refers to excessive buying and selling.) Retooling a portfolio that consists mainly of mutual funds is much easier than one that consists of lots of individual stocks and bonds. Most major mutual fund companies have a broad spread of different funds that emphasize different themes, and they make it very easy, often cost-free, to switch between different funds in their smorgasbord. I'll say more about this later when I discuss asset allocation.

It is time for the mathematical model. To reiterate, the basic assumptions are:

- You're in it for the long haul. Don't even think about pulling out money on an interim basis.
- No churning of your portfolio. Most of your acquisitions will be in the buy-and-hold mode.
- Dividends are reinvested. Set it up that way when you open the account and resist any temptation to alter it.
- Taxes are either deferred or paid for with separate funds. This is important, as it will allow for the compounded growth of your portfolio in the most advantageous manner.
- The investment amount is increased every year.

Since this is a long-term program, postulating a 7% annual return is appropriate. In this book, we have often taken 3% as a reasonable estimate for the annual inflation rate. Therefore, let's assume you increase your investment allotment by that percent each year. What we have now is very much like the regular deposit model we developed in Chapter 2, except that the amount deposited each year is growing by 3%. You may benefit from looking back at that discussion. I will essentially repeat it now, allowing for the increased investment amount each year. The pertinent sections in that chapter are entitled "Making 'Cents' Out of the Plan by Chopping It into Chunks" and "Magic Numbers Again."

THE ANALYSIS

As we have done many times, we'll do the analysis in a way that easily generalizes and helps us to see what's going on, while at the same time allowing the math wizards to develop a simple formula for computing the values in general circumstances. The key idea, as in Chapter 2, is to separate out the different chunks of money that are invested in different years. Let's assume an initial investment of $100 in Year 1. That amount is increased by 3% every year, and everything is growing at a compounded rate of 7%. The original $100 investment grows to $\$100 \times 1.07 = \$107$ at the end of the first year, at which time we invest another

$\$100 \times 1.03 = \$103$. So at the start of the second year, the investment account contains $\$107 + \$103 = \$210$. At the end of the second year it compounds at 7% to yield $\$210 \times 1.07 = \$224.70$. That's enough of that. Let's go directly to the general analysis. For simplicity, we describe what happens with a five-year plan. If we think only about the fate of the original \$100 invested on the first day of the program, we know how to compute what that will grow into in five years. We are experts at that computation already: the original deposit of \$100 will be worth

$$\$100 \times 1.07^5 = \$140.26$$

at the end of five years. Next, what about the \$103 that was invested at the beginning of the second year? It has four years to grow. At the end of the plan it will be worth

$$\$100 \times 1.03 \times 1.07^4 = \$135.01.$$

Let's do one more round. How much is invested at the start of the third year? Since we are increasing the investment amount by 3% every year, that amount will be $\$100 \times 1.03 \times 1.03 = \$100 \times 1.03^2 = \$106.09$. That amount has three years to grow, so it will eventually become

$$\$100 \times 1.03^2 \times 1.07^3 = \$129.96.$$

Now you should see how to compute the value of the deposits that are made at the beginning of Years 4 and 5. Each will have one less year to grow and so will be worth at the end of the five-year period

$$\$100 \times 1.03^3 \times 1.07^2 = \$125.11,$$

$$\$100 \times 1.03^4 \times 1.07^1 = \$120.43,$$

respectively. The grand total in the account will be equal to the sum of the five different chunks, namely

$$\$140.26 + \$135.01 + \$129.96 + \$125.11 + \$120.43 = \$650.77.$$

Let's spell it out again. If you invest at the beginning of every year for five successive years, \$100—adjusted up by 3% per year, and assuming a return of 7% annually—the investment at the end of five years will be worth

$$\$100 \times 1.07^5 + \$100 \times 1.03^1 \times 1.07^4 + \$100 \times 1.03^2 \times 1.07^3 + \$100 \times 1.03^3 \times 1.07^2 + \$100 \times 1.03^4 \times 1.07^1.$$

Now you should be able to see what will happen over the course of n years: you will have a sum of as many terms as there are years, and each term will be \$100 multiplied by two numbers: first, 1.03 raised to the powers 0, 1, 2, 3, up to and including $n - 1$; and second, 1.07 raised to the powers $n, n - 1, \ldots$ down to 1. This is sort of a double reverse geometric series. Thank goodness the mathematicians can add this one up. As usual, if you are brave enough to want to see the algebra involved:

Click on *Double Geometric Series* under "Mathematical Demonstrations and Special Features."

In fact, if you invest D dollars initially, inflate it by s every year, and the investment returns r annually, then at the end of n years, the investment will be worth

$$FinalValue = D[(1 + r)\frac{(1 + r)^n - (1 + s)^n}{r - s}].$$

Do you see that we have encountered yet another magic number? The expression in the square bracket above is a magic number. If you multiply it by an initial investment D, the product represents the amount that D will grow into in n years, assuming an annual return r and an inflation (of the amount you are investing annually) rate of s. Note that the magic number depends on three variables: the length of the program, the rate of return, and the rate at which the annual investment inflates.

In the specific example we presented above, the relevant numbers were: $n = 5, r = 0.07, s = 0.03$, and $D = \$100$. Note that in that case the formula becomes,

$$100[(1 + 0.07)\frac{(1 + 0.07)^5 - (1 + 0.03)^5}{0.07 - 0.03}] = 650.77,$$

which agrees with the figure we computed above by adding up the chunks.

MAGIC NUMBERS—YET AGAIN

I shall now repeat the concluding paragraph of the "Magic Numbers Again" section of Chapter 2 (slightly modified) because it emphasizes the central point of the book. Namely, the principle of a magic number appears for an escalating regular investment just as it did for a regular deposit account, a lump sum account, a loan, etc. This principle is a key concept in the book, and it reveals that many of the formulas that govern the computations of your (financial) life have a common thread. Of course, the actual formula for the magic number will not concern you very much, as you are likely not going to remember it. As long as you have access to the arithmetic machine on the Web site, you can do the computation in every case. And so you can do whatever comparative analysis you desire in attempting to set up your long-term investment program. This illustrates the book's fundamental premise: This is exactly the kind of financial decision-making you need to do. Moreover, nobody taught you why you should do it, much less how you should do it. My goal has been to rectify that deficiency, in virtually all matters of your financial life—not just your long-term investment fund. Have I been successful?

A TABLE OF MAGIC NUMBERS FOR LONG-TERM INVESTMENT GAINS

Table 12.1 gives the magic numbers for an escalating investment program for various escalation rates and numbers of years. It presumes a 7% annual return. You can use the entries in the table to compute long-term investment gains by multiplying the initial amount invested by the magic number. Thus, if you start your investment program with an initial investment of $1,000, escalate your contribution by 3% annually, and achieve an annual return of 7%, then you will have $16,672, $55,201, $138, 699, or $313,307 after ten, twenty, thirty, or forty years, respectively. Moreover, if you can start instead with $5,000, then your investment portfolio's value in forty years would be more than $1.5 million. Note that in the latter instance, since $1.03^{40} = 3.26$, in the fortieth year of the program you will contribute $5,000 × 3.26 = $16,300, still a very modest number compared to the eventual worth of the portfolio. To illustrate the model using some other numbers, you can read from Table 12.1 that an initial $1,000

Table 12.1
Magic numbers for long-term gains (for an escalating regular annual investment account) assuming a 7% growth rate

	Number of Years			
Escalation Rate	10	20	30	40
0%	14.7836	43.8652	101.0730	213.6096
1.5%	15.6922	49.0805	117.6839	256.0304
3%	16.6715	55.2006	138.6986	313.3072
4%	17.3664	59.8687	155.8226	362.8526
5%	18.0967	65.0767	176.0317	424.4941

investment would yield $49,081 after twenty years at a 1.5% escalation rate and $424,494 after forty years at a 5% escalation rate. In the first row of the table, I have included some numbers for a 0% escalation rate, that is, when the annual amount invested is kept constant. The model then becomes exactly the same as the regular deposit model in Chapter 2, and you will note that the numbers in the columns for ten and forty years agree precisely with the corresponding entries in Table 2.1.

IMPLEMENTATION

Now that you are aware of the potential in a regular escalating investment model, you are probably contemplating more practical issues, such as:

What should I buy? How much of it? What else? How much should I devote to stocks and how much to bonds? Where do I buy these?

There are no "one answer fits all" responses to these questions. Only you can determine the best answers for your particular situation. But I will provide some guidelines and suggestions. I will first make some general observations, then a more concrete set of recommendations.

For many of you, the answers to the above questions lie in your employer's cafeteria plan. You may have the option to participate in a 401(k) plan, or a company profit-sharing plan, or some other tax-deferred plan that is primarily directed toward retirement. If so, there is probably a selection of mutual funds from which you must make your investment choices. Look at the data the plan supplies on past performance of these funds; talk to friends, coworkers, and financial advisers (if you have them); do some research on the Web or in the library. Pick a spread of funds that spans the gamut from very conservative to very aggressive; choose across several different sectors of the market; balance the choice of funds that emphasize growth (probably stock funds) with those that emphasize income (probably bond funds). I'll say something more specific on balance below when I talk about asset allocation and diversification. If you don't have access to an employer-sponsored plan, then you may be able to get into a (perhaps non tax-deferred) plan through a professional or union organization. Some community or religious organizations or social clubs sponsor plans. Finally, you can set up a self-directed IRA or a Keogh plan if you are self-employed. What I am suggesting is that regardless of your employment situation, there are ample investment opportunities available. Finding the best vehicle for yourself may require some research on your part. In fact, the hardest parts of the whole venture are summoning the will to start and then maintaining the discipline to persevere. You will find that the choices of what/how much to buy and sell are less taxing (no pun intended) than the decision to start and not stop.

RECOMMENDATIONS

- Start immediately. A glance at Table 12.1 reveals the consequences of delay. You accumulate more than double in forty years what you amass in thirty years. If you procrastinate, you could waste a decade in which you are earning a good salary. Your forty-year window shrinks to thirty surprisingly quickly.
- Devote as much as you can to the program. That is easier said than done, of course. As we have seen throughout the book, there are many tugs on your financial resources—many of them totally legitimate and compelling. It's just a matter of paying yourself first. Establish your investment program and set the bar as high as your budget will allow.
- Make sure to escalate the amount you invest annually—another recommendation that is easier said than done. Pay raises are wonderful; they give you the opportunity to do some things that may not have been possible earlier. You can't devote your entire raise to your investment program, but be sure to allocate some of it. And then what about the years when your income might stagnate or decline? Escalating your investment program at those times is especially challenging. Well, maybe a small increment is possible—to be compensated for by a larger than normal one in a good year yet to come.
- Structure your investment program in a tax-deferred setting if at all possible. This should be easy for those of you who are self-employed or have access to an employer cafeteria program. Otherwise, recent tax changes have expanded other opportunities. Limits on IRAs have gone up. These are easily set up and administered by a bank, broker, or mutual fund company. Annuities are another possibility. (Actually, I view annuities with some suspicion. They are complicated and difficult for amateurs to understand, and too often they do not deliver as promised. If you want to pursue that avenue, I recommend a great deal of research and comparison.) If you can't find a tax-free environment, then I recommend that you try to pay any taxes due on your investments (dividends and capital gains) with money from your regular budget, that is, your salary or other noninvestment income. In this way, you can still preserve your dividend reinvestment setup, and the full compounding effect of your investment program is maintained. This is another challenging requirement, but one I highly recommend, and by now you should understand the critical importance of compounding and its salutary effects on your portfolio.

In the next list, I deliver on the promise to discuss asset allocation and diversification.

- Virtually all financial advisers will preface any discussion of allocation with the recommendation that you have six months of cash stashed away for an unexpected emergency: unemployment, sudden illness, a lawsuit, need to pay ransom, whatever. Exactly how to determine how much cash you might need for six months is not always so simple, and why six months and not, say, a year is an unanswered question. Some say the amount of your cash stash should equal your total take-home pay for six months. That seems as good a criterion as any to me. Whatever amount you think is appropriate, you should have that amount of money in cash—meaning in the bank, in the mattress, in a money market fund, someplace where the funds are liquid and immediately available. (In Chapter 5, I took a more liberal stance toward the meaning of "liquid." You have to find your own comfort level.)

- Now, let's slightly oversimplify matters and assume all of your investments fall into one of two categories: first, stocks or equities, and second, bonds, CDs, or notes. This requires that you understand all of your mutual fund holdings well enough to classify them into one of the two categories. Now, what is the "ideal" proportion between the two that should describe your portfolio? Well, there are a few well-known *asset allocation* models. A very popular one is: Subtract your age from 110; that's the percentage of your investments that should be in stocks, with the remainder in bonds. Some models use 100 instead of 110. Some incorporate the cash stash in the bond allocation. The moral is clear: the younger you are, the more risk you can afford and the more aggressively oriented can be your portfolio. Stocks are more volatile than bonds, but the returns are higher. If you have a longer investment window, you can afford the greater risk in pursuit of the greater return. Note that the 110 model says that at age 60, you should have a 50–50 allocation of stocks and bonds. Here is a somewhat different way to break it down that is more closely tied to when you need your money, rather than to your age. If you are more than 10 years out from needing the money, you can have the bulk, say two-thirds or three-fourths in aggressive stock investments. As that number 10 shrinks, you have to transfer more and more of your funds to safer investments (e.g., bonds). However, if you expect to be around for a while, you should never move all of it to the safe house. You should always keep a minimum, say one-fourth, in growth—for inflation never sleeps.
- Now that we've answered the question of how much stocks and how much bonds, we come to the issue of which stocks and which bonds. Here's a helpful approach to that question. The economy has lots of sectors: technology, communications, insurance, industrials, finance, health, transportation, defense, and retail being among the most easily identifiable. There are other ways to cut up the pie: large, mid, and small cap—that is, according to the size of the capital resources of a firm. Another method is to recognize the dichotomy between *growth* and *value* (with, roughly speaking, the former meaning stocks of companies that are projected to grow in earnings and profits in the future, and the latter meaning companies that are already well positioned but undervalued currently for some reason). My recommendation: pick a few, say a half dozen, and spread your portfolio across those sectors. This is called *diversification*. It has one great advantage: since different sectors often move out of phase with each other, diversification minimizes risk. It may on occasion limit gains, but the benefits far outweigh the limitations.

- Diversifying your investments is easier if they are in mutual funds rather than individual stocks and bonds. As I explained, you can transfer between different funds in the same mutual fund company easily and cheaply. Buying and selling stocks is more complicated and much more costly. So a natural question arises: Should all of your portfolio be in mutual funds? For many people, that is the simplest strategy. However, I recommend that you buy a modest number of individual stocks and bonds. The reason: It is more fun and engages the intellect more actively. Following an individual stock is much more interesting than tracking the net asset value of a mutual fund. I certainly have had fun, and agony, doing so over the years. Also, trying to gauge the worth of a single stock is more stimulating than evaluating the net asset value of a mutual fund. Nevertheless, I think that your portfolio should emphasize mutual funds—if so, it will be easier, safer, and simpler to implement some of the preceding recommendations. Just not as much fun. The same comment applies to bonds. Buy yourself one or two corporate or muni bonds. Don't make it your first purchase; wait until you have more assets. Don't forget to reinvest the dividends.
- Finally, don't try to time the market. You are certain to lose unless you are willing to devote an inordinate number of hours per week to research on investments. (Do you really have the time for that?) Even if you devote the hours, you may still come out on the short end. To wit:

I have been dealing with the same stockbroker for more than twenty years. He is intelligent, well informed, articulate, and extremely solicitous of my financial needs and concerns. He has given me a great deal of advice, always carefully thought out and presented, over the years. And I would say that he has been right more often than he has been wrong—*but not by much*. Amazingly, in spite of the fact that he does this work full-time for a living, many of his recommendations have turned out to be clunkers. My point is that dealing with a stockbroker is a little like gambling. The odds in my dealings with my broker are that it will be better for me to follow his advice than not, but only by a sliver. Over the long haul, it works out well for me. Do you have the fortitude to stay with your own advice over the long haul? I doubt it. The first bad move will spook you and cause further bad errors. As I said, leave the decisions to professionals. If you don't want to establish a long-term relationship with a broker, then stick mainly with mutual funds.

FURTHER OBSERVATIONS

By now you have certainly noticed that I have filled a whole chapter with quantitative and qualitative advice on investing without recommending a single specific stock, bond, company, or mutual fund. Those choices are yours. I am here just to lay out the general parameters that should guide your choices and to deliver the arithmetic goods that will help you project into the future. Continuing in that mode, I will conclude the chapter with a broad set of what I would call observations, more so than recommendations, on important matters pertaining to investing.

1. *Choice of broker/adviser.* If you can't arrange an investment program that is mostly automated, for example, in an employer cafeteria plan, then you have three choices: a real broker, a discount broker, or the Internet. I have already given you my philosophy of how it works with a real broker. With a discount broker, trades cost you much less money, but you don't get any meaningful advice. If you invest over the Internet—or, horror of horrors, day trade—then you should be aware that most people doing that have been getting slaughtered.
2. *Churning.* If you do get involved with a broker, be alert to the possibility of her steering you into a churning course. Believe it or not, there are brokers out there who only want to gyrate your portfolio so that they can generate commissions.

Beware, also. If you are doing your own trading on the Internet, you can very easily fall prey to self-churning.

3. *Dollar-cost averaging.* If your investments are regular and automated, for example, through payroll deduction or even via your own personal systematic purchases, then you are engaging in what the experts call dollar-cost averaging. This refers to the fact that you're not plunking down funds one time to buy a stock, bond, or mutual fund. You are buying the equity over the course of time, paying different prices during the year and thus some average price per share for what you purchase over the year. Financial advisers make a big deal out of this. I'm not so impressed. They say that if prices go up, you are buying into a winner; if prices drift down, since you're getting the stock at a low price, you've lowered your average cost. Poppycock. If the price went up during the year, I would wish that I had bought all of what I now own at the beginning of the year. And if prices went down, then it would clearly have been better to buy it all at the end of the year. But you can't have it both ways. Nor might you be able to have it either way. That is, you probably couldn't buy it all at the beginning of the year because you didn't have the cash. And even if you could save up to buy it all at the end of the year, what if prices go up—as indeed you hope they will? I think that the merit of regular disciplined investing is not dollar-cost averaging, but rather that your budget permits it and it results in the accumulation of assets as the years go by in as relatively a painless way as possible.
4. *Preferred stock.* These vehicles are like a cross between a stock and a bond. They trade like stocks, often pay a high dividend, the stock price doesn't move much, and if the company goes broke the preferred stockholders are in

line for the scraps ahead of the regular stockholders. I have done quite well with these over the years. Although, to be honest, I'm never totally sure whether to categorize them as stocks or bonds. For the record, I list them among my stocks.

5. *Company stock.* Your employer's plan likely includes your company's stock as an option. Some plans allow for only the company stock. Nevertheless, you should not load up on company stock. It's the old "all the eggs in one basket" problem. Certainly your company's stock can play a role in your portfolio, but no more than say 20%. Remember: diversification! The folks who had nothing but Enron stock (a company that went belly-up a few years ago) in their retirement portfolios will attest to the wisdom of that observation.
6. *Mutual fund capital gains.* There's a nasty little feature of mutual funds of which you should be aware. You know that if you buy a stock for $100 and sell it for $110, then you have a capital gain of $10 (per share). If you hold the stock for less than a year, the $10 counts as income, same as your salary, bank interest, or dividends. If you hold it for more than a year, then the profit is called a long-term capital gain and taxed at a lower rate. Since mutual funds buy and sell stocks constantly, they incur capital gains. The tax laws force them to pass along those gains to you—on paper, not in real dollars—even if you have not sold your mutual fund shares. So each year, you may have to declare some phantom capital gains by funds that are sitting in your portfolio. Of course, you get to add those amounts to your cost basis when you do finally sell your mutual fund shares, but that may be far into the future. This is clearly a flaw in the U.S. tax laws. So what else is new! With individual stocks, you only incur gains when you actually sell. Oh well, this is a disadvantage of mutual funds. It's more than compensated for by the advantages, so you'll just have to learn to live with it.
7. *Other investment vehicles.* I have not allotted any space for the other investments that I described earlier in the chapter. If you want to pursue some of those, then you'll need to figure out how much space to allocate for them in your portfolio. But here's a related question: What about your house and other personal possessions? Aren't they assets? Yes, they are, but not monetary assets. Enjoy 'em if you got 'em. But unless you are sitting on a mansion that you plan to liquidate at some point and then live in a cheap condo, you shouldn't be counting your house as a financial investment. Your house is an appreciating asset, but it's not an entry in your investment ledger. You should be living in your house because you love it, not because you expect it to make you money—even if it does in the end, by the way.

☺ When I was in graduate school, I had a fellowship and my wife worked full-time. We actually had some extra money, and so we tried our hand for the first time at investing. We bought a mutual fund that appreciated nicely over the next few years. But when rough economic times hit in the

> early 1970s, the price fell, and, not surprisingly, we panicked—we sold it. At that time, we were completely preoccupied with young children, a budding academic career, new houses and cars. We did no investing again for nearly a decade—a mistake that we will regret for the rest of our lives. Over the last twenty years, we have managed to establish a regular and somewhat disciplined approach to investing, although only in the last ten years or so have we devoted the attention to the issue that it warrants. Things went rather well throughout the 1980s and 1990s. But like almost everyone, I got caught up in the tech fervor of the late 1990s and allowed my portfolio to get somewhat too skewed in that direction. Naturally, I was hurt by the "tech bust," but not as badly as many of my acquaintances who were not paying any attention to diversification. I remain optimistic that I will recoup these losses (actually, I have come a long way back in the last year) and that the principles laid out in this chapter, which I have followed reasonably faithfully, will keep me moving forward for many years.

I hope that the main lesson you will take from this important chapter is that a regular, sustained investment program is crucial for your long-term financial health and, if pursued vigorously and aggressively, will even lead you down a path toward financial wealth. But it requires perseverance. You must be in it for the long haul. You cannot be spooked by the years in which the market is floundering. Also, keep it simple: stocks, bonds, and primarily mutual funds. Use investment clubs, sensible friends and relatives, and reputable advisers to keep you informed and motivated. Finally, don't fixate on your portfolio. Pay it close heed, but only during a modest portion of your waking hours. Remember: wealth is also measured in terms of family, friends, home, career, and avocations.

YOUR NEW COMPUTATIONAL SKILLS

How to compute the final worth of an escalating, regular investment program, given that you know the starting amount, the annual return, the annual escalating rate, and the length of the program.

CHAPTER 13

Retirement

Now that we've devoted a whole book to methods and schemes for accumulating money, we will see in this last chapter how long it will take you to dispose of it. For young readers, I know that thinking about retirement is very difficult—it seems so far in the future. Well, I have news for you: Retirement comes around faster than you can imagine. I hope that I have succeeded in showing you how procrastination in planning for it can cost you a lot of money. But if you take planning seriously and pursue a regular, aggressive investment program, you can succeed in building up quite a nest egg.

At the cusp of retirement, one has to contemplate how to put that nest egg to use. Is it big enough? If not, how long will it last? We will answer those and related questions in this chapter. Truthfully, this material may resonate more strongly with senior readers than with young ones. But as I have cautioned throughout the book, forewarned is forearmed. Regardless of your age, if you know what's coming, you'll be better prepared to deal with it.

RETIREMENT FACTORS

If you've gotten this far, you know how to accumulate some money toward your retirement. Will it be enough? How much do you need? Those are very tricky questions that have been addressed by numerous authors. You won't be surprised to learn that those authors have espoused many different answers. But virtually any book on the subject will contain a statement such as: You need a retirement income equal to at least x% of your preretirement net income. There are two problems with that statement: the variable amount x and the meaning of the phrase "net income." Net income is sometimes defined as take-home pay, sometimes as after-tax income, and sometimes even as twelve times average monthly expenses. And the quantity x may vary from as low as 50% to as much as 85%. I am somewhat dubious of these prescriptions. Based on my observations of friends and relatives in retirement, I would say the following:

Unless you plan a dramatically different lifestyle, a precipitous drop in your expenses upon retirement is not necessarily something you should expect. True, your expenditures on work clothes, commutation, professional dues, and other directly work-related expenses will definitely decrease. You may also expect to devote fewer resources toward savings, investments, and insurance. But expenses such as food and household expenditures will stay the same. And other expenses may actually increase—for example, health care, entertainment, travel, gifts (for grandchildren). After all, you have this newfound free time. In American society, filling up time more often than not involves pouring out money.

Another factor to consider is taxes. In general, your tax burden should decrease. There are additional income tax exemptions triggered by the acquisition of senior status. Increased health costs may result in more tax deductions or credits. Some communities offer real estate tax breaks to the elderly. And I'm sure all of you have seen this assertion many times: You'll be in a lower tax bracket because your income will be lower. I've had a lot of financial objectives in my life, but being in a lower tax bracket has never been one of them. Don't misunderstand me—taxes are way too high in the United States, and both the tax rates and income brackets should be lowered. But I'm not holding my breath. If the only way I can lower my bracket is to lower my income, then that is an objective I shall not pursue. I think it is awful that much of the working population of America is under the misguided assumption that they're going to be OK in their old age because, first, their lower income will lower their taxes, and second, because Social Security will take care of their remaining needs.

In summary, you will probably need less income in retirement than you needed preretirement. How much less may not be as great as the "experts" would lead you to believe. In principle, having the same income in retirement as in preretirement would be lovely. That may not be feasible, but you certainly should shoot for an x closer to 85% than to 50%.

SOURCES OF RETIREMENT INCOME

Now let's move toward a computation. Look at your preretirement income. What will replace it? Usually, there are three sources:

1. Any benefits you receive from defined benefit retirement plans.
2. Your government welfare—er, ahem, I mean Social Security.
3. The income thrown off from the retirement nest egg that you accumulated over the years via your investment program.

Defined benefit retirement plans are those where you pay some formulaic amount over the years, and at retirement there is a formulaic benefit payout. The contribution will typically be a percentage, say 5%, of your salary. The payout may be something like 2% of your preretirement salary times the number of years you contributed to the plan. The funding for the plan comes from your (and your fellow coworkers) contributions, often supplemented by employer contributions, all of which have been invested by the plan administrators during your working years. Defined benefit retirement plans were once very common in both corporate America and the public sector. They are almost extinct in the private sector now but still fairly common in the public sector, although benefits have been curtailed substantially. Also, professional organizations and unions sometimes make these kinds of plans available to their members. These plans were, and some still are, excellent opportunities for those who are eligible. If you have one available, I hope you are participating. Your plan administrator should be able to give you a projection of your potential retirement benefit.

Social Security is also a formulaic plan. The amount of your benefit is determined by your age, marital status, salary over the years, and the period of time in jobs subject to FICA taxes. The contribution is 6.2% of your gross salary up to a maximum that is adjusted annually. Currently, the maximum is approximately $87,000. Incidentally, your employer has to contribute the same amount on your behalf. In recent years, the Social Security Administration has been mailing annual statements containing a record of your past contributions and anticipated future benefits. Perhaps you received one recently. If not, you can call the Social Security Administration to obtain the information—but be prepared to be patient with the service you receive.

Your next task is to add up the projected annual benefits from items 1 and 2 in the list above. Then subtract that figure from x% of your preretirement income—where presumably you have decided what is the minimum x you can tolerate. I will call the resulting difference your annual *shortfall;* it is the amount you need to generate annually in supplemental income by means of the investment nest egg you have accumulated. You now have two numbers staring you in the face:

S = your annual shortfall. As explained, this is the amount you need to make up because the total of your defined benefit and Social Security benefit incomes falls short of your needed retirement income, which you've set at x% of your preretirement income.

E = the nest egg that you amassed through investments, which will be used to generate funds to address the shortfall.

DO YOU HAVE ENOUGH MONEY?

The obvious questions are:

1. Will E generate S in the first year of your retirement?
2. Is E big enough to generate S annually for the rest of your life?
3. If in addition we allow for inflation, is E large enough to generate the inflation-adjusted annual supplement that you need?

4. Will you have to deplete *all* of E over the remainder of your life, or will you be able to leave something to your heirs?

We will build two models for answering these questions—one that ignores inflation and one that allows for inflation. The second model is the one that is really critical for you, but we will also pursue the first because it is instructive and helpful for understanding the second. These models are much simpler than those you will find in popular retirement books or software. The one produced by the investment/mutual fund firm T. Rowe Price is very typical. It's an excellent product, but in using it you must make so many choices and compute so many variables that the amateur has difficulty understanding what's going on. The models here will be much more transparent, and only very slightly less accurate than the T. Rowe Price model.

A RETIREMENT MODEL THAT IGNORES INFLATION

So, let's start with a model that ignores inflation. You've decided that S is your annual need or shortfall. Your nest egg E awaits your instruction in order to generate S. Is E enough to throw off S annually? To answer, we need to know what rate of return to expect. We've already agreed that 7% is the typical result of a balanced portfolio. But as you age, you convert your portfolio to safer status, thereby likely decreasing its rate of return. Therefore, let's take 6% as the expected rate of return on your retirement nest egg E. We'll allow for different choices later. So for E to generate S every year, 6% of E had better be equal to or bigger than S. Mathematicians write

$$.06E \geq S.$$

Dividing through by.06, we see that this inequality says the same thing as

$$E \geq S/.06 = 16.67S.$$

That means your nest egg must be at least 16.67 times the size of your annual shortfall. To put that in perspective, it means that if you need to make up a shortfall of \$10,000 per year, then your nest egg must be greater than or equal to \$166,700. Table 13.1 presents other values.

Now what if, heaven forbid, your nest egg is not big enough? That is, what happens if

$$E < S/.06?$$

Then 6% of E will be less than S, so when you remove S from your nest egg during the first year of retirement to make up your shortfall, your nest egg will not

Table 13.1
Nest egg needs, based on a 6% return rate

Annual Shortfall (S)	Required Nest Egg (E)
\$10,000	\$166,700
\$25,000	\$416,750
\$50,000	\$833,500
\$100,000	\$1,667,000

generate enough return to replace S and the total amount in the nest egg at the beginning of the second year will be less than what it was originally. The situation will accelerate, and eventually you will deplete your nest egg. In how many years? Let's figure it out.

Now bear with me as the math is going to get a little bit thick. Each year, the retirement portfolio will earn 6% but then be decreased by the removal of the annual shortfall. This will decrease the balance each year, and our job is to figure out when that balance vanishes entirely. Table 13.2 shows how much is left in the nest egg at the end of each year.

The last formula in Table 13.2 describes what's left of the nest egg after n years. By now, you should recognize the geometric series. If we add it up, we get

$$1.06^nE - (S/.06)(1.06^n - 1).$$

So the question at hand is for which value of n will the last expression reduce to zero? That is, we have to solve the equation

$$1.06^nE - (S/.06)(1.06^n - 1) = 0$$

for n in terms of E and S. This is a little more complicated than the equations we have met thus far in the book, because the variable we need to solve for appears as an exponent in the equation. We can't do it by simple arithmetic, but mathe-

Table 13.2
A declining nest egg, based on a 6% return rate

End of Year	Contents of Nest Egg
0 (the original amount)	E
1	$1.06E - S$
2	$1.06(1.06 - S) - S = 1.06^2E - 1.06S - S$
3	$1.06(1.06^2E - 1.06S - S) - S = 1.06^3E - 1.06^2S - 1.06S - S$
n	$1.06^nE - 1.06^{n-1}S - \cdots - 1.06S - S =$ $1.06^nE - S(1.06^{n-1} + \cdots + 1.06 + 1)$

maticians figured out how to do it long ago. The answer is in terms of logarithms, a subject you should have encountered in high school. The answer is

$$n = \frac{\ln(\frac{S}{S - .06E})}{\ln(1.06)} \qquad \text{(Formula 13.1)}$$

The symbol "ln" stands for *natural logarithm*. It may appear on the calculator you have in your drawer. If not, it's not a catastrophe as you can, as usual, get the output of the formula by using the Web site. So let's give a few illustrative examples of the values of n that emerge for reasonable choices of S and E. Suppose your shortfall is S = \$20,000. As you may recall, this means that your defined benefit plus Social Security income is projected to fall \$20,000 short of the total annual retirement income that you need. Note that 16.67 × \$20,000 = \$334,000. So if you have that amount or more in your nest egg (and there is no inflation), you are set for life. But if you have only E = \$250,000, say, then the result of plugging those values into Formula 13.1 yields

$$\frac{\ln(\frac{20000}{20000 - .06 \times 250000})}{\ln(1.06)} = 23.79.$$

Your nest egg in this instance would last nearly 24 years before you have to fall on your sword, or at least show up at the door of one of your kids. If you had half as much, that is, \$125,000 as a nest egg, it would only last 8 years. And if all you had accumulated was \$75,000, then you have a mere $4\frac{1}{3}$ years before the apocalypse. Here are two more illustrations:

- If the shortfall is \$40,000 and the nest egg is \$600,000, you're OK for $39\frac{1}{2}$ years. (That's a long time, reflecting the fact that \$600,000 is pretty close to 16.67 × \$40,000 = \$666,800, which would last forever.)
- If the shortfall is \$100,000 and the nest egg is \$1 million, your money will last for $15\frac{3}{4}$ years. Is that long enough? I don't know. Do you?

You can do some estimating and plug in your own numbers if you:

 Consult the Web site. (See the *Retirement Calculator*.)

RESTRUCTURING THE MODEL

Here's another way to structure the logarithmic formula that is much less dependent on specific numbers. We know that for a particular value of the shortfall S, the amount needed so that your money lasts forever is $16.67S$. That is the ideal nest egg. So let us write

$$I = 16.67 \times S.$$

Now suppose your true nest egg E is some fraction of that amount, such as one-half or three-quarters. We can write that as

$$E = \alpha \times I,$$

where the Greek letter α stands for the fraction. Now notice what happens when we plug these equations into Formula 13.1; we get a new formula for the number of years your money lasts, namely,

$$n = \frac{\ln(\frac{1}{1-\alpha})}{\ln(1.06)}. \quad \text{(Formula 13.2)}$$

The new formula depends only on the fractional amount α, not on the variables S or E. So now you can compute how long your money will last as soon as you identify what fraction of the ideal nest egg you managed to amass. Looking back at the examples above, since \$250,000 is almost precisely three-quarters of \$334,000, it should be that accumulating 75% of what you need ought to last about 24 years. And similarly, since \$1,000,000 is 60% of \$1,667,000, 60% should buy you approximately $15\frac{3}{4}$ years. These observations are borne out in Table 13.3.

Table 13.3
How long your nest egg will last, based on a 6% return rate

The Fraction (α) Represented by the Quotient of the Actual Nest Egg Divided by the Ideal Nest Egg	Number of Years the Nest Egg Lasts
1/10 = 0.10	1.81
1/5 = 0.20	3.83
1/4 = 0.25	4.94
1/3 = 0.33	6.96
2/5 = 0.40	8.77
1/2 = 0.50	11.90
3/5 = 0.50	15.73
2/3 = 0.67	18.85
3/4 = 0.75	23.79
4/5 = 0.80	27.62
9/10 = 0.90	39.52

For example, you can read from this table that if you manage to accumulate a retirement portfolio that is 50% of the ideal portfolio, then that amount will last you just under twelve years. But I reiterate: this observation and the numbers in Table 13.3 emerge from a model that ignores inflation and presumes a 6% annual return on the retirement portfolio. Table 13.4 gives some numbers associated with different rates of return.

Whoa! Is there something wrong here? For higher rates of return, your money should last longer—or so it would seem. Is something counterintuitive going on here? Actually, no. Here is the explanation. Suppose you have a shortfall of $30,000. Then at a 6% return, your ideal nest egg I is a cool half-million dollars, $I = \$30{,}000/.06 = \$500{,}000$. Now suppose you only accumulate one-half of it, that is, $E = \$250{,}000$. Then we know, from either Table 13.3 or Table 13.4, that the nest egg will last 11.9 years. But now suppose the rate of return is only 5%. Then your ideal nest egg I is greater, in fact $I = \$30{,}000/.05 = \$600{,}000$. In order for α to remain at one-half, you must now accumulate $300,000. Not surprisingly, the greater amount lasts longer—specifically, 14.21 years according to Table 13.4. On the other hand, you can easily confirm (with the Web site, for instance) that if you still only accumulate $250,000 toward a $30,000 shortfall and the return rate is 5%, then your nest egg will only last 11 years—less than the 11.9 years it lasts with a 6% return.

Table 13.4
The number of years a nest egg will last, depending on the fraction of the ideal nest egg accumulated and the rate of return

	Rate of Return			
The Fraction (α) Represented by the Quotient of the Actual Nest Egg Divided by the Ideal Nest Egg	**3%**	**5%**	**6%**	**7%**
1/10 = 0.10	3.56	2.16	1.81	1.56
1/5 = 0.20	7.55	4.57	3.83	3.30
1/4 = 0.25	9.73	5.90	4.94	4.25
1/3 = 0.33	13.72	8.31	6.96	5.99
2/5 = 0.40	17.28	10.47	8.77	7.55
1/2 = 0.50	23.45	14.21	11.90	10.24
3/5 = 0.60	31.00	18.78	15.73	13.54
2/3 = 0.67	37.17	22.52	18.85	16.24
3/4 = 0.75	46.90	28.41	23.79	20.49
4/5 = 0.80	54.45	32.99	27.62	23.79
9/10 = 0.90	77.90	47.19	39.52	34.03

A RETIREMENT MODEL THAT ACCOUNTS FOR INFLATION

All of the preceding assumes, as stipulated, that inflation is ignored. On the other hand, *taxes* are not ignored. The presumption is that taxes are one of your expenses in retirement, as of course they are preretirement (Oh boy are they!), and they are included in the budgetary analysis that resulted in your shortfall amount. But now let's get real and include inflation in the model. If you really are going to be spending ten, twenty, or more years in retirement relying on your nest egg, you can't discount inflation over that long a period.

If we include inflation in the model, then the amount of your annual shortfall is no longer a static figure; it will increase every year due to inflation. So we need to assign an inflation rate. Throughout the book I have used 3% as a good historical figure for annual inflation. In the rest of this chapter, I will use 2%. Why the decrease? There are three reasons. First of all, I have already indicated that the government's official inflation figures are widely regarded as being overstated. Second, I think it is fair to say that the stuff that retirement folks consume is not subject to inflation to the same degree as the stuff consumed by nonretirees—with the exception of health care. Just think of early-bird specials as opposed to BMWs. Finally, the elderly are better at pulling in their belts than are young working people. Now, if we return to the standard 6% retirement portfolio, then a 2% inflation rate means that you are not free to use all of the 6% return for annual income. You must set aside 2% of it to grow your portfolio in order to deal with the increasing prices of the goods and services your retirement income is intended to purchase. That leaves you with a net 4% return for your shortfall. Clearly, the practical effect of including inflation in the model is that it is going to increase the size of the target, that is, the ideal nest egg, and thereby diminish the number of years your actual nest egg will last if you can't hit the target. Thus, if your shortfall is $20,000 upon retirement, then your ideal nest egg will be

$$\$20{,}000/.04 = \$500{,}000$$

instead of the $334,000 it was when inflation was discounted. Said otherwise, since 1/.04 = 25, your nest egg needs to be 25 times the size of your shortfall (rather than 16.67 times) in order for your nest egg to generate the inflation-adjusted shortfall you require for the rest of your life. Let's repeat Table 13.1, but this time using the larger multiplying factor, namely 25. Note that the ideal nest egg numbers in Table 13.5 are 50% higher than the corresponding numbers in Table 13.1

To reiterate, of the 6% thrown off by your nest egg, 4% of it will supply your shortfall income. The other 2% is reinvested in your portfolio, so that in the second year you can repeat the process and accommodate the new shortfall, which has swollen by 2%—and so on every year. But as before, we must deal with the

Table 13.5
Nest egg needs based on a 6% return rate with 2% set aside to cover inflation, leaving an effective 4% return rate

Annual Shortfall (*S*)	Ideal Nest Egg (*I*)
$10,000	$250,000
$25,000	$625,000
$50,000	$1,250,00
$100,000	$2,500,000

fact that the nest egg you actually accumulate may be less than the ideal nest egg you need. Once again, how long will it last? The math for dealing with that question is a little more complicated than what we have seen thus far in the chapter. I'll spare you the details and just give you the formulas.

The first formula is the analog of Formula 13.1. If your actual nest egg E generates a 6% return, with 2% devoted to dealing with inflation in order to address an annual shortfall S, then it will last n years, where

$$n = \frac{\ln(\frac{S}{S - .04E})}{\ln(\frac{1.06}{1.02})} \qquad \text{(Formula 13.3)}$$

Similarly, the analog of Formula 13.2 is given as follows. If you have a 6% return in a 2% inflationary economy, then if your actual nest egg is α times the ideal nest egg (the latter being 25 times the shortfall), then your nest egg will last n years, where

$$n = \frac{\ln(\frac{1}{1 - \alpha})}{\ln(\frac{1.06}{1.02})} \qquad \text{(Formula 13.4)}$$

Here α is a number between 0 and 1.

Next we give a table that mirrors Table 13.3. Table 13.6 indicates the life of a nest egg in an inflationary economy for different values of α.

Oh, oh, the numbers here are larger than the numbers in Table 13.3, which is counterintuitive. The explanation is similar to the one that explained the changes caused by different return rates. Namely, when inflation is not ignored, the ideal nest egg is now 25 times the shortfall, rather than 16.67 as it was without inflation. Therefore, the actual nest egg must be larger to maintain the fractional value α. For example, if you have an actual nest egg of $450,000 and a

Table 13.6
How long your nest egg will last, based on a 6% return rate and a 2% inflation rate

The Fraction (α) Represented by the Quotient of the Actual Nest Egg Divided by the Ideal Nest Egg	Number of Years the Nest Egg Lasts
1/10 = 0.10	2.74
1/5 = 0.20	5.80
1/4 = 0.25	7.48
1/3 = 0.33	10.54
2/5 = 0.40	13.28
1/2 = 0.50	18.02
3/5 = 0.60	23.82
2/3 = 0.67	28.56
3/4 = 0.75	36.04
4/5 = 0.80	41.84
9/10 = 0.90	59.86

shortfall of $30,000, then the nest egg will last 39.52 years without inflation, but only 23.82 years if inflation is figured in. That is because $450,000 is 90% of the no-inflation ideal nest egg of 16.67 × $30,000 = $500,000 (see Table 13.3), but only 60% of the inflation ideal nest egg of 25 × $30,000 = $750,000 (see Table 13.6). I leave it to you to use the Web site to do more comparisons on the number of years to address the same shortfall with the same nest egg, both with and without inflation. Needless to say, in the real world you must rely on Table 13.6 and Formulas 13.3 and 13.4, rather than Table 13.3 and Formulas 13.1 and 13.2.

Now we reinterpret the information we have gleaned from our models to supply the answers to the four questions we asked in the section "Do You Have Enough Money?"

1. Clearly, E will generate S in the first year of retirement if $E \geq S$. But of course we hope to spend more than one year in retirement, so
2. E will generate S annually forever if $E \geq S/r$, where r is the return you achieve on your retirement portfolio. We have used $r = .06$ as typical. Note that $S/.06 = 16.67S$, $S/.05 = 20S$, and $S/.04 = 25S$. Thus, depending on your rate of return, you need between 16.67 and 25 times the size of your shortfall. But this ignores inflation, so
3. Allowing for inflation, E will generate S annually forever provided

$$E \geq \frac{S}{r-i},$$

where r is the return rate and i is the inflation rate.

4. If $E < S/(r-i)$, then you have to use the Web site to compute how many years your nest egg will last, where you can specify either the actual nest egg and your annual shortfall, or the ideal nest egg and the fraction of it you managed to accumulate.

I apologize if I've made it all sound so cut and dried by emphasizing the numbers at the expense of the human equation. In fact, many elderly people live in terror at the prospect of outliving their resources. Huge unexpected expenses such as extended nursing home stays can wreak havoc with retirement projections. This is a real and legitimate fear, and I do not mean to minimize or trivialize it. That said, I emphasize that the prime goal of the models and tables in this chapter is twofold: (1) if you are young, to give you some motivation to take retirement planning seriously, and to give you some financial targets at which to aim; and (2) if you are elderly and more or less know what your S and E are/will be, to give you some realistic numbers to use in trying to decide whether you are secure or not, and whether you need to make some adjustments to your expenditures and/or your investment strategy.

There is an alternate approach that the elderly might adopt. Instead of taking the nest egg and shortfall as given and computing the number of years until you become a ward of the state (as we have done), you could postulate the number of years that you anticipate enjoying financial independence and then compute how much your nest egg will permit you to spend every year. I realize that deciding a priori how long you are going to live might be seen as macabre, but it's a rational point of view—and the math is interesting. In fact, this change of point of view means that, mathematically, you look at the equation that comes before Table 13.2 and instead of solving for n in terms of S and E, you solve for S in terms of E and n. The result is

$$S = \frac{1.06^n E}{\left(\frac{1.06^n - 1}{.06}\right)}.$$

But of course you really should take inflation into account, and in that case the formula becomes

$$S = \frac{1.06^n E}{\left(\frac{1.06^n - 1.02^n}{.04}\right)},$$

where we have taken, as usual, 6% as the rate of return and 2% as the inflation rate. If you prefer to do things this way, then you can use the Web site to compute some values. Here are two:

if $n = 20$, $E = \$500{,}000$, then $S = \$37{,}267$;

if $n = 15$, $E = \$1{,}000{,}000$, then $S = \$91{,}238$.

As I have told you, I am one of the "fortunate" ones who has a good defined benefit retirement plan. The parameters of my plan are not too dissimilar from what I laid out above in the section "Sources of Retirement Income." But there are two big constraints on my plan—indeed on virtually any defined benefit plan—that do not apply to your retirement nest egg. Namely, to collect any benefits under the plan, first I have to be retired, and second I have to be alive. Neither applies to your nest egg. You can use (some of) the income from your nest egg before you retire, and your heirs can use it, or the nest egg itself, after you die. However, like Social Security, I can only collect via a defined benefit retirement plan in the interval between my retirement and my death. (Well, there is a caveat in that my wife can continue to collect some benefits as a surviving spouse but my children cannot. Philosophically, the benefits stop at my demise; if I choose a survivor option, the plan adjusts my benefit down so that actuarially the plan pays out the same total whether I have a survivor option or not—but let's not go into those details here.) Anyway, clearly, a highly desirable goal is to maximize the interval of eligibility. That suggests early retirement at one end and long life at the other. Early retirement is an option, but my plan enforces severe benefit penalties if I choose it. And while maximizing the other end is surely a goal with which all can identify, it is something we usually cannot control. Like many people with these plans, I think about this dilemma often. Do I really want to maximize my interval of eligibility? Of course, the question only pertains to the front end; the back end is an uncontrollable event. But I confess that even as the crunch time of impending retirement bears down on me, indecision reigns.

Before I close this personal section, I would to like offer some highly subjective advice. Obviously, one should be cautious about giving advice on situations that one has not yet experienced. But in watching family and friends negotiate the shoals of retirement, I would submit three recommendations for those of you planning retirement:

1. Have at least one major new activity that you intend to pursue. It should be something fresh and exciting, perhaps an activity that you always wanted to pursue but never had the time or chance. Or it might

be something completely spontaneous, never before contemplated but eagerly anticipated when conceived.

2. Have at least one old activity that you plan to continue or renew. It might be something you tried once but never devoted enough energy or time to. Or it might be an important activity in your current life that you enjoy and intend to pursue even more ardently.
3. Take care of your health; you are going to need it when you retire.

Retirement can be dangerous. Too often retirees are alone, with diminished physical and/or mental capacities, and husbanding limited but precious resources. Such people are easy prey, and too many scams are perpetrated on the elderly. You need to be vigilant and careful. Your friends and relatives, especially your children, are your first line of defense in protecting your interests. Mend your fences if you are going to count on these important resources in retirement.

WHAT YOU LEARNED IN THIS BOOK

It's time now to draw this journey through your financial life to a close. Finances, that is, money, plays a big role in your life. You need to be in control of your money in order to use it effectively and intelligently. To do so you need to plan and have the tools to make intelligent decisions. That demands doing some arithmetic on occasion. If you can do it yourself, then I hope I have shown you the right questions to ask and steered you toward the right math to do in order to answer the questions. If you can't do the math yourself, then at least you should have gleaned from the book what decisions you need to be making, and then you can use the resources on the Web site to do the arithmetic. To sum up, here are the things we learned how to do in this book—either by hand, with a calculator, or electronically via the Web site:

- Compute the value of an account into which has been deposited a specific sum of money that has been accumulating interest for a specific number of years at a specific rate, compounded at a specific frequency (Chapter 1).
- Compute the value of an account into which has been deposited a specific sum of money at specified regular intervals for a specific number of years, and that has been earning interest at a specific rate, compounded at a specific frequency (Chapter 2).
- Compute the precise future cost of an item knowing its current price and the projected rate of inflation, and compute the effect of income taxes on your rate of return on an investment using your marginal tax rate (Chapter 3).
- Compute the future value of a regular deposit investment account when it enjoys tax-deferred status and understand the role of both the principal and the interest in such an account on your income taxes (Chapter 4).

- Compute your freedom quotient, that is, the quotient of your after-tax salary divided by your gross salary, or alternatively, the quotient of your after-tax income (the difference between your gross income and your total tax paid) divided by your gross income (Chapter 5).
- Compute the monthly payment on a typical home or car loan, given that you know the amount borrowed, the loan rate, and the length of the loan (Chapter 6).
- Compute the monthly payment on a typical car lease, given that you know the capital cost, the residual value, the interest rate or money factor, and the length of the lease (Chapter 7).
- Compare the monthly costs of a homeowner with a renter for comparable level properties, and how much mortgage a specific monthly allotment will support (Chapter 8).
- Understand that insurance is a bet and what the nature and possible outcomes of such a bet entail (Chapter 9).
- Understand your credit card bill by being able to compute the monthly interest charges and minimum payment due (Chapter 10).
- Understand the nature of gambling, how odds are computed, and why gambling is such a bad practice (Chapter 11).
- Compute the final worth of an escalating, regular investment program, given that you know the starting amount, the annual return, the annual escalating rate, and the length of the program (Chapter 12).
- Compute the size of the nest egg you need to accumulate in order to offset any shortfall in retirement income, and compute how long that nest egg will last if it is insufficient to generate all the income you need annually (Chapter 13).

So, in closing, educate yourself about finances and money; do the math, using the Web site if necessary; and make informed decisions. Good luck.

YOUR NEW COMPUTATIONAL SKILLS

How to compute the size of the nest egg you need to accumulate in order to offset any shortfall in retirement income, and how to compute how long that nest egg will last if it is insufficient to generate all the income you need annually.

Index

About the Author

RON LIPSMAN is Professor of Mathematics and Associate Dean of the Physical Sciences College, University of Maryland. The author of more than 70 mathematical research articles and co-author of eight technical books, he has over 35 years of experience in teaching, tutoring, and advising students and colleagues alike on issues related to mathematics, computing, and financial management.